Bengali for Foreigners

(Revised Second Edition)

Basic grammar
Basic vocabulary with sentences
Secondary vocabulary
English - Bengali - transliteration

Edited by
BROTHER JAMES

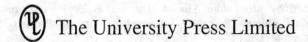 The University Press Limited

The University Press Limited
Red Crescent Building
114 Motijheel C/A
P. O. Box 2611
Dhaka 1000
Bangladesh

Temporary Relocation Address
Red Crescent House
61 Motijheel C/A (5th floor)
Dhaka 1000
Fax : (88 02) 9565443
E-mail: upl@bangla.net
Website: www.uplbooks.com

First published 1978
Revised second edition 1982
Third impression 1987
Fourth impression 2004

Cover design by Tofazzal Hossain

ISBN 984 05 1045 2

Published by Mohiuddin Ahmed, The University Press Limited, Red
Crescent Building, Dhaka 1000, Printed at Elora Art Press, 635 North
Shahjahanpur, Dhaka.

CONTENTS

PART—I
Grammar

ii

GRAMMAR

Lesson 1
INTRODUCTION

The contents of this book are the simplified and easier portions of two books printed in 1956 : "English–Bengali Grammar and Basic–Secondary Vocabulary with sentences (English–Bengali)"

The less common and harder parts of the earlier grammar are omitted. The sentences in the examples have been considerably simplified and put into colloquial form.

The first 30 lessons are the most basic, but one's needs will dictate one's choices. .

In effect, the vocabulary is a basic, most common one. In practice the emphasis should always be on *Bengali* words, sentences and grammar rather than on English words, expressions and grammar. This will result in one's *thinking and speaking in Bengali*. Speaking in Bengali with Bengalis is the easiest, cheapest and best way of learning their language. To do so, the rudiments of grammar and vocabulary are necessary. This book tries to provide them.

Acquaint yourself well with the entire contents : the table of contents, the grammar chapter titles and what is involved in the enlargement, the extent of the basic vocabulary and the sentences, the secondary vocabulary without sentences, the extensive index. Sometimes the table of contents will be more useful than the index. If you don't find a word you're looking for in either vocabulary, look for a similar word or a synonym. Some words, like **across** and **through**, are treated in the grammar.

A basic—secondary vocabulary is easily stretched. There's no need to learn, in the early stages, the negative form of words—just add না n*a* to the word.

Talk—and listen. Use new words and phrases *as* you learn them. Vary your studying by memorizing words, phrases, sentences. Repeating them to yourself helps ; writing them out is another aid. With a little effort and practice you can start communicating with others.

If you intend to stay in Bangladesh for a year or two or more, have some reliable Bengali mark your Bengali—to—English dictionary. A check mark (√) in front of common words and phrases will be very helpful.

Lesson 2

PRONUNCIATION

The vowels :

initial form	internal form	symbol	like		examples
আ	া	*a*	a	in father	আম *am*
অ ৹	(inherent)	a	a	in paw/caw	কর kara
ই ৹	ি	i	i	in nib	ইহা ih*a*
ঈ	ী	ee	ee	in thee	বাড়ী b*aree*
উ	ু	u	u	in put	উপর upar
ঊ	ূ	oo	oo	in fool	দূর door

The vowels :

initial form	internal form	symbol	like		examples
এ	◌	ে	e	e in then	এত eta
ও	ে া	o	o	in oblique/ obey	ও o that
ঐ	ৈ	ai/ oi	oy	in toy	ঐখানে oikhane
ঔ	ৌ	au/ ow	ow	in know/go	ঔষধ aushadh

Notes : ● এ e, this, and এ e in এটা eta is lengthened into ei, eita. Also, medial e in সে she and সেটা sheta is lengthened into shei, sheita.

● The final অ aw in a verb sounds like a soft or short o : karbo, jabo, karo, balo, kalo, chhoto, bhalo. It often has a similar sound internally, especially before a syllable having ি i : jodi, kkhoti, proti.

● Medial ি i in chini, firi...is longer. ae is like a held or exaggerated a in hat, batter, back, though in hurried conversation it is more like e in let, beg.

The consonants :

	symbol	used in	translit.	meaning
ক	k	কাক	kak	crow
খ	kh	খালি	khalee	empty
গ	g	গমন	gaman	going
ঘ	gh	ঘর	ghar	house/room
চ	ch	চা	cha	tea
ছ	chh (often s in B. D.)	আছে	achhe	(he/she) is
জ	j (often z in B. D.)	জল	jal	water
ঝ	jh	ঝড়	jhar	storm
ঙ, ন	n	না	na	no

The consonants :

	symbol	used in	translit.	meaning
প	p	পাপ	p*a*p	sin
ফ	f	ফল	fal	fruit
ব	b	বাগান	b*a*g*a*n	garden
ভ	bh	ভাল	bh*a*la	good/well
ল	l	লাল	l*a*l	red
য	j	যাই	j*a*i	I go
য়	y	যায়	j*a*y	he/she goes
		kariy*a*/kari*a*		doing
হ	h	হাত	h*a*t	hand
ম	m	মা	m*a*	mom/mother
র	rolled r	রস	rash	juice
	European r			

ড়	*r*	বড়	bar*a*	pronounced with
ঢ়	*r*	দৃঢ়	dreer*a*	the tongue against the upper palate

*শ	sh	শেষ	shesh	end — This s is
*স	sh	সব	shab	all — often pron. like Eng. s
ষ	sh	শেষ	shesh	end

ক্ষ, though it is k ক + sh ষ, it is pronounced as a held kh খ, hence it is marked kkh.

Dentals : These are pronounced like many similar European/Latin letters—with the tongue touching the inside of the upper teeth.

ত	t	তিনি	tini	he (honorific)
থ	th	থাকা	th*a*k*a*, much like *th* in thin, thigh
দ	d	দান	d*a*n, much like *th* in then, the
ধ	dh	ধান	dh*a*n, much like *th* in that, their

* In combination with other consonants, শ sh and স sh are sometimes pronounced as s :—স্থান sth*a*n, বিশ্রাম bisr*a*m.

Palatals : These are pronounced with the *tongue touching* the hard palate (roof of the mouth).

ট	*t*	টাকা	*taka* close to *t* in ticket
ঠ	*th*	ঠিক	*thik* aspirated form of *t*
ড	*d*	ডাল	*dal* like doll, tongue back farther
ঢ	*dh*	ঢাল	*dhal* aspir. form of *d*

These should be practised till they are mastered.

Palatal t, th, d, dh—ট ঠ ড ঢ—as well as ড়—are printed in italics. So too is the n that indicates the nasal sound of and আকার, *akar* (the letter আ or its symbol া).

Lesson 3

MAKING SENTENCES

In Bengali the subject comes first, the verb last, the object in between. (Words in brackets may be left out.)

আমি পড়ি।	*Ami pari.*	I read/study.
আমি বই পড়ি।	*Ami bai pari.*	I read (a) book(s).
সে মাছ কিনে/বেচে।	*She machh kine/beche.*	He/she buys/sells fish.
আমি জনকে দেখি।	*Ami Johnke dekhi.*	I see John.
আমি তোমাকে দেখি।	*Ami tomake dekhi.*	I see you.
তুমি আমাকে দেখ।	*Tumi amake dekha.*	You see me.

Modifiers come before the words they modify.

[আমি] নূতন বই চাই।	*(Ami) nootan bai chai.*	I want a new book.
এখানে/সেখানে বস।	*Ekhane/shekane basha.*	Sit here/there.
আমি ছেলে/মেয়ে...	*Ami chhele/meye...*	I am a boy/girl....
আমি ভাল/গরীব [আছি]।	*Ami bhalo/gareeb ( ).*	I am good/poor.
সে আমার ভাই/বোন [আছে]।	*She amar bhai/bon ( ).*	He/She (is) my brother/siste

[তুমি] কি চাও ?   (Tumi) ki ch*a*o ?   What do (you) want ?
[আমি] ভাল বই চাই । (*A*mi) bh*a*lo boi ch*a*i. (I) want a good book.

Lesson 4

VERB CHART

(a) Simple Present Tense—Simple Verbs

Root + ই i/অ a/এ e   1st/2nd/3rd person

1.	আমি *a*mi, I	করি kari	do, make
		কিনি kini	buy
	আমরা *a*mr*a*, we	পারি p*a*ri	can
		দেখি dekhi	see
2.	তুমি tumi, you	কর kara	do, make [কর্ kar root]
		কিন kina	buy [কিন্ kin "]
	তোমরা tomr*a*. you	পার p*a*ra	can [পার্ p*a*r "]
		দেখ, dekha	see [দেখ dekh "]
3.	সে, she, he, she, it	করে kare	does, makes
	তা t*a*, it	কিনে kine	buys
	তারা t*a*r*a*, they	পারে p*a*re	can, is (are) able
		দেখে dekhe	sees

Simple Present Tense—double-vowel roots (in effect)

1.	আমি *a*mi, I	যাই j*a*i, go		নেই nei, take	
	আমরা *a*mr*a*, we	পড়াই par*a*i. teach		দেই dei, give	
		দেখাই dekh*a*i, show		হই hai, be, become	
2.	তুমি tumi, you	যাও j*a*o, go		নাও n*a*o	
	তোমরা tomr*a*, you	পড়াও par*a*o, teach		দাও d*a*o	
		দেখাও dekh*a*o, show		হও ho	
3.	সে she, he, she, it	যায় j*a*y, goes		নেয় ney	
	তা t*a*, it	পড়ায় par*a*y, teach(es)		দেয় dey	
	তারা t*a*r*a*, they	দেখায় dekh*a*y, show(s)		হয় hay	

(h)   Simple Future—*   root + ব, ba ; বে be ; বে be

1.   আমি ami, I   কর্‌ব karba   * যাব jaba
                         কিন্‌ব kinba   দেখাব dekaba
      আমরা amra, we   পার্‌ব parba   দিব diba
                         দেখ্‌ব dekhba   হ'ব haba হইব haiba
2.   তুমি tumi, you   কর্‌বে karbe   যাবে jabe যাইবে jaibe
                         কিন্‌বে kinbe   দেখাবে dekhabe
      তোমরা tomra, you পার্‌বে parbe   দিবে dibe
                         দেখ্‌বে dekhbe   হ'বে habe হইব haiba
3.   সে she, he, she, it কর্‌বে karbe   যাবে jabe
      তা ta, it   কিন্‌বে kinbe   দেখাবে dekhabe
      তারা tara, they   পার্‌বে parbe   দিবে dibe
                         দেখ্‌বে dekhbe   হ'বে habe হইবে haibe

(c)   **Present Perfect Tense**—often used for English Past
(L. 26)

Root + ছি chhi/ছ chha/ছে chhe or এছি echhi/এছ echha/এছে echhe.

1.   I, we   করছি karchhi করেছি echhi গেছি gechhi গিয়েছি gechhi
      e. g. did, have, have done   giyechhi
               কিনছি kinchhi কিনেছি „   দেখাইছি dekhaichhi
                                          দেখিয়েছি dekhiyechhi
               পারছি parchhi পেরেছি „   দিছি dichhi দিয়েছি
                                          diyechhi
               দেখছি dekhchhi দেখেছি „   হ'ছি ha(i)chhi হয়েছি
                                          hayechhi
2.   you,   করছ karchha   করেছ echha গেছ gechha গিয়েছ
      you   giyechha
               কিনছ kinchha   কিনেছ   „   দেখাইছ dekhaichha
                                          দেখিয়েছ dekhiyechha.

---

* In Bangladesh it is not uncommon to hear the complete verb forms : যাইব jaiba ; পাইব paiba ; দেখাইব dekhaiba. Though written—ba (baw) and—be, in practice these are **bo** and **bei** (as in the English word **bay**)

8

পারছ *par*chha পেরেছ ,, দিছ dichha দিয়েছ diyechha.

দেখছ *dekh*chha দেখেছ ,, হইছ haichha হয়েছ hayechha.

3. he, she, করছে *kar*chhe করেছে echhe গেছে gechhe গিয়েছে giyechhe

it, কিনছে *kin*chhe কিনেছে ,, দেখাইছে dekh*a*ichhe দেখিয়েছে dekhiyechhe

they, পারছে *par*chhe পেরেছে ,, দিছে dichhe দিয়েছে diyechhe

দেখছে *dekh*chhe দেখেছে ,, হইছে haichhe * হয়েছ hayechhe

Lesson 5

THE SUBJECT

The subject may be a noun, pronoun, verbal noun or infinitive.

A mango is sweet.	They come here.
আম মিষ্টি ।	তারা এখানে আসে ।
*A*m mish*t*i.	T*ara* ekh*a*ne *a*she.
Walking is good.	Being idle is not good.
বেড়ান ভাল [ ] ।	অলস হওয়া ভাল না ।
Be*r*an bh*a*la.	Alas haoya bh*a*la n*a*.
Today's lesson is long.	This reading/lesson is/feels/ seems good.
আজকার পড়া লম্বা ।	এই পড়া ভাল লাগে ।
Ajk*a*r par*a* lamb*a*.	Ei p*ara* bh*a*la l*a*ge.

* More standard colloquial verb forms can be found in the appendix. See TENSES.

I like to play ·· It feels good to ···

খেলতে ভাল লাগে ।

Khelte bhala lage.

[ ]—Empty brackets signify the verb *to be* is not expressed.

Lesson 6

THE NOMINATIVE CASE, THE PREDICATE NOMINATIVE CASE

A predicate noun is one connected with the subject by some Yorm of the verb *to be* or a similar verb expressed or understood. It agrees with its subject in case and, when possible, in gender also. [   ] *To Be* not expressed.

She is my sister.

সে আমার বোন [   ] ।

She amar bon.

Those are goats.

ও গুলি ছাগল ।

O gule chhagal.

He/she was my friend.

সে আমার বন্ধু ছিল ।

She amar bandhu chhila.

I am a man.

আমি মানুষ [আছি] ।

Ami manush (achhi)

John is a good boy.

জন ভাল ছেলে [আছে] ।

Jan bhala chhele (achhe).

They are students (boys/girls).

তারা ছাত্র/ছাত্রী ।

Tara chhatra/chhatree. m/f

He is not my brother/father.

সে আমার ভাই/বাবা ··· না ।

She amar bhai/baba ... na.

Lesson 7

THE PLURAL NOUNS

A noun in Bengali is not placed in the plural if the plurality is capable of being understood from the context.

All men will die.

There are no eggs in the market/bazar.

সব মানুষ মরবে ।

Shab manush marbe.

বাজারে ডিম নাই/নেই ।

Bazare dim nai/nei.

The flowers in the garden look beautiful.

He and I are friends.

বাগানে ফুল দেখতে সুন্দর ।

Bagane ful dekhte shundar.

সে ও আমি বন্ধু ।

She o ami bandhu.

many students (m)

his clothes

অনেক ছাত্র

anek chhatra

তার কাপড়

tar kapar

the bird(s) in the woods

There are eggs on the table.

বনের পাখী

baner pakhee

টেবিলের উপরে ডিম আছে ।

Tebiler upare dim achhe.

Lesson 8

THE APPOSITIVE—NOUN IN APPOSITION

The appositive is a noun explaining or defining another noun denoting the same person or thing. When a noun in Bengali stands in apposition another it precedes the principal noun. It agrees with the appositive noun in case and, when possible, in gender also.

the city of Dacca

The boy John lives/stays here.

ঢাকা শহর

Dhaka shahar

জন ছেলেটি এখানে থাকে ।

Jan chheleti ekhane thake.

Here the river Padma is very wide.

my uncle George

এখানে পদ্মা নদী খুব চওড়া ।

Ekhane padda nadee khub chowra.

আমার জর্জ মামা

amar Jorj mama

I never saw Rabindranath the poet.

● কবি রবীন্দ্রনাথকে কখনও দেখি নাই/নি ।

Kobi Rabindronathke kokhano dekhi nai/ni.

Singing is my greatest pleasure.

গান গাইতে আমার সবচেয়ে বড় আনন্দ ।

Gan gaite amar shab cheye bara ananda.

Lesson 9
THE OBJECT—THE ACCUSATIVE /OBJECTIVE CASE

In Bengali the object immediately precedes the transitive verb, while in English it usually follows it.

Clean your teeth.	I know Gopal.
দাঁত পরিষ্কার কর ।	আমি গোপালকে চিনি ।
Dant parishkar kara.	Ami Gopalke chini.
He calls me.	I call him.
সে আমাকে ডাকে ।	আমি তাকে ডাকি ।
She amake dake.	Ami take daki.
I'll do it today.	Rabin sings a song.
আমি তা আজ করব ।	রবীন গান গায় ।
Ami ta aj karbo.	Rabeen gan gay.

Bring (the) tea. I want sugar. Forgive me.

চা আন ।   চিনি চাই ।   আমাকে ক্ষমা কর ।

Cha ana.   Chini chai.   Amake khhama karo.

Lesson 10
THE DATIVE CASE—INDIRECT OBJECT

The dative case is used with a verb implying a gift or transfer to some person, or, in other words, the case of the indirect object.

● The case ending is after the principal noun.

When there are two objects, that which carries the inflection কে ke usually comes first.

I shall give you a book.

আমি তোমাকে বই দিব ।

Ami tomake bai dibo.

Tell me a story.

আমাকে একটি গল্প বল ।

Amake ekti galpa bala.

Write him a letter (to him).

তার কাছে চিঠি লেখ/লিখ ।

Tar kachhe chithi lekha/likha.

Teach me a song.

আমাকে একটি গান শিখাও ।

Amake ekti gan shikhao.

I brought him a pen (for him).

আমি তার জন্য একটি কলম

আনলাম ।

Ami tar janna ekti kalam anlam.

Buy a book for me.

আমার জন্য একটি বই কিনে আন ।

Amar janna ekti bai kine ana.

Note : Verbs that may take কে ke as indirect objects are : ask, buy [taka deo], tell, give, hand [hate kario deo], teach, lend, read [pario shunao], write [chithi deo], sing to [gan shunao].

Lesson 11

DATIVE CASE—The translation of certain English datives into Bengali.

When a transitive or neuter verb in English is followed by *to* denoting motion *towards* an object, Bengali does not use the dative case.   It uses some word denoting locality with the genitive case, or simply uses the locative.

Go to the garden.

বাগানে যাও ।

Bagane jao.

I went to my mother and asked for a taka.

আমি মায়ের কাছে গিয়া একটি টাকা চাইলাম/চালাম ।

Ami mayer kachhe giya ekti taka chailam/chalam.

We pray to God for help.

আমরা ঈশ্বরের কাছে সাহায্য প্রার্থনা করি ।

*Amra Eeshsharer k*a*chhe sh*a*h*o*jja pr*a*rthan*a kari.

She/he goes to school five times a week.

সে সপ্তাহে পাঁচবার স্কুলে যায় ।

She shapt*a*he p*a*nchb*a*r skule j*a*y.

I go to Dacca once a month.

মাসে একবার ঢাকায়/ঢাকা যাই ।

M*a*she ekb*a*r *Dhakay/Dh*a*ka j*a*y.

NOTE :—These verbs go with GEN.+কাছে k*a*chhe : sell, throw, bring to, write to [লেখ lekha]

These verbs go with GEN.+জন্য janna, buy make [b*a*n*a*o toy*a*r kara], leave [r*a*khi*a j*a*o], bring [as a favour], find, sing for [g*a*n g*a*o].

Lesson 12
PERSONAL POSSESSIVE OR GENITIVE OF POSSESSION

The possessive in Bengali is always expressed by the genitive case of the personal pronoun, instead of the special pronominal forms found in some languages.

Our washerman does good work.

আমাদের ধোপা ভাল কাজ করে ।

*Am*a*der dhop*a bh*a*lo k*a*j kare.

Please sweep my room.

আমার কামরায় দয়া করিয়া ঝাড়ু দিও ।

*Am*a*r k*a*mr*a*y doy*a kariya jh*a*r u dio.

What is/are his objection(s) ?

তার আপত্তি কি ? (কি কি ?

T*a*r *a*patti ki ? [ki ki ?

My dog goes with me.

আমার কুকুর আমার সঙ্গে যায় ।

*A*m*a*r kukur *a*m*a*r shange jay.

at your convenience

তোমার সুবিধার মত

tom*a*r shubidh*a*r mata

What is his/her salary ?

তার বেতন কত ?

T*a*r betan kata ?

his/her home/book

তার বাড়ী/বই

t*a*r b*a*ree/bai

Lesson 13

DECLARATIVE SENTENCE—THE SENTENCE

An examination of the sentence structure shows that the chief difference between the Bengali sentence and the English sentence is in the order of the words. In Bengali/B*a*ngl*a* the main verb comes at the end of the sentence. The position of the words in an affirmative declarative sentence is as follows : (1) the subject with its qualifying words , (2) the object, if there is any , (3) the predicate with its qualifying words. Negative sentences are formed by adding না n*a* to the end of the affirmative sentence ; or, if the verb in the affirmative sentence is the present tense of আছে *a*chhe, by changing it to না n*a*.

You give me much rice.

তুমি আমাকে অনেক ভাত দেও/দাও ।

Tumi *a*m*a*ke anek bh*a*t deo/d*a*o.

He reads his new books.

সে তার নূতন বই পড়ে ।

She t*a*r nootan boi pa*r*e.

We bring our books to school.

আমরা আমাদের বই স্কুলে আনি ।

*A*mr*a* *a*m*a*der bai skule *a*ni.

It is good news.

ইহা ভাল খবর ।

T*a*/ih*a* bh*a*la khabar.

The bed was small. (bedstead)
খাট ছোট ছিল ।
Khaṭ chhoṭa chhila.

My clothes (are) torn.
আমার কাপড় ছিঁড়া [আছে] ।
Amar kapar chhinra
(achhe).

Lesson 14

THE SENTENCE : SEVERAL NOUNS IN THE SAME CASE

When several nouns are in the same case and governed by the same verb, the case ending is added after the last only (see also lesson 8).

I do not go out because of the wind and rain.
বাতাস ও বৃষ্টির জন্য আমি বাইরে যাই না ।
Batash o brishṭir janna ami baire jay na.

He used to live in this city with Joseph and Mariyam.
তিনি যোসেফ ও মরিয়মের সঙ্গে এই শহরে বাস করতেন ।
Tini Joshef o Mariyamer shange ei shahare bash karten.

I shall find dad, mom and (my) sister there.
আমি বাপ, মা ও বোনকে সেখানে পাইব/পাব ।
Ami bap, ma o bonke shekhane paiba/paba.

This is for John and you.
I shall go to Dacca and
Comilla,
এটা জন ও তোমার জন্য ।
আমি ঢাকা ও কুমিল্লায় যাব ।
Eta Jon o tomar janna.
Ami Dhaka o Kamilay jaba

Lesson 15

THE SENTENCE : QUALIFYING WORDS

A qualifying word usually precedes the word it qualifies, Adjectives used attributively always precede the words they qualify. The same rule applies to all other parts of speech which qualify other words, be they nouns in the genitive, past participles or adverbs.

He reads (is reading) his new book.

সে তার নূতন বই পড়ে ।

She t*a*r nootan bai pa*r*e,

It is good news,

ভা/ইহা ভাল খবর ।

T*a* ih*a* bh*a*la khabar,

Where were you for so long/so many days ?

এত দিন কোথায় ছিলে ?

Eta din koth*a*y chhile ?

Read well/study hard,

ভাল মত পড় ।

Bh*a*la mata pa*r*a,

How is it that you know this ?

তু মি ইহা/তা কেমনে জান ?

Tumi ih*a*/t*a* kemne j*a*no ?

Don't drink bad water,

খারাপ জল খাইও/খেয়ো না ।

Kh*a*r*a*p jal kh*a*io/kheyo n*a*.

Speak slowly/softly.

আস্তে আস্তে কথা কও ।

*A*ste *a*ste kath*a* kao.

Red paint/colour	white paper	two boys/girls
লাল রং	সাদা কাগজ	দুইটি ছেলে/মেয়ে
l*a*l rang	sh*a*d*a* k*a*gaj	dui*t*i chhele/meye

Lesson 16

THE VERB *TO HAVE* (Case I) OWNERSHIP—
GEN. + আছে *a*chhe

To express ownership the subject of the English sentence is placed in the genitive in Bengali, the object in the nominative case with the proper tense of আছে *a*chhe. If the sentence is clear without আছে *a*chhe, it is omitted. [ ]

I have a cow.

আমার গাভী আছে ।

*A*m*a*r g*a*bhee *a*chhe.

He/She has a goat.

তার একটি হাগল [আছে] ।

T*a*r ek*t*i chh*a*gal [*a*chhe].

You have one pair of shoes and two pair of socks.

তোমার একজোড়া জুতা ও দুই জোড়া মোজা [আছে] ।

Tom*a*r ek jo*ra* jut*a* o dui jo*ra* moj*a* [*a*chhe].

The fisherman has only one net.	[had......
জেলেটির কেবল একটি জাল [আছে] ।	[ছিল······
Jele*t*ir kebal ek*t*i jal [*a*chhe].	[chhila...

I have some leisure now.

আমার এখন কিছু অবসর [আছে].

*A*m*a*r ekhan kichhu abshar [*a*chhe].

The knife has a good/fine/sharp edge.

ছুরিটির ভাল ধার [আছে] ।

Chhuri*t*ir bh*a*la dh*a*r [*a*chhe].

Negative :

He has no ink/book/cow/mother......	[had no...
তার কালি/বই/গাভী/মা...... নাই/নেই ।	[ছিল না
T*a*r k*a*li/bai/g*a*bhee/m*a*......n*a*i/nei.	[chhila n*a*

Lesson 17

THE VERB *TO HAVE* (Case II) POSSESSION—
GEN.+ আছে *a*chhe.

In the sentence which states that someone is in possession of the property of another, the subject (the possessor) is in the genitive governed by the Postpositions, কাছে k*a*chhe, near and the actual owner placed in the simple genitive of possession and the proper tense of আছে *a*chhe.

The man has my cow.	He has my book.
লোকের কাছে আমার গরু আছে ।	তার কাছে আমার বই আছে ।
Loker k*a*chhe *a*m*a*r garu *a*chhe.	T*a*r k*a*chhe *a*m*a*r bai *a*chhe.

2—

The boatman has my luggage in his boat.

মাঝির নৌকার ভিতরে আমার মাল [আছে] ।

Majhir noukar bhitare amar mal [achhe].

I have your pen and his.

আমার কাছে তোমার ও তার কলম [আছে] ।

Amar kachhe tomar o tar kalam [achhe].

Lesson 18

THE USE OF আছে achhe, including cases where আছে achhe is translated "it is" ; "there is" and "there are". Omission of same when it can be understood.

There are fishes in the pond.

পুকুরে মাছ আছে ।

Pukure machh achhe.

There is someone there.

সেখানে কেহ আছে ।

Shekhane keha achhe.

There's food on the table.

টেবিলে খাবার আছে ।

Tebile khabar achhe.

I am/was with him/her. [...will be]

আমি তার সঙ্গে [আছি]/ছিলাম । [থাকব] ।

Ami tar shange [achhi]/chhilam. [thakbo]

It is mine/yours/his/hers...

ইহা/তা আমার/তোমার/তার [   ]

Iha/ta amar/tomar/tar [   ]

It is a very small house.

এইটি খুব ছোট ঘর ।

Eiti khub chhota ghar.

There is much dust in my room.

আমার কামরায় অনেক ধুলা [আছে] ।

Amar kamray anek dhoola [achhe].

There's no doubt about it.

এ বিষয়ে সন্দেহ নাই/নেই ।

E bishaye shandeha nai/nei.

There's no reason to cry.

কাঁদবার কারণ নাই/নেই ।

Kandbar karan nai/nei.

It's too bad.

দুঃখের বিষয় ।

Dukher bishay.

What is this ?   Your book.

এটা কি ?   তোমার বই ।

Eta ki ?   Tomar boi.

What is your name ?

তোমার নাম কি ?

Tomar nam ki ?

This/it is for you.

এটা তোমার জন্য [   ] ।

Eta tomar janna [   ].

I am tired/happy/lazy/fat/black — dark...

আমি ক্লান্ত/সুখী/অলস/মোটা/কাল/...

Ami klanta/sukhee/alash/mota/kala...

How is your mother ?

তোমার মা কেমন [আছে] ?

Tomar ma keman [achhe] ?

It is easy to do.

এ কাজ করা সহজ ।

E kaj kara shahaj [V. Noun.]

The verb TO BE is often omitted in Bengali where it is understood (*present tense*)—unless there is *only* the subject and predicate or when TO BE is emphasized.

He/she is my brother/sister/friend/companion.

সে আমার ভাই/বোন/বন্ধু/সাথী...... ।

She amar bhai/bon/bandhu/shathee... .

He/she is not my brother/sister...

সে আমার ভাই/বোন...না/[নয়] ।

She amar bhai/bon...na [nay].

You are not my brother/sister...

তুমি আমার ভাই/বোন...না [নও] ।

Tumi amar bhai/bon...na [nao].

I am not your/his/her friend.

আমি তোমার/তার বন্ধু...না [নই] ।

Ami tomar/tar bandhu...na [nai].

It is now night/winter/cold/hot...

এখন রাত/শীতকাল/ঠাণ্ডা/গরম...

Ekhan rat/sheetkal/thanda/garam...

It is easy to learn Bengali.

বাংলা [ভাষা] শিখা সহজ ।

Bangla [bhasha] shikha shahaj.

Lesson 19

THE USE OF হওয়া haoya — be, become, happen

I was afraid/doubtful/troubled/ill···

আমার ভয়/সন্দেহ/কষ্ট/অসুখ··· হইল/হল ।

*A*ma*r* bhay/shandeha/kash*t*a/asukh···haila/hala.

It's time to go···	It got/is warm/hot···
যাবার সময় হইছে/হয়েছে ।	গরম হইছে/হয়েছে ।
*Ja*ba*r* shamay haichhe/hayechhe.	Garam haichhe/hayechhe.
It is raining.	[It] is finished/late···
বৃষ্টি হইতেছে/হচ্ছে ।	শেষ/দেরি···হইছে/হয়েছে ।
Brish*t*i haitechhe/hachchhe.	Shesh/deri···haichhe/ hayechhe
If you come, I'll be happy.	This will do.
যদি আস, সুখী হব ।	এতে হবে ।
Jadi *a*sha shukhee haba.	Ete habe.
I won't get taller/bigger.	It didn't rain.
আরও লম্বা হব না ।	বৃষ্টি হল না ।
*A*ro lamb*a* haba n*a*.	Brish*t*i hala n*a*.
I got angry/mad/	I made a mistake.
আমার রাগ হইল ।	ভুল হইছে/হয়েছে ।
*A*ma*r* r*a*g haila.	Bhool haichhe/hayechhe.
It is hard to write.	I got no food.
লিখতে কষ্ট হয় ।	আমার খাওয়া হল না ।
Likhte kash*t*a hay.	*A*ma*r* kh*a*oya hala n*a*.
It's a storm/cyclone···	
ঝড়/তুফান······হইছে/হয়েছে ।	
Jha*r*/tuf*a*n···haichhe/hayechhe.	

Study lessons 18 and 19 carefully.

Lesson 18—be, remain, exist, be in a condition.

Lesson 19—be, become, happen, occur.

You'll hear BOTH : hoba/haiba ; hobe/haibe ;/hala/hailo···

Lesson 20

NEGATIVE SENTENCES

নয় nay ; না na—corresponding to the English words NOT/NO.

Although the first form given is used in writing at times, the second form is always used in colloquial Bengali. (See the lesson dealing with the negative of verbs in the past tenses). It should be noted that the verb *to be* in the negative past takes the ordinary logical form of ছিল না chhila na.

He will not leave college.

সে কলেজ ছাড়বে না ।

She kolej chharbe na.

They don't eat meat/milk/vegetables.

তারা মাংস/দুধ/শাক-শব্জি খায় না ।

Tara mangsha/dudh/shak-shabji khay na.

My pen was here.
আমার কলম এখানে ছিল ।
Amar kalam ekhane chhila.

My pen was not here.
আমার কলম এখানে ছিল না ।
Amar kalam ekhane chhila na.

I don't go there.
(আমি) সেখানে যাই না ।
(Ami) shekhane jai na.

He doesn't come here.
সে এখানে আসে না ।
She ekhane ashe na.

Aren't you reading/studying ? Don't you read ?
পড় না ?
Para na ?

I don't get fever.
আমার জ্বর হয় না ।
Amar jjar hay na.

See TENSES for more negatives. Others are scattered throughout the grammar.

Lesson 21

INTERROGATIVE SENTENCES

In general the interrogative sentences are formed by adding the particle কি ki to the end of a affirmative sentence unless there is an interrogative adverb or pronoun ordinarily in conversation simple inflection of the voice (as in English) suffices for the কি ki.

Will (you) go there?

[তুমি] সেখানে যাবে ?
(Tumi) shekhane jabe ?

Do you/did you/will you have paper ?

তোমার কাগজ আছে/ছিল/হবে ?
Tomar kagaj achhe ?/chhila ?/habe ?

May I go now ?/later ?

এখন/পরে যাইতে/যাতে/যেতে পারি ?
Ekhan/pare jaite/jate/jete pari ?

Will they come home ?

তারা বাড়ী আসবে ?
Tara baree ashbe ?

Did he/she go to Faridpur ?

সে ফরিদপুর গেছিল/গিয়েছিল ।
She Faridpur gechhila/giyechhila ?

How many cows/much money did you have ?

তোমার কয়টা গরু/কত টাকা ছিল ?
Tomar kayta garu/kata taka chhila ?

Did you ever go there ?

(তুমি) সেখানে কখনও গেছিলে/গিয়েছিলে ?
(Tumi) shekhane kakhano gechhile/giyechhile ?

Too, কি ki is not used with the interrogative adverbs ঃ কোথায়, কই kothay, kai, where ; কখন, কবে kakhan, kabe, when ; কেন kena why etc. or with the interrogative pronouns q. v.—who, which, what, whom,

Lesson 22

INTERROGATIVE SENTENCES IN THE NEGATIVE

Negative interrogative sentences are formed by adding না–কি *na*-ki to the end of the affirmative sentence. In conversation কি ki is omitted.

Is he/she not a good boy/girl?

সে ভাল ছেলে/মেয়ে না [নয়] ?

She bhala chhele/meye na [nay] ?

Am I not a man/human being ?

আমি মানুষ না [নই] ?

*A*mi m*a*nush n*a* [nai] ?

Didn't he/she go ?

সে যায় নাই/নি ?

She j*a*y n*a*i/ni ?

Won't he/she go ?

সে যাবে না ?

She j*a*be na ?

Aren't you a good boy/girl ?

তুমি ভাল ছেলে/মেয়ে না [নও] ?

Tumi bh*a*la chhele/meye
n*a* [nao] ?

He/she didn't go.

সে যায় নাই/নি ।

She j*a*y n*a*i/ni.

Aren't you working ?

কাজ কর না ?

K*a*j kara n*a* ?

Didn't you do the work ?

কাজ কর নাই/নি ?

K*a*j kara n*a*i/ni ?

See TENSES for more negatives.

Lesson 23

IMPERATIVE SENTENCES : COMMAND, ADMONITION

These express a command or admonition. The pronoun is usually not expressed. To obtain the proper inflection in speaking put the accent on the syllable before the না n*a* when না n*a* is used.

Very quietly / very softly/slowly ! come ; come, don't delay !

খুব আস্তে আস্তে ! আস/এস ; আস/এস না, দেরী করিও না !

Khub *a*ste *a*ste ! *a*sha/esha ; *a*sha/esha n*a* deri kario n*a* !

Don't come here/go there.

এখানে আসিও না/এস না/যাইও/যেয়ো না ।

Ekh*a*ne *a*shio n*a*/esha n*a*/j*a*io/jeio n*a*.

Mix the water and flour well.	Come here.	Go there.
জল ও ময়দা ভাল করিয়া/করে মিশাও ।	এখানে আস ।	সেখানে যাও ;
Jal o mayd*a* bh*a*la kari*a*/k*a*re mish*a*o.	Ekh*a*ne *a*sha.	Shekane j*a*o.

Do this now.	Do this later.
এই কাজ কর ।	এই কাজ করিও ।
Ei k*a*j kara.	Ei k*a*j kario.

See lessons 29 and 30 for more imperative sentences.

Lesson 24

IMPERATIVE : ENTREATY

When the negative word না n*a* is used with the present imperative, it often adds the idea of entreaty ; so also, at times does the future imperative.

Won't you have a seat ?

বস না; বসবে/ বসবেন না ?

Basha n*a*; bashbe/bashben n*a* ?

Please eat.	If you eat, I'll be pleased.
খাও/খান না ।	খাইলে/ খেলে সুখী হব ।
Kh*a*o/khan/n*a*.	Kh*a*ile/ khele/shukhee haba.

Keep quiet

চুপ কর না ।

Chup kara na.

Come on in.

ভিতরে আস/এসো না ।

Bhitare asha/esha na.

See also lessons 29 and 30.

Lesson 25

TENSE—Simple present tense   do   do   he does

করি   কর   করে

kari   karo   kare

(a) To make a statement about the present without calling attention to the incompleteness or continuity of the action, and at the same time without denying it.

He/She knows Bengali.

সে বাংলা জানে ।

She Bangla jane.

I see/can see him/her.

আমি তাকে দেখতে পাই ।

Ami take dekhte pai.

(b) To express natural habitual actions or general truths :

It rains in the rainy/monsoon season.

বর্ষাকালে বৃষ্টি হয় ।

Barshakale brishti hay.

He/she lies/tells lies.

সে মিথ্যা কথা বলে ।

She miththa katha bale.

(c) As a historic present :

It was in that year that he/she was born.

সে বৎসরই তার জন্ম হয় ।

She batshar–i tar janma hay

(d) To express deliberation or possibility :

What am I to do ?

কি করি ?

Ki kari ?

What can be done ? L . 82

কি করা যায় ? (?)

Ki kara jay ? (?)

(e)   In quoting authors or other people **:**

Jesus says...	He says···
যীশু বলেন···	সে বলে/তিনি বলেন...
Jishu balen···	She bale/tini balen···

(f)   A simple present followed by না *na* shows a present negative. If followed by নাই/নি *nai/ni*, it represents the negative of the simple past, the past, perfect or the present perfect :

He doesn't come here.	He/she didn't come here.
সে এখানে আসে না ।	সে এখানে আসে নাই/নি ।
She ekh*a*ne ashe n*a*.	She ekh*a*ne *a*she n*a*i/n*i*.

Lesson 26

TENSE :   PRESENT PERFECT

করছি karchhi	করছ karchha	করছে karchhe
করেছি karechhi	করেছ karechha	করেছে karechhe

(a)   To describe a finished action the results of which continue in the present.

That's what I've come to tell you.

তোমাকে তাই/এ কথা বলতে আসছি/এসেছি ।

Tom*a*ke t*a*i/e kath*a* balte ashchhi/eshechhi.

(b)   OFTEN where English uses the simple past.

I came here yesterday.

আমি কাল এখানে আসছি/এসেছি ।

*A*mi k*a*l ekh*a*ne *a*shchhi/eshechhi.

Mangoes have come out in the bazar.	[did not
বাজারে আম উঠছে/উঠেছে ।	[উঠ নাই/নি
B*a*z*a*re *a*m u*th*chhe/u*th*echhe.	[u*th*e n*a*i/ni

Only 40 boys came to school.

মাত্র ৪০/চল্লিশ জন ছাত্র স্কুলে আসছে/এসেছে ৮

Matra challish jan chhatra skule ashchhe/eshechhe.

He swept my room this morning.

সে সকালে আমার কামরায় ঝাড়ু দিছে/দিয়েছে ।

She shakale amar kamray jharu dichhe/diyechhe.

   (c) OFTEN where English uses AM, IS, ARE with an adjective or past participle.

The door is closed.

দরজা বন্ধ হইছে/হয়েছে

Darja bandha haichhe/hayechhe.

The work is done.

কাজ শেষ হইছে/হয়েছে ।

Kaj shesh haichhe/hayechhe.

I made a mistake.

ভুল হইছে/হয়েছে ।

Bhul haichhe/hayechhe.

A mistake was made.

I didn't make a mistake.

ভুল হয় নাই/নি ।

Bhul hay nai/ni. (Neg.)

Lesson 27

TENSE : SIMPLE FUTURE

করব karba   করবে karbe   করবে karbe.

   (a) To express action that will take place after a lapse of time.

I shall meet him/her tomorrow.

কাল তার সঙ্গে আমার দেখা হবে ।

Kal tar shange amar dekha habe.

I won't give him/her anything.

আমি তাকে কিছু দিব না ।

Ami take kichhu diba na.

He/she will go home tomorrow.

সে কাল বাড়ী যাবে ।

She kal baree jabe.

সে/ও

she/o

They will come by the 5 o'clock train.

তারা/ওরা পাঁচটার গাড়ীতে আসবে ।

T*a*ra/ora p*a*nch*t*ar g*a*r eete *a*shbe.

(b) Sometimes used as an English conditional.

If a tiger came, I would run away.

বাঘ যদি আসত, আমি পলাইয়া যাইতাম   [আসলে]

B*a*gh jadi *a*shta, *a*mi pal*a*iy*a* jait*a*m.   [*a*shle]

(c) In the 3rd person honorific form to express a polite request — a future imperative.

If you see him, tell him this.

তার সঙ্গে দেখা হলে, তাকে এ কথা বলবেন ।

*T*ar shange dekh*a* hale, t*a*ke e kath*a* balben.

(d) With a following imperative.

Come AND have some tea.

চা খাবেন, আসুন ।

Ch*a* kh*a*ben, *a*shun.

SEE lesson 89 for the future continuous tense.

Lesson 28

PRESENT IMPERATIVE

লেখ lekha ; লেখেন lekhen ; লেখুন lekhun ; লেখুক lekhuk

(a) To denote a wish or command to be complied with at once.

Go, come.	Listen.	say (it) ; I'll see (if you know).
যাও/আস/এস ।	শুন ।	বল দেখি ।
j*a*o *a*sha/esha.	Shuna.	Bala dekhi.

People say.   what do they say?   let them say.

লোকে বলে।   কি বলে?   বলুক।

Loke bale.   ki bale?   baluk.

Say right now what you have to say.

আপনার যা বলবার তা এখনই বলুন। (তোমার...বল।)

Apnar ja balbar ta ekhan-i balun. (tomar...balo.)

(b) না na added to the present imperative has the force of won't you···? Do···

Do tell me.   Do sit down.

বল না।   বস না।

Bala na.   Basha na.

(c) না na before উক uk or উন un makes it negative.

May it not be so!   God forbid!

এমন না হোক/হউক!   ঈশ্বর না করুন।

Eman na hok/hauk!   Eeshshar na karun!

(d) The negative of the first and third person of the present imperative may be expressed by putting যেন না jena na before the present simple.

May I never do such a thing.

এমন কাজ (আমি) যেন কখনও না করি।

Eman kaj (ami) jena kakhano na kari.

Don't let him come today.

সে যেন আজ না আসে। তিনি...আসেন।

She jena aj na ashe. Tini...ashen.

Lesson 29

TENSE : FUTURE IMPERATIVE

লেখবে lekhbe.

(a) To denote a wish or command to be complied with at some future time.

It won't do if you come today, come tomorrow.
আজ আসলে হবে না, কাল আসবে/আসবেন ।
Aj ashle habe na, kal ashbe/ashben.

If you see him/her, tell him/her this.
তার সঙ্গে দেখা হলে, এ কথা বলবে/বলবেন ।
Tar shange dekha hale, e katha balbe/balben.

  (b) If na না is added, it becomes a prohibition.

Don't tell him/her anything.
তাকে কিছু বলবে/বলবেন না ।
Take kichhu balbe/balben na.

Don't hit him/her.
তাকে/ওকে মারবে না ।
Take/oke marbe na.

Don't buy that
তা কিনবে না ।
Ta kinbe na.

Lesson 30

THE ACCUSATIVE WITH CAUSATIVES

  With causative verbs two accusatives/objectives are some—
times used.

  NOTE ON CAUSATIVE VERBS : দেখা dekha, দেখান
dekhan * ;

  See—show ; eat—feed , learn—teach , do—make...do , sit—
set ; rise—raise etc.

He/she showed me the boy.
সে আমাকে/আমারে ছেলে [টি]কে দেখাইল ।
She amake/amare chhele(ti)ke dekhaila.

  * There are very many : rub, shake, move, raise, make,
bear, stop, mix, explain, inform, ring, join, increase, graze,
sink...

I'll make you (do the) work.

তোমা দিয়া কাজ করাইব/করাব ।

   Toma diya kaj karaibo/karabo.

Inform the police...

পুলিশকে ...জানাও ।

   Pulishke...janao.

I read him a story.

তাকে একটি গল্প পড়িয়া/
পড়ে শুনালাম ।

Take ekti galpa
pariya/pare
shunalam.

He made me listen to the song.

সে আমাকে গান শুনাল ।

She amake gan shunala.

She/he explained the
sum to me.

সে আমাকে অঙ্ক বুঝাল ।

She amake anka
bujhala.

Lesson 31

DEFINITIVE PARTICLES

(May be deferred)

In English when a noun is in the plural it is expressed by adding certain suffixes, whereas in Bengali (with regard to inanimate nouns) the plural is generally understood and certain suffixes are added to express the singular.

The tree is in the garden.

বাগানে গাছ[টি] আছে ।

Bagane gachh[ti] achhe.

Your garden is very beautiful.

তোমার/আপনার বাগান[টি] খুব
সুন্দর ।

Tomar/apnar bagan[ti] khub
shundar.

Chase that sheep away.

ও/ঐ ভেড়াটা তাড়াইয়া/তাড়িয়ে দেও ।

O/oi bhe*rata ta*r*a*iya/ta*ri*ye
deo.

His/her room is quite small

তার ঘরটি বেশ ছোট ।

T*a*r ghar*ti* besh chho*ta*.

I can't find the shoe/pen...

জুতাটি/কলমটি...খুঁ‌জিয়া/খুঁ‌জে পাইতেছিনা / পাচ্ছিনা ।

Jut*ati*/kalam*ti*...khu*n*jiy*a*/khu*n*je P*a*itechhin*a*/pachhin*a*.

Often these are omitted in conversation.

Lesson 32

DEFINITIVE PARTICLES, টা *ta* CONNOTES CONTEMPT. DISLIKE, BIGNESS, UGLINESS.

(May be deferred.)

Call the coolie.   ......

কুলীটাকে ডাক ।   কুলীকে ডাক ।

Kulee*take dak*.   Kuleeke *dak*.

He is a bad man.

সে একটা দুষ্ট লোক ।

She [ek*ta*] dush*ta* lok.

Kill the mosquito.   ......

মশা[টাকে] মার ।   মশা মার ।

Mash*a*[*ta*ke] m*a*ra.   Masha m*a*ra

The garden is not/no good.

বাগান[টা] ভাল না ।

B*a*gan[*ta*] bh*a*la n*a*.

Lesson 33

DEFINITIVE PARTICLES

(May be deferred)

(These are little used colloquially) খানি kh*a*ni AND খানা kh*a*n*a* have the same distinctions as টি *ti* AND টা *ta*. They are used principally with objects whose surface is the most important part.

There is a knife on the table.

এক খানা ছুরি টেবিলের উপরে [আছে] ।

Ek kh*ana* chhuri *t*ebiler upare [*a*chhe].

He gave me a 5 taka note.

সে আমাকে একখানি পাঁচ টাকা নোট দিল ।

She *a*make ek kh*a*ni p*a*nch t*a*ka no*t* dila.

a chair	the bed (stead)	a large stone
এক খানা চেয়ার	খাট খানা	এক খানা বড় পাথর
ek kh*ana* chey*a*r	kh*at* khana	ek kh*ana* ba*r*a p*a*thar
the house	a few books	a book
ঘর খানা	কয়েক খানা বই	এক খানা বই
ghar kh*ana*	kayek kh*ana* bai	ek kh*ana* bai
two books		
দুইটি/দুইখানা বই		
dui*t*i/dui kh*ana* bai		

Lesson 34

(May be deferred)

ACCUSATIVE CASE WITH THE PARTICLES টি *t*i OR টা *t*a OR খানা kh*ana* etc. When the particles are affixed to nouns in the accusative the inflection কে ke is always used. (Often left out colloquially).

They caught the thief.	Call the coolie.
তারা চোর[টা]কে ধরিয়া/ধরে ফেলল ।	কুলী[টা]কে ডাক ।
T*a*ra chor[*t*a]ke dhariya/dhare fella.	Kulee[*t*a]ke *d*aka.
Kill the mosquito.	Call the boy/girl...
মশা[টা] মার ।	ছেলে[টা]কে/মেয়ে[টা]কে ডাকিয়া/ ডেকে আন ।
Mash*a*[*t*a] m*a*ra.	Chhele[*t*a]ke/meye[*t*a]ke *d*akiya/*d*eke *a*na.

Kill the mad dog.

পাগলা কুকুরটা   মারিয়া/মেরে ফেল ।

Pagla kukurta   mariya/mere fela.

Lesson 35

NOMINATIVE APPOSITIVE

When an article is represented as being full of or essentially constituted of a thing, we find instead of the English genitive a nominative appositional construction. The distinction between this appositive nominative and the genitive of material must be carefully noted. Lesson 39 q. v.

a jar of water
এক কলসী জল
ek kalshee jal

a box of books
এক বাক্স বই
ek baksha bai

a tin of oil
এক টিন তৈল/তেল
ek tin toil/tel

three cups of tea
তিন কাপ/পেয়ালা চা
tin kap/peyala cha

I want a glass of water/milk······
এক গ্লাস জল/দুধ······চাই
ek glass jal/dudh……chai

two bottles of ink
দুই দোয়াত কালি
dui doyat kali

a bucket of water
এক বালতি জল
ek balti jal

a spoonful of sugar
এক চামচ চিনি
ek chamach chini

a sack of grass
এক বস্তা ঘাস
ek basta ghash

WEIGHTS and MEASURES are formed this way.

a seer of milk

এক সের দুধ

ek sher dudh

a maund of rice

এক মণ চাউল

ek man chaul

six yards of cloth.

ছয় গজ কাপড়

chhay gaj kapar

a seer/2 lbs of sugar

এক সের চিনি

ek sher chini

Lesson 36

GENITIVE—often used where English uses IN.

a lot of houses in that town

সে শহরের অনেক ঘর

she shaharer anek ghar

the boys/girls in/of this school

এই স্কুলের ছেলেরা/মেয়েরা

ei skuler chhelera/meyera

a beggar in the street/road

রাস্তার ভিক্ষুক

rastar bhikkhuk

NOTE : There is a GENITIVE/ACCUSATIVE of Compulsion or Duty. It is treated in Lesson 84 under INFINITIVE : Compulsion or Duty—have to/must. The GENITIVE or the ACCUSATIVE/OBJECTIVE case may be used.

I must go now.

আমার এখন যাইতে/যেতে/ হয় ।

Amar ekhan jaite/jete/ hay.

Lesson 37

GENITIVE of purpose—(or use)

Used where English uses a NOUN as a modifier.

milk bucket

দুধের বালতি

dudher balti

walking stick

বেড়াইবার লাঠি

beraibar lathi

playing field

খেলার মাঠ

khelar math

writing ink	eating/dining room	rice field
লেখবার কালি	খাবার ঘর	ধানের ক্ষেত
lekhbar kali	khabar ghar	dhaner khhet

lamp oil	luggage/baggage cart/ train	letter/writing paper
বাতির তেল/তৈল	মালের গাড়ী [মাল	চিঠির কাগজ
batir tel/toil	maler garee [mal	chithir kagaj

coal mine	cotton/cloth mill	invitation to tea
কয়লার খনি	কাপড়ের কল	চা'র নিমন্ত্রণ
kaylar khani	kaparer kal	cha'r nimantran

drinking water	letter box
খাবার জল	চিঠির বাক্স
khabar jal	chithir baksha

Lesson 38

GENITIVE OF DESCRIPTION

Where English uses a noun as an adjective, very often Bengali/Bangla employs the **genitive, possessive case.**

flower garden	village watchman	idle words
ফুলের বাগান	গ্রামের চৌকিদার	কথার কথা
fuler bagan	gramer choukidar	kathar katha

examination day	white of the egg	by the riverside
পরীক্ষার দিন	ডিমের সাদা অংশ	নদীর ধারে
pareekkhar din	dimer shada angsha	nadeer dhare

well water	5 o'clock train	floor of the room
কুয়ার জল	পাঁচটার গাড়ী	ঘরের মেঝ
kuyar jal	panchtar garee	gharer mej

book shop	stomach/tooth ache	eyelid
বইয়ের দোকান	পেটের/দাঁতের ব্যথা	চোখের পাতা
baiyer dok*a*n	pe*t*er/d*a*nter beth*a*	chokher p*a*ta
street corner	pump water	
রাস্তার কোণ(া)	কলের জল/পানি	
r*a*st*a*r kon(*a*)	k*a*ler jal/p*a*ni	

Lesson 39

GENITIVE OF MATERIAL

iron pipe	gold watch	lemon juice	cardboard box
লোহার পাইপ	সোনার ঘড়ি	লেবুর রস	কাগজের বাক্স
loh*a*r p*a*ip	shon*a*r gha*r*i	lebur rash	k*a*gajer b*a*ksha
ink spot	silver spoon	mud house	tin
কালির দাগ	রূপার চামচ	মাটির ঘর	টিনের
k*a*lir d*a*g	roop*a*r ch*a*mach	m*a*tir ghar	*t*iner
bamboo matting		wooden box/chair...	
বাঁশের বেড়া		কাঠের বাক্স/চেয়ার...	
b*a*nsher be*r*a		k*a*th*e*r b*a*ksha/chey*a*r...	

Lesson 40

GENITIVE OF MEASUREMENT (Including Gen. of Time and Gen. of Price/Cost).

a day's journey	a month's vacation	two weeks' work
এক দিনের পথ	এক মাসের ছুটি	দুই সপ্তাহের কাজ
ek diner path	ek m*a*sher chhu*t*i	dui shapt*a*her k*a*j
five–year old boy	a stone's throw away	a 4-hour trip
পাঁচ বৎসরের ছেলে	এক ঢিলের পথ	চার ঘন্টার রাস্তা
p*a*nch batsharer chhele	ek *dh*iler path	ch*a*r ghan*t*ar r*a*st*a*

a man/woman of 80
আশি বৎসরের বুড়া/বুড়ি
ashi batsharer bura/buri

a 40-taka sari
চল্লিশ টাকার শাড়ী
chalish takar sharee.

2 takas' worth of mangoes
দুই টাকার আম
dui takar am

SEE also : Locative of Price lesson 67.
L. 41—60 postpopitions with GEN.

Lesson 41

✸–GENITIVE with মধ্যে maddhe—among, between, within.

Who is in the house ? within 2 days   among you
ঘরের মধ্যে কে ?   দুই দিনের মধ্যে   তোমাদের মধ্যে
gharer maddhe ke ? dui diner maddhe tomader maddhe

within an hour   within 20 miles
এক ঘন্টার মধ্যে   কুড়ি মাইলের মধ্যে
ek ghantar maddhe kuri mailer maddhe

between 2 words   within a minute   among yourselves
শব্দ দুইটির মধ্যে   এক মিনিটের মধ্যে   তোমাদের মধ্যে
shabda duitir maddhe ek miniter maddhe   tomader maddhe
mark to point out Postpositions in the
Vocabulary section.

Lesson 42

— GENITIVE with পাছে pachhe/পিছনে pichhane—behind, in back of.

behind the wall   behind me/the tree/school
দেওয়ালের পাছে   আমার/গাছের/স্কুলের পাছে
deoyaler pachhe   amar/gachher/skuler pachhe

NOTE : পাছে pachhe is also (1) an adverb, meaning *behind*
and (2) a conjunction meaning *lest*, so that...not.

Lesson 43

—GENITIVE with ভিতরে bhitare—*in, inside of, into*

There is no one in the room.
ঘরের ভিতরে কেহ নাই/নেই ।
Gharer bhitare keha n*a*i/nei.

within the house/indoors
বাড়ীর ভিতরে
b*a*reer bhitare

within a week
এক সপ্তাহের ভিতরে/মধ্যে
ek shapt*a*her bhitare/maddhe

Go into the room.
ঘরের ভিতরে যাও ।
Gharer bhitare j*a*o.

in the mind
মনের ভিতরে
maner bhitare

Adj. ভিতর দিক্—*the inner side*

Lesson 44

— GENITIVE with সঙ্গে shange ; সাথে sh*a*the—*with*

He/she will go with me.
সে আমার সঙ্গে যাবে ।
She *a*m*a*r shange j*a*be.

Meet me at 8 in the morning.
আমার সঙ্গে সকাল আটটায় দেখা করবে ।
*A*m*a*r shange shakal *a*tt*a*y dekh*a* karbe.

Henry went home with his father.
হেনরী তার বাবার সঙ্গে বাড়ী[তে] গেছে/গিয়েছে ।
Henree t*a*r b*a*b*a*r shange b*a*ree(te) gechhe/giyechhe.

John comes here with him/her.
জন তার সঙ্গে এখানে আসে ।
Jan t*a*r shange ekh*a*ne *a*she.

Lesson 45

— GENITIVE with বিরুদ্ধে biruddhe—*against.*

I shall not go there against the wishes of my parents.
[আমি] আমার বাপ-মায়ের ইচ্ছার বিরুদ্ধে সেখানে যাব না ।
[*A*mi] *a*m*a*r b*a*p-m*a*yer ichchh*a*r biruddhe sekh*a*ne j*a*ba n*a*.

I have no complaint against him/her.

তার বিরুদ্ধে আমার কোন নালিশ নাই/নেই ।

T*a*r biruddhe *a*m*a*r kona n*a*lish n*a*i/nei.

He/she speaks/talks against me.

সে আমার বিরুদ্ধে কথা বলে/কয় ।

She *a*m*a*r biruddhe kath*a* bale/kay.

Lesson 46

— GENITIVE with কাছে k*a*chhe ; নিকটে nik*a*t*e,*—near, by, to,

Sit by me.

আমার কাছে বস ।

*A*m*a*r k*a*chhe basha.

Come to me.

আমার নিকট আস/এস ।

*A*m*a*r nik*a*t *a*sha/ esho.

Go to him/her.

তার কাছে যাও ।

T*a*r k*a*chhe j*a*o.

I'm going to the doctor.

আমি ডাক্তারের কাছে যাব ।

*A*mi *d*akt*a*rer k*a*chhe j*a*bo.

near the field/river/house/bazar/school...

মাঠের/নদীর/বাজারের/স্কুলের...কাছে

m*a*th*e*r/nodeer/b*a*j*a*rer/skul*e*r...k*a*chhe

I got the book from Badal.

বাদলের কাছে বই[খানা] পাইছি/পেয়েছি ।

B*a*daler k*a*chhe boi[kh*a*n*a*] p*a*ichhi/peyechhi.

I'll get (he owes me) taka 10 from him.

তার কাছে দশ[টি] টাকা পাব ।

T*a*r k*a*chhe dash(*t*i) *t*ak*a* p*a*ba.

I have no money.

আমার কাছে টাকা নাই/নেই ।

*A*m*a*r k*a*chhe *t*ak*a* n*a*i/nei.

Lesson 47

— GENITIVE with নীচে neeche—under, below, beneath.

There is a frog under the table.   He is below me in the class.

টেবিলের নীচে একটি ব্যাঙ আছে ।   ক্লাসে সে আমার নীচে [থাকে] ।

Tebiler neeche ekti beng achhe.   Klashe she amar necche
                                        (thake).

There are ten men under the tree.

গাছের নীচে দশটি লোক আছে ।

Gachher neeche dash(ti) lok achhe.

Lesson 48

— GENITIVE with বাইরে baire —out, outside of, out of.

He/she is outside of the house/out of doors.

সে ঘরের বাইরে [আছে] ।

She gharer baire (achhe).

The children play outside of the school.

ছেলেমেয়েরা স্কুলের বাইরে খেলে ।

Chhelemeyera skuler baire khele.

Put it outside of the house.   That's beyond his work (duty).

ঘরের বাইরে রাখ ।   সেটা তার কাজের বাইরে ।

Gharer baire rakha.   Sheta tar kajer baire [ ].

Lesson 49

— GENITIVE with চারিদিকে charidike—(a) round, on four sides.

They stood around me.

তারা আমার চারিদিকে দাঁড়াইল/দাঁড়াল ।

Tara amar charidike danraila/danrala.

Water is all around an island.

দ্বীপের চারিদিকে জল থাকে ।

Ddeeper charidike jal thake.

I looked around me, but found no one.

আমার চারিদিকে তাকাইয়া/তাকিয়ে কাকেও দেখলাম না ।

[ ] Amar charidike takaiya/takiye kakeo dekhlam na.

They ran round the school.

তারা স্কুলের চারিদিকে দৌড়াইয়া আসল/দৌড়িয়ে এল ।

Tara skuler charidike dauraiya ashla/dauriye ela.

Lesson 50

GENITIVE with সামনে shamne—in front of [before ; place]

in front of the door/house/school/...

দরজার/ঘরের/স্কুলের/...সামনে

darjar/gharer/skuler/...shamne

Ask pardon in front of everyone.

সকলের সামনে   /মাফ চাও ।

Shakaler shamne   /maph chao.

I appeared before the judge.

আমি জজের [বিচারকের] সামনে উপস্থিত হইলাম/হলাম ।

[Ami] jajer [bicharoker] shamne upasthit hailam/halam.

Lesson 51

— GENITIVE with মত mata—like.

like today/God/honey/a son/a baby...

আজকের/ঈশ্বরের/ মধুর/ছেলের/শিশুর...মত

ajker/Eessharer/madhur/chheler/shishur...mata

a man after my own heart	He/she looks like you.
আমার মনের মত মানুষ	দেখতে সে তোমার মত [ ] .
*a*m*a*r maner mata m*a*nush	Dekhte she tom*a*r mata [ ].

Lesson 52

— GENITIVE with বদলে badale—instead of, in place of.

I came instead of him/her.	He/she will work instead of me.
তার বদলে [আমি] আসলাম/এলাম ।	সে আমার বদলে কাজ করবে ।
T*a*r badale [*a*mi] *a*shl*a*m/el*a*m.	She *a*m*a*r badale k*a*j karbe.
Work instead of playing.	I took tea instead of rice.
খেলার বদলে কাজ কর ।	ভাতের বদলে চা খাইছি/খেয়েছি ।
khel*a*r badale k*a*j kara.	Bh*a*ter badale [*a*mi] ch*a* khaichhi/kheyechhi,

Lesson 53

— GENITIVE with পরে, পর pare, par—after (time)

Come after 3 o'clock.	after that	after this
তিনটার পরে আস/এস ।	তার পর	এর পরে
Tin*t*ar pare *a*sha/esha.	t*a*r par	er pare

Go home after you do the work/after working.

কাজের পরে বাড়ী যাবে ।

K*a*jer pare b*a*ree j*a*be.

Who came after you ?

তোমার পরে কে আসছে/এসেছে ?

Tom*a*r pare ke *a*shchhe/eshechhe ?

after school/eating/tiffin/resting/......

স্কুলের/খাওয়ার/টিফিনের/বিশ্রামের/...পরে

skuler/kh*a*oy*a*r/*t*ifiner/bisr*a*mer/...pare

Lesson 54

— GENITIVE with আগে *age*—before (time)

Come before 3 o'clock.

তিনটার আগে আস/এস ।

Tint*a*r *a*ge *a*sha/esha.

Come before school.

স্কুলের আগে আস/এস ।

Skuler *a*ge *a*sha/esha.

Who will come before you ?

তোমার আগে কে আসবে ?

Tom*a*r *a*ge ke *a*shbe ?

Bathe before going.

যাওয়ার আগে স্নান করবে ।

J*a*oy*a*r *a*ge sn*a*n karbe.

I'll come before he/she goes.

তার যা.ওয়ার/যাবার আগে [আমি] আসব ।

T*a*r j*a*oy*a*r/j*a*b*a*r *a*ge [*a*mi] *a*shba.

before this

এর আগে

er *a*ge

Lesson ·55

— GENITIVE with জন্য janna—for, on behalf of, because of.

I could not come earlier because of rain.

বৃষ্টির জন্য আগে আসতে পারি নাই/নি ।

Brish*t*ir janna *a*ge *a*shte p*a*ri n*a*i/ni.

I'll buy milk for the baby.

শিশুর জন্য দুধ কিনব ।

Shishur janna dudh kinba.

for taka 10

দশ টাকার জন্য ।

dash t*a*k*a*r janna.

For the sake of peace he/she kept quiet.

শান্তির জন্য সে চুপ করিয়া/করে রইল/রল ।

Sh*a*ntir janna she chup kariy*a*/kare raila/rala.

for myself/himself

আমার/তার নিজের জন্য

*a*m*a*r/t*a*r nijer janna

for this reason/therefore

এই জন্য

ei janna

Lesson 56

GENITIVE with চেয়ে, cheye — than — comparison.

He/she is taller than I am/than me.
সে আমার চেয়ে লম্বা ।
She amar cheye lamba.

bigger than this
এর চেয়ে বড়
er cheye ba a

He/she is younger than I,
সে আমার চেয়ে ছোট ।
She amar cheye chhota.

less than 5 taka
পাঁচ টাকার চেয়ে কম
panch takar cheye kam

This is the tallest tree.
এই গাছ[টা] সব চেয়ে লম্বা/ উচু ।
Ei gachh[ta] shab cheye lamba/uchu.

Lesson 57

— GENITIVE with উপরে upare ; উপর upar — on, upon, above, over.

He/she is above me in class.
ক্লাসে সে আমার উপরে [ ] ।
Klashe she amar upare [ ].

on the box/hill/ground/desk/
road (on the surface)
বাক্সের/পাহাড়ের/মাটির/ডেক্সের/রাস্তার
উপর
baksher/paharer/matir/desker/
rastar upar

The clock is on the wall.
ঘড়িটা দেওয়ালের উপর [ ] ।
Ghari[ta] deoyaler upar [ ].

over my head
আমার মাথার উপরে
amar mathar upare

Are you angry with me ?
[তুমি] আমার উপরে রাগ কর ?
[Tumi] amar upare rag kara ?

He is over six years old.
তার বয়স ছয় বৎসরের উপর ।
Tar bayash chhay batsharer upar.

Lesson 58

— GENITIVE with বিষয়ে bishaye—about, concerning.

I know nothing about him/her.　　Don't worry about me.

তার বিষয়ে আমি কিছু জানি না ।　　আমার বিষয়ে চিন্তা করিও না ।

Tar bishaye ami kichhu jani na.　　Amar bishaye chinta kario na.

He/she wants to know about the job/work.

সে কাজের বিষয়ে কিছু জানতে চায় ।

She kajer bishaye kichhu jante chay.

about this/that (or in this matter...)

এ/সে বিষয়ে

e/she bishaye

Lesson 59

— GENITIVE with দিকে dike—toward(s), in the direction of.

Look at/toward me.　　He is for me/on my side.

আমার দিকে চাও/তাকাও ।　　সে আমার দিকে ।

Amar dike chao/takao.　　She amar dike.

On all sides.　　In which direction ?　　to the left/right

সকল দিকে ।　　কোন্ দিকে ?　　বাঁ/ডান দিকে

Shakal dike.　　kon dike ?　　ban/dan dike

this/that way

এই/সে দিকে

ei/she dike

Lesson 60

— GENITIVE with কারণে karane—because of.

because of the rain　　because of illness

বৃষ্টির কারণে　　অসুখের কারণে/জন্য

brishtir karane　　ashukher karane/janna

for this/that reason

এই/সেই কারণে

ei/shei karane

Lesson 61 a.

POSTPOSITION পর্যন্ত Parjanta—till, until, upto [not declined]

upto/till the end/head/ten o'clock/tomorrow...

শেষ/মাথা/দশটা/কাল...পর্যন্ত

shesh/matha/dashta/kal...parjanta

Lesson 61 b.

বিনা bina—without

without/beside you/him/religion...(NOMINATIVE)

তুমি/সে/ধর্ম...বিনা

tumi/she/dharma...bina

without fault/reason/fees/money (free)/need/order...

বিনা দোষে/কারণে/বেতনে/পয়সায়/কাজে/হুকুমে...

bina doshe/karane/betane/payshay/kaje/hukume...

I can't do without you.

তুমি বিনা চলতে পারিনা।

Tumi bina chalte parina.

without permission

বিনা অনুমতিতে

bina anumatite

Lesson 61 c.

GENITIVE পাশে pashe—at the side of, beside

at the side of/beside the river/pond/me/road...

নদীর/পুকুরের/আমার/রাস্তার...পাশে

nadeer/pukurer/amar/rastar...pashe

Lesson 61 d.

GENITIVE তলায় talay—at the foot of.
at the foot of/below the tree/hill...
গাছের/পাহাড়ের...তলায়/তলে
gachher/paharer...talay/tale

Lesson 61 e.

কাছ থেকে—kachh theke—from.
from me/him/her/them... (a person)
আমার/তার/তাদের...কাছ থেকে
amar/tar/tader...kachh–theke

Lesson 61 f.

GENITIVE···ভিতর দিয়া, উপর দিয়া bhitar diya, upar diya—
through, across.
through/across the field/jungle/village...
মাঠের/জঙ্গলের/গ্রামের···ভিতর দিয়া/উপর দিয়া/দিয়ে
mather/jangaler/gramer···bhitar diya/upar diya/diye

Lesson 62

POSTPOSITION—ছাড়া chhara—without, except, besides, but.

without sin/you/an umbrella···	besides this book
পাপ/তুমি/ছাতা... ··ছাড়া	এই বই ছাড়া
pap/tumi/chhata······chhara	ei bai chhara
except tea/water······	except or but me/him–her/them/laugh/eat···
চা/জল···ছাড়া	আমি/সে/তারা/হাসা/খাওয়া···ছাড়া
cha/jal···chhara	ami/she/tara/hasha/khaoya···chhara

There is no one without sin.

পাপ ছাড়া লোক নাই/নেই ।

Pap chhara lok nai/nei.

I have nothing except/but/besides this.

এইটা ছাড়া আমার আর কিছু নাই/নেই ।

Eita chhara amar ar kichhu nai/nei.

No one went except/but/besides me.

আমি ছাড়া আর কেহই যায় নাই/নি ।

Ami chhara ar keha-i jay nai/ni.

The girl does nothing but laugh.

মেয়েটি হাসা ছাড়া কিছুই করে না ।

Meyeti hasha chhara kichhu-i kare na.

Lesson 63

INSTRUMENTAL CASE—দিয়া diya—by means of, by which.

The instrumental case expresses either the agent or the instrument by which an action is effected. In English these are usually expressed by the prepositions—by, with or through.

with a pen/knife/stick/fork/spoon/shoe···

কলম/ছুরি/লাঠি/কাঁটা/চামচ/জুতা···দিয়া/দিয়ে

kalam/chhuri/lathi/kanta/chamach/juta···diya/diye

by boat/cycle/car—train/launch/plane···

নৌকা/সাইকেল/গাড়ি/লঞ্চ/প্লেন ···/দিয়া/দিয়ে

nauka/saikel/gari/lanch/plen···diya/diye

with soap/water/bricks/powder/scissors···

সাবান/জল-পানি/ইট/পাউডার/কাঁচি···দিয়া/দিয়ে ।

shaban/jal-pani/it/paudar/kanchi···diya/diye.

4—

Wipe it with a cloth.

কাপড় দিয়া/দিয়ে মুছিয়া/মুছে দাও ।

Kapar diya/diye muchhiya/muchhe dao.

Dry the ink with a blotter.

ব্লাটিং দিয়া/দিয়ে কালি শুকাও ।

Bloting diya/diye kali shukao.

Sharpen the pencil with a knife.

ছুরি দিয়া/দিয়ে পেন্সিল কাট/কেটো ।

Chhuri diya/diye pensil kata/keto.

I eat with my hand.

আমি হাত দিয়া/দিয়ে খাই ।

Ami hat diya/diye khai.

I talk with my mouth.

মুখ দিয়া কথা বলি ।

Mukh diya katha bali.

LOC.—Through his efforts they won the games.

তার চেষ্টায় ওরা খেলায় জিতল ।

Tar chestay ora khelay jitla.

Lesson 64

ABLATIVE CASE—FROM—থেকে theke, হইতে haite, হতে hate.

This case indicates the person, thing or place from which the subject is removed or obtained.—Milne.

Leaves fell from the tree. (off)

গাছ থেকে পাতা পড়ল ।

Gachh theke pata parla.

I'll go away from here. (this place)

এখান থেকে চলিয়া/চলে যাব । (এই স্থান/যায়গা)

Ekhan theke chaliya/chale jabo.

I have been saved from a terrible misfo tune/danger.

ভয়ানক বিপদ থেকে রক্ষা পাইছি/পেয়েছি ।

Bhayanak bipad theke rakkha paichhi/peyechhi.

Women did not go out of their houses.   (used to)

স্ত্রীলোক বাড়ী থেকে বাইর হইত/হত না ।

Strilok b*a*ree theke b*a*ir haita/hata n*a*.

He/she got out of/down from/off the train···

সে গাড়ি থেকে নামল ।

She ga*r*i theke n*a*mla.

I got 100 taka from him/her.

* তার কাছ থেকে/কাছে থেকে এক শ' টাকা পাইছি/পেয়েছি ।

T*a*r k*a*chh theke/k*a*chhe theke ek sha *taka* p*a*ichhi/peyechhi.

   (In colloquial Bengali থেকে theke is used for হইতে haite—
Milne.) It is also used for চেয়ে cheye, *than* ;

more than that

ওর চেয়ে/থেকে বেশী

o*r* cheye/theke beshee

Lesson 65

THE LOCATIVE CASE—PLACE WHERE, TO/INTO WHICH

   The locative case denotes place or thing where or wherein.
In English this case is recognized by the prepositions *in*, *into*
and *at*–তে te, য় y after 'া, *a* ; ে, e after consonants.

I stayed at home.	To what town did he go ?
আমি বাড়ীতে রইলাম ।	সে কোন্ শহরে গেছে/গিয়েছে ?
*A*mi b*a*rite rail*a*m.	She kon shahare gechhe/giyechhe ?
He/she fell into the river	He/she swept my room. (in···)
সে নদীতে পড়িয়া/পড়ে গেল ।	সে আমার কামরায় ঝাড়ু দিছে/দিয়েছে ।
She nadeete pa*r*iy*a*/	She *a*m*a*r k*a*mr*a*y jh*a*ru dichhe/
pa*r*e gela.	diyechhe.

   * with থেকে theke the Loc.   ending of adverbs is dropped ;
কোথা থেকে ? koth*a* theke ? From where ?...

in the boat/garden/water/school/sky...

নৌকায়/বাগানে/জলে-পানিতে/স্কুলে/আকাশে...

naukay/bagane/jale–panite/skule/akashe...

The book has 50 pages. (L. 70)   Fill the tins with water.

বইটিতে/বইয়ে পঞ্চাশটি পাতা আছে ।   টিনগুলিতে জল ভর ।

Baitite/baiye panchasti pata   Tin gulite jal bhara.
achhe.

He/she hurt his/her eye.

সে তার চোখে আঘাত/ব্যথা পাইছে/পেয়েছে ।

She tar chokhe aghat/betha paichhe/peyechhe.

NOTE :   Compare Lesson 36 and 65.

Lesson 66

LOCATIVE—used for Instrumental Colloquially.

by mail   on foot   by bus/train/cycle···

ডাকে   পায়ে   বাসে/গাড়িতে/সাইকেলে··

dake   paye   base/garite/saikele...

Cut it with your teeth.   I hear with my ears.

দাঁতে কাট ।   আমি কানে শুনি ।

Dante kata.   Ami kane shuni.

You can do it with his help = It can be done...

তার সাহায্যে করা যায় ।

Tar shahajje kara jay.

By this mind and body will stay fit.

তাতে শরীর ও মন ভাল থাকবে ।

Tate shareer o man bhala thakbe.

   Additional LOCATIVE uses :

This is good for nothing.   He agreed to that/it.

এটা কোন কাজে লাগে না ।   তাতে সে রাজি হল !

Eta kona kaje lage na.   Tate she raji hala.

I have no objection to that.
ভাতে আমার আপত্তি নাই/নেই ।
Tate amar apatti nai/nei.

with his permission
তার অনুমতিতে
tar anumatite

I did the work with great
difficulty.
এ কাজ অতি কষ্টে করলাম ।
E kaj ati kashte karlam.

What's the good of this ?
এতে লাভ কি ?
Ete labh ki ?

I went empty–handed.
আমি খালি হাতে গেলাম ।
Ami khali hate gelam.

busy with work
কাজে ব্যস্ত
kaje besta

by God's grace
ঈশ্বরের/খোদার দয়ায়
Eeshsharer/
khodar dayay

Lesson 67

LOCATIVE OF PRICE

How much did it cost to build this house ?
কত টাকায় এ ঘরটি উঠান হইছিল/হয়েছিল ?
Kata takay e gharti uthan haichhila/hayechhila ?

Good meat sells at 20 taka a seer. (2 lbs.)
ভাল মাংস কুড়ি টাকায় পাওয়া যায় ।
Bhala mangsha   kuri   takay paoya jay.

I bought this cloth for 20 taka.
বিশ টাকায় এই কাপড় কিনছি/কিনেছি ।
Bish takay ei kapar kinchhi/kinechhi.

free of charge	for a taka	eggs 2 taka for 4
এম্নে/অমনি	এক টাকায়	ডিম এক হালি দুই টাকা
emne/amni	ek takay	dim ek hali dui taka

Lesson 68

LOCATIVE with certain words—FULL OF, COVERED WITH

full of tigers	covered with dirt	wet with rain
বাঘে ভরা	ময়লায় ঢাকা	বৃষ্টিতে ভিজা
Baghe bhara	maylay *dhaka*	bristite bhija

The school is full of students.

স্কুল ছাত্রে/ছাত্রীতে ভরা [ ] ।

Skul chhatre/chhatreete bhara [ ]. m./f.

The tank/pond/river...is full of water.

পুকুর/নদী...জলে-পানিতে ভরা [ ] ।

Pukur/nadee...jale-panite bhara [ ]. (nodee)

covered with jewels/snow...	wet with sweat
রত্নে/তুষারে...ঢাকা	ঘামে ভিজা
ratne/tushare...*dhaka*	ghame bhija

Lesson 69

LOCATIVE of TIME

in the morning/afternoon/evening...

সকালে/বিকালে/সন্ধ্যায়...

shakale/bikale/shanddhay...

at dawn/noon/10/night/midnight/10 a. m./...

ভোরে/দুপুরে/দশটায়/রাত্রে/দুপুর রাত্রে/সকাল দশটায়...

bhore/dupure/dashtay/ratre/dupur ratre/shakal dashtay

last year/month/week...

গত বৎসর/মাস/সপ্তাহ OR গত বৎসরে/মাসে/সপ্তাহে...

gata batshar/mash/shaptaha OR gata batshare/mashe/shaptahe...

next year...

আগামী বৎসর...   (choice as above.

agamee batshar...   (choice as above.

THESE NON–LOCATIVES ARE LIKE THE ACCUSATIVE OF TIME

I shall stay there a day/a week/a month/a year/...

সেখানে একদিন/এক সপ্তাহ/এক মাস/এক বৎসর...থাক্‌ব ।

Shekh*a*ne ek din/ek shapt*a*ha/ek m*a*sh/ek batshar...th*a*kba.

Lesson 70

LOCATIVE with HAVE, আছে *a*chhe.

"The room has doors" denotes neither ownership nor possession but merely location. It is translated by the locative case of the subject, the nominative case of the object and the proper *tense* of আছে *a*chhe.

The room has doors/chair/space/windows...

ঘরে দরজা/চেয়ার/জায়গা/জানালা...আছে ।

Ghare darj*a*/chey*a*r/j*a*yg*a*/jan*a*l*a*...*a*chhe

This cloth has many holes.

এ কাপড়ে অনেক ছিদ্র আছে ।

E k*a*pa*r*e anek chhidra *a*chhe.

* The river has no water = There is no water in...

নদীতে জল নাই/নেই ।

Nadeete jal n*a*i/nei.

There's no oil in the lamp.

বাতিতে তেল নাই/নেই ।

B*a*tite tel n*a*i/nei.

There is no water in...

Nodeete...

Lesson 71

GERUND in ইবার ib*a*r + কথা, kath*a*—SUPPOSED TO. আছে *a*chhe is often understood. The subject in English becomes genitive and modifies কথা kath*a* in Bengali. The gerund in ইবার ib*a*r is a genitive of purpose modifying কথা kath*a*.

* Similar sentences in L. 18.

I'm supposed to go. [i. e.—There is word of my going.]

আমার যাবার কথা আছে ।

Amar jabar katha *a*chhe.

I was supposed to go/come/eat...

আমার যাবার/আসার/খাইবার–খাবার...কথা ছিল ।

Amar jabar/ashar/khaibar–khabar...katha chhila.

We are to eat at 3 o'clock.

তিনটার সময় আমাদের খাবার কথা [ ] । খাওয়ার কথা ।

Tin*tar* shamay *amader* khabar katha [ ]. kh*a*oyar katha.

You weren't supposed to do this (work).

তোমার এ কাজ করবার কথা ছিল না ।

Tom*ar* e k*a*j karb*ar* kath*a* chhila n*a*.

SEE also L. 80—VERBAL NOUN in GENITIVE.

Lesson 72

NOUN + GERUND IN ইবার ib*ar*—DESCRIPTIVE GENITIVE

When used with a noun or pronoun it becomes a kind of descriptive genitive.

I have somethi॒g to say/do/write...

আমার কিছু বলবার/করবার/লেখবার...আছে ।

*A*m*a*r kichhu balb*ar*/karb*ar*/lekhb*ar*...*a*chhe.

drinking water/play ground/spending money

খাবার জল/খেলবার মাঠ/খরচ করবার টাকা

kh*a*b*ar* jal/khelb*ar* m*ath*/khorach karb*ar* *ta*ka.

There's no need to go there.

সেখানে যাবার দরকার নাই/নেই ।

Shekh*a*ne j*a*b*a*r dark*a*r n*a*i/n*a*i.

He had to do it.

তার এ কাজ করবার দরকার ছিল ।

T*a*r e k*a*j karb*ar* dark*a*r chhila.

I have to go to **Dacca**.

আমার ঢাকা যাবার দরকার ।

*Am*ar *Dhaka* j*a*b*a*r d*a*rk*a*r.

Lesson 73

GERUND IN ইবার ib*a*r + POSTPOSITION/PREPOSITION

after it rained	after the thief fled	before sun up
বৃষ্টি হবার পর	চোর পলাবার পর	সূর্য উঠবার আগে
brish*t*i hab*a*r pa*ı*	chor pal*a*b*a*r par	shoorja u*th*b*a*r *a*ge

worth seeing	not worth seeing	worth living in
দেখবার মত	দেখবার মত না	থাকবার মত
dekhb*a*r mata	dekhb*a*r mata n*a*	th*a*kb*a*r mata

'There's no song worth singing, no gift worth giving.''— Tagore

"গাবার মত হয়নি কোন গান, দিবার মত হয়নি কিছু দান ।"

G*a*b*a*r mata hay ni kona g*a*n, dib*a*r mata hay ni kichhu d*a*n.

while he was dying	before going home
তার মরবার সঙ্গে সঙ্গে/সময়	বাড়ী যাবার আগে
t*a*r marb*a*r shange shange	b*a*ree j*a*b*a*r *a*ge

Lesson 74

GERUND IN ইবার ib*a*r PURPOSE

The form ইবার ib*a*r is employed with জন্য janna [or without it] to denote purpose. It either modifies a noun or is predicated of a noun and takes no subject. It is often used for the Infinitive of Purpose.

I came to look/see.
দেখবার আসছি/এসেছি ।
Dekhbar ashchhi/eshechhi.

I went to buy cloth.
কাপড় কিনবার জন্য গেছি/গিয়েছি ।
Kapar kinbar janna gechhi/
giyechhi.

to see the patient
রোগী দেখবার [জন্য]
rogee dekhbar [janna]

I don't wish to work.
আমার কাজ করবার ইচ্ছা নাই/নেই ।
Amar kaj karbar ichchha nai/nei.

What do you have to say ?
তোমার কি বলবার আছে ?
Tomar ki balbar achhe ?

There is no one to help him.
তার সাহায্য করবার কেহ নাই/নেই ।
Tar shahajja karbar keha nay/nei.

I want a key to open the lock/door.
আমি তালা/দরজা খুলবার চাবি চাই ।
Ami tala/darja khulbar chabi chai.

time to go
যাবার সময়
jabar shamay.

Lesson 75

1. **VERBAL NOUN : NOMINATIVE**—(The verb form found in the dictionary word lists.)

Semi-impersonal constructions are very common in Bengali.   Here the attention is drawn rather to sensing the idea ভাব bhab of the verb'than to its subject. In fact, in indigenous grammars, besides the Active and Passive Voice, there is shown a ভাববাচ্য bhabbachcha, a Sense Voice, in which the action of the verb is itself practically the subject.

I've finished eating.
আমার খাওয়া হইছে/হয়েছে ।
Amar khaoya haichhe/
hayechhe.

I'm not going.
আমার যাওয়া হবে না ।
Amar jaoya habe na.

We will play now.
আমাদের এখন খেলা হবে ।
Amader ekhan khela habe.

They will come here.
তাদের এখানে আসা হবে ।
Tader ekhane asha habe.

Where are you going ?
তোমার কোথায় যাওয়া হইতেছে/হচ্ছে .
Tomar kothay jaoya haitechhe/ hachchhe ?

I didn't lie down last night.
আমার রাত্রে শোয়া হয় নাই/নি ।
Amar ratre shoya hay nai/ni.

Lesson 76

II. VERBAL NOUN

Should, ought to are expressed by the verbal noun, the subject in the genitive case, and উচিত—uchit.

I should go/ought to go.
আমার যাওয়া উচিত ।
Amar jaoya uchit.

I should have gone.
আমার যাওয়া উচিত ছিল ।
Amar jaoya uchit chhila.

You should not write like this.
তোমার এমনে/এভাবে লেখা উচিত না ।

Tomar emne/e bhabe lekha uchit na.

You ought to read this book.

তোমার এ বই পড়া উচিত ।
Tomar e bai para uchit.

I ought not to go
আমার যাওয়া উচিত না ।
Amar jaoya uchit na.

What should I do ?
আমার কি করা উচিত !
Amar ki kara uchit ?

We should love our parents.
আমাদের পিতা-মাতাকে/বাপ-মাকে ভালবাসা উচিত ।
Amader pita-matake/bap- make bhalabasha uchit.

What to do ? What's to be done ?
কি করি ? কি করব ?
or ki kari ? ki karba ?

Lesson 77

III. **VERBAL NOUN—NOMINATIVE CASE**—walking/
to walk

This may be used in place of the English infinitive or the
verbal noun. In the present tense আছে *achhe* is omitted. [ ]

Walking/to walk [is] good.	This is hard to do.
বেড়ান ভাল [ ] ।	এ কাজ করা কঠিন ।
Ber*a*n bh*a*la.	E k*a*j kar*a* ka*th*in.
It is easy to say but hard to do.	Stealing is a sin.
বলা সহজ ; করা কঠিন ।	চুরি করা পাপ ।
Bal*a* shahaj ; kar*a* ka*th*in [ ].	Churi kar*a* p*a*p,

I don't like to fish.

মাছ ধরা আমার ভাল লাগে না ।

M*a*chh dhar*a* *a*m*a*r bh*a*la l*a*ge n*a*.

I have no wish to go there. [see INFIN.]

সেখানে যাওয়া আমার ইচ্ছা নাই/নেই ।

Shekh*a*ne j*a*oy*a* *a*m*a*r ichchh*a* n*a*i/nei.

It is unjust to speak like this.

এ রকম কথা বলা অন্যায় ।

E rakam kath*a* bal*a* ann*a*y.

Lesson 78

IV. **VERBAL NOUN**—খাওয়া kh*a*oy*a*, যাওয়া j*a*oy*a*, etc.—
OBJECTIVE CASE ː eating/to eat ; going/to go, etc.

He didn't think stealing is bad.

সে চুরি করাকে খারাপ মনে করে নাই/নি ।

She churi kar*a*ke kh*a*r*a*p mane kare n*a*i/ni.

Talking to God is called prayer.

ঈশ্বরের কাছে কথা বলাকে প্রার্থনা বলে ।

Eeshsharer kachhe katha balake prarthana bale.

I think it fitting to go there today.

আমি আজ সেখানে যাওয়াকে উপযুক্ত/উচিত মনে করি ।

Ami aj shekhane jaoyake upajukta/uchit mane kari.

I didn't think it good to do that.

আমি সেটা করাকে ভাল মনে করি নাই/নি ।

Ami sheta karake bhala mane kari nai/ni.

Lesson 79

V. VERBAL NOUN—পর্যন্ত parjanta, till—is a postposition which takes the NOMINATIVE CASE. (Some authors say this verbal noun is in the oblique case). Used with the verbal noun in the negative, it expresses *until*. (Literally translated : "up to the time this does *not* happen...") না—na + verbal noun + পর্যন্ত parjanta.

I won't work till I have eaten.

না খাওয়া পর্যন্ত কাজ করব না ।

Na khaoya parjanta kaj karba na.

I don't wind my watch until it stops.

ঘড়ি না থামা পর্যন্ত চাবি দেই/দিই না ।

Ghari na thama parjanta chabi dei/dii na.

Stay here till I come.

আমার না আসা পর্যন্ত এখানে থাক ।

Amar na asha parjanta ekhane thaka.

SEE also the participle in ইয়া iya to translate *until, unless.* L. 108.

Lesson 80

VI. VERBAL NOUN—Expresses MUST, AM SUPPOSED. This verbal noun, in the genitive, modifies a NOUN. The genitive of the verbal noun in ইবা ib*a* is often preferred to this genitive.

There is no need to go there.

সেখানে যাওয়ার দরকার নাই/নেই ।

Shekh*a*ne j*a*oy*a*r dark*a*r n*a*i/nei.

He/she had to do that work.

তার সে কাজ করার দরকার ছিল ।

T*a*r she k*a*j kar*a*r dark*a*r chhila.

I have to go there   (There is need of...)

আমার সেখানে যাওয়ার দরকার ।   [আছে *a*chhe left out]

*A*m*a*r shekh*a*ne j*a*oy*a*r dark*a*r.

I am supposed to go there.

আমার সেখানে যাওয়ার দরকার [আছে] ।

*A*m*a*r shekh*a*nə j*a*oy*a*r dark*a*r [*a*chhe].

time to go.

যাওয়ার সময়

j*a*oy*a*r sham*a*y

I was supposed to go there.

আমার সেখানে যাওয়ার কথা ছিল ।

*A*m*a*r shekh*a*ne j*a*oy*a*r kath*a* chhila.

I came to eat.

খাওয়ার/খাবার জন্য আসলাম ।

kh*a*oy*a*r/kh*a*b*a*r jann*a* *a*shl*a*m.

Also : before/after/for...going

Ram had better go than stay.

যাওয়ার আগে/পরে/জন্য...

j*a*oy*a*r *a*ge/pare/jann*a*...

রাম থাকার চেয়ে যাওয়া ভাল ।

R*a*m th*a*k*a*r cheye j*a*oy*a* bh*a*la.

Lesson 81

VII VERBAL NOUN—in the LOCATIVE —shows CAUSE. The subject of the verbal noun is in the nominative.

He was angry with me FOR SAYING so/that.

এ কথা বলায় সে আমার উপর রাগ করেছে/করছে ।

E kath*a* bal*a*y she *a*m*a*r upar r*a*g karechhe/karchhe.

You have nothing to do about our going or not going.

আমাদের যাওয়া ও না যাওয়ায় তোমার কিছু আসে যায় না ।

Amader jaoya o na jaoyay tomar kichhu ashe jay na.

Due to my father's illness I couldn't go out.

আমার বাবার অসুখ হওয়ায় আমি বাইর হতে পারি নাই/নি ।

Amar babar ashukh haoyay ami bair hate pari nai/ni.

The road was muddy on account of the rain.

বৃষ্টি হওয়াতে রাস্তা কাদা হইয়া/হয়ে গেল ।

Brisṭi hoayate rasta kada haiya/haye gela.

since the sky was clear...	since it was dark...
আকাশের অবস্থা ভাল থাকাতে...	অন্ধকার হওয়াতে...
akasher abastha bhala thakate...	*andhakar haoyate...*

Lesson 82

VIII VERBAL NOUN—হওয়া *haoya* ; যাওয়া *jaoya* etc.—
NOMINATIVE—PASSIVE VOICE.

Though the English passive voice is only awkwardly translated into Bangla/Bengali, there is in Bengali a very common
form of the passive voice.

In the bazar books/fish/vegetables...can be had/are available.

বাজারে বই/মাছ/সব্জী...পাওয়া যায় ।

Bajare bai /machh/shabjee...paoya jay.

That can't be done.	It can easily be seen.
তা করা যায়/যাবে না ।	তা সহজে দেখা যায় ।
Ta kara jay/jabe na.	*Ta shahaje dekha jay.*

These pictures can't be given away.

এই ছবি দেওয়া যায় না।

Ei chhabi deoya jay na.

I can't hear you.

তোমার কথা শুনা যায় না।

Tomar katha shuna jay na.

He isn't/his words aren't easily understood.

তার কথা সহজে বুঝা যায় না।

Tar katha shahaje bujha jay na.

This pen is impossible.

এই কলমে লেখা যায় না।

Ei kalame lekha jay na.

You can go by this path/road/way.

এই পথ দিয়া [পথে]/রাস্তায় যাওয়া যায়।

Ei path dia [pathe]/rastay jaoya jay.

It can be

It will be possible to go tomorrow.

কাল যাওয়া যাবে।

Kal jaoya jabe.

All this is known.

এই সব জানা আছে।

Ei shab jana achhe.

All has been said.

সব বলা হইছে/হয়েছে।

Shab bala haichhe/hayechhe.

The work is being done.

কাজটা করা হইতেছে/হচ্ছে।

Kajta kara haitechhe/hachchhe.

God can't be seen.

ঈশ্বরকে দেখা যায় না।

Eeshsharerke dekha jay na

You can't go in rain like this.

এরকম বৃষ্টিতে যাওয়া যায় না।

E rakam bristite jaoya jay na.

The matter has long been known.

বিষয়টি অনেক দিন জানা গেছে/গিয়েছে।

Bishayti anek din jana gechhe/giyechhe.

He has been killed/he died.

সে মারা গেল।

She mara gela.

you'll be killed

মারা পড়বে

mara parbe

The boy has been punished.

ছেলেকে শাস্তি দেওয়া হইছে/হয়েছে ।

Chheleke shasti deoya haichhe/
hayechhe.

I have been beaten soundly.

আমাকে খুব মারা হইছে/হয়েছে ।

Amake khub mara haichhe/
hayechhe.

The boy/girl will be admitted to our school.

ছেলেকে/মেয়েকে আমাদের স্কুলে ভর্তি করা হবে ।

Chheleke/meyeke amader skule bharti kara habe.

The flower/fruit has been picked.

ফুল তোলা হইছে/হয়েছে ।   ফল পাড়া হইছে/হয়েছে ।

Ful tola haichhe/hayechhe.   Fal para haichhe/hayechhe.

He has been written to.

তাকে লেখা হইছে/হয়েছে ।

Take lekha haichhe/hayechhe.

The work is finished/done.

কাজ [শেষ] করা হইছে/হয়েছে ।

Kaj [shesh] kara haichhe/
hayechhe.

He's/she's been told.

তাকে বলা হইছে/হয়েছে ।

Take bala haichhe/hayechhe.

The lamp has been lit.

বাতি জ্বালান হইছে/হয়েছে ।

Bati jjalana haichhe/hayechhe.

(One) can't go by this road.

এই রাস্তা দিয়া/দিয়ে যাওয়া যায় না ।

Ei rasta diya/diye, jaoya
jay na.

John has been fined.

জনকে জরিমানা করা হইছে/হয়েছে ।

Janke jarimana kara haichhe/
hayechhe.

The sum has been worked out/done.

অংক কষা হইছে/হয়েছে ।

Anka kasha haichhe/hayechhe.

The letter has been written.

চিঠি লেখা হইছে/হয়েছে ।

Chithi lekha haichhe/hayechhe.

Many things were said.

অনেক কথা বলা হইছে/হয়েছে ।

Anek katha bala haichhe/
hayechhe.

He didn't go.

তার যাওয়া হল না ।

Tar jaoya hala na.

English is taught here.

এখানে ইংরাজী শিখান হয় ।

Ekhane Ingrajee shikhan hay.

He can't be found.

তাকে পাওয়া যায় না ।

Take paoya jay na.

6—

I won't be able to go.

আমার যাওয়া হবে না ।

*A*ma*r* jaoya habe n*a*.

***General Note* :** "If the English sentence is passive, it should be restated as an active voice sentence in Bengali." This is especially true in colloquial Bengali.

***NOTE* :**—Two other ways of expressing a passive idea :—
(i) with a causative verb—ভরা bhar*a*, fill ; ভরান bhar*a*n, cause to be filled, (2) an adjective + করা kar*a*, do/make or হওয়া haoy*a*, be/become—ভরতি করা bharti kar*a*, admit (to school) ; ভরতি হওয়া bharti haoy*a*, be admitted ; নষ্ট করা nash*t*a kar*a*, spoil/destroy ; নষ্ট হওয়া nash*t*a haoy*a*, be spoiled/ destroyed etc.

Lesson 83

INFINITIVE—I—Compulsion or Duty—HAVE TO, MUST. GEN./ACC./LOC. + INFINITIVE

We have to go there.

আমাদের সেখানে যাইতে/ যেতে হবে ।

*A*ma*d*er shekh*a*ne j*a*ite/ jete habe.

You must keep quiet.

তোমার/তোমাদের চুপ করতে হয়/ হবে ।

Tom*a*r/tom*a*der chup karte hay/habe.

I must go right now.

আমার এখনই সেখানে যাইতে/যেতে/ যাতে হবে ।

*A*ma*r* ekhani shekh*a*ne j*a*ite/ jete/j*a*te habe.

To see is to believe.

দেখলেই বিশ্বাস করতে হয় ।

Dekhle—i bishsh*a*sh karte hay.

They didn't know what to do/
they had to do.

কি করতে হবে, তারা তা জানত না ।

Ki karte habe, tara ta janta na.

He had to come.

তার আসতে হইছে/হয়েছে ।

Tar ashte haichhe/hayechhe.

To see him is to love him.

তাকে দেখলেই ভালবাসতে হয় ।

Take dekhle-i bhalabashte hay.

They have to do this.

তা তাদের করতে হয় ।

Ta tader karte hay.

Lesson 84

INFINITIVE— II—Ability, Permission.

Nomin. **+** INFIN. $\begin{cases} \text{+ পারা } para\text{—can, may, be able} \\ \text{+ জানা } jana\text{—know} \end{cases}$

He/she knows how to swim.

সে সাঁতার কাটতে জানে ।

She shantar katte jane.

Ram Babu knows how to write
poetry.

রাম বাবু কবিতা লেখতে জানেন ।

Ram Babu kabita lekhte janen.

I can't do it/I am not able
to do it.

তা আমি করতে পারি না ।

Ta ami karte pari na.

I can do it.

তা আমি করতে পারি ।

Ta ami karte pari.

He/she can make you laugh.

সে তোমাকে হাসাইতে/হাসাতে পারে ।

She tomake hashaite/hashate pare.

He/she can speak English/write a letter.

সে ইংরেজী বলতে জানে/চিঠি লেখতে জানে ।

She Ingrejee balte jane/chithi lekhte jane.

Lesson 85

INFINITIVE—III—Nomin. + INF. + চাওয়া chaoya want,
wish

+ ইচ্ছা করা ichchha kara,
wish, will

+ রাজি হওয়া raji howa,
be agreeable

I want/wish to go...stay/read/sing.
আমি যাইতে/ যেতে...থাকতে/পড়তে/গান করতে...চাই ।
Ami jaite/ jete... thakte/parte/gan karte...chai.

Lila wishes/wants to come with us.
লীলা আমাদের সঙ্গে যাইতে/যেতে ইচ্ছা করে ।...চায় ।
Leela amader shange jaite/jete ichchha kare. ...chay.

Do you want to come in/go out ?
ভিতরে আসতে চাও ? ··বাইরে যাইতে/যেতে চাও ?
Bhitare ashte chao ?...baire jaite/jete chao ?

I too want to go. I'm willing to go with you.
আমিও যাইতে/যেতে চাই । [আমি] তোমার সঙ্গে যাইতে রাজি আছি ।
Ami-o jaite/jete chai. [Ami] tomar shange jaite raji achhi.

They don't want to work/aren't willing to work.
তারা কাজ করতে রাজি না ।
Tara kaj karte raji na.

I want to see him/meet him/her.
তাকে দেখতে চাই/তার সঙ্গে দেখা করতে চাই ।
Take dekhte chai/Tar shange dekha karte chai.

Lesson 86

INFINITIVE—IV—Permit or Allow or Forbid

Nomin. + Acc. + INFIN. + দেওয়া deoy*a*.

I let him/her go/come/read...

আমি তাকে যাইতে/আসতে/পড়তে...
দিলাম ।

*A*mi t*a*ke j*a*ite/*a*shte/p*a*rte...
dil*a*m.

Let him/her do [it].

তাকে [তা] করতে দেও ।

T*a*ke [t*a*] karte deo.

He/she didn't let me come
in/go out.

সে আমাকে ভিতরে আসতে/বাইরে
যাইতে দেয় নাই/নি ।

She *a*m*a*ke bhitare *a*shte/
b*a*ire j*a*te dey n*a*i/ni.

Let me do my work.

আমাকে আমার কাজ করতে
দেও/দাও ।

*A*m*a*ke *a*m*a*r k*a*j karte deo/
d*a*o.

Lesson 87

INFINITIVE—V—Purpose—Nomin. + INF. + Some Verb of
purpose or action—come, go, sit...

He/she goes to play/sing/tell the news...
সে খেলতে/গান করতে/খবর জানাতে...যায় ।
She khelte/gan·karte/khabar j*a*n*a*te...j*a*y.

The girl has gone to the river to get water.   (bring
মেয়েটি জল আনতে নদীতে গেছে/গিয়েছে ।
Meye*t*i jal *a*nte nadeete gechhe/giyechhe.

He came to see/meet me.   to tell the truth...
সে আমাকে দেখতে আসল ।   সত্য কথা বলতে গেলে ...
She *a*m*a*ke dekhte *a*shla.   satta kath*a* balte gele...

I shall go for a walk.   to bathe/to see mom
আমি বেড়াতে যাব ।   স্নান করতে/মাকে দেখতে
*A*mi be*r*ate j*a*ba.   sn*a*n karte/m*a*ke dekhte

They sat down to eat/talk/listen...
তারা খাইতে/খেতে/আলাপ করতে/শুনতে...বসল ।
T*a*r*a* kh*a*ite/khete/*a*l*a*p karte/shunte...bashla.

Lesson 88

INFINITIVE—VI—Acquisitiveness—To get, To do something
Nomi.+INFIN.+পাওয়া p*a*oy*a*

I will get to go there.	I didn't get to eat/drink water/play...
সেখানে যাইতে/যেতে/যাতে পাব ।	খাইতে-খেতে/জল খাতে-খেতে/ খেলতে...পাই নাই/নি ।
Shekh*a*ne j*a*ite/jete/j*a*te p*a*ba.	Kh*a*ite-khete/jal kh*a*te-khete/ khelte...p*a*i n*a*i/ni.

Last night I didn't get a chance to sleep.
গত রাত্রে আমি ঘুমাতে পাই নাই/নি ।
Gata r*a*tre *a*mi ghum*a*te p*a*i n*a*i/ni.

He/she is nowhere to be found.
তাকে কোথাও পাওয়া যায় না/যাইতেছে-যাচ্ছে না ।
T*a*ke koth*a*o p*a*oy*a* jay n*a*/j*a*itechhe-jachchhe n*a*.

I didn't get to see him/the play/the movie…
আমি তাকে/নাটক-ড্রামা/সিনেমা...দেখতে পাই নাই/নি ।
*A*mi t*a*ke/n*a*tak-d*r*ama/sinem*a*...dekhte p*a*i n*a*i/ni.

Lesson 89

INFINITIVE—VII—Continuity in the future : keep doing
FUTURE CONT. TENSE—Nomi.+INFIN.+থাকা–th*a*ka

He/she will not listen, he/she will keep on talking.
সে শুনবে না, কথা বলতে থাকবে ।
She shunbe n*a*, kath*a* balte th*a*kbe.

I'll read the letter ; keep on arranging.
আমি চিঠি পড়ি ; তুমি মিলাইতে/মিলাতে থাক ।
*A*mi chi*th*i pa*r*i ; tumi mil*a*ite/mil*a*te th*a*ka.

Tomorrow morning it will keep raining.

কাল সকালে বৃষ্টি হইবে/হতে থাকবে ।

Kal shakale brishṭi haite/hate thakbe.

I'll be waiting for you there.

আমি তোমার জন্য সেখানে অপেক্ষা/দেরি করতে থাকব ।

Ami tomar janna shekhane apekkha/deri karte thakba.

The bird will continue singing a while longer.

পাখীটা আরও কিছু কাল [ক্ষণ] গাইতে/গেতে থাকবে ।

Pakhiṭa aro kichhu kal [kkhan] gaite/gete thakbe.

There will be a light burning till you come.

তুমি না আসা পর্যন্ত আলো জ্বলতে থাকবে ।

Tumi na asha parjanta alo jjalte thakbe.

Lesson 90

INFINITIVE—VIII—Like, Love—
Nomin. + INFIN. + ভালবাসা, bhalabasha.

I like to play/eat/pray/sleep...

আমি খেলতে/খাইতে/খেতে/প্রার্থনা করতে...ভালবাসি ।

Ami khelte/khaite/khete/prarthana karte...bhalabashi.

Cats like to eat fish and milk.

বিড়াল মাছ ও দুধ খাইতে-   /খেতে ভালবাসে ।

Biral machh o dudh khaite-   /khete bhalabashe.

Rahim does not like to read/study.

রহিম পড়তে ভালবাসে না ।

Rahim parte bhalabashe na.

He liked/used to like to walk by the riverside,

সে নদীর ধারে বেড়াইতে/   ভালবাসত ।

She nadeer dhare beraite/   bhalabashta.

Lesson 91

INFINITIVE—IX—Refuse, Tell, Order, Forbid
Nomin + INFIN. + Verb

Tell/order him to come here.

তাকে এখানে আসতে বল/[আদেশ কর] ।

Take ekhane ashte bala/[adesh kara],

He made me go.

সে আমাকে যাইতে/   যেতে বাধ্য করল ।

She amake jaite/   jete badhdha karla,

He forbade me to leave.

সে আমাকে যাইতে/   যেতে নিষেধ করল ।

She amake jaite/   jete nishedh karla.

Lesson 92

INFINITIVE—X—Sense : See, Hear
Nomin. + INFIN. + দেখা dekha, শুনা shuna.

I saw him reading/playing/praying...

আমি তাকে পড়তে/খেলতে/প্রার্থনা করতে...দেখলাম ।

Ami take parte/khelte/prarthana karte...dekhlam.

I heard him/her singing/talking...

তাকে গান করতে/কথা বলতে...শুনছি/শুনেছি ।

Take gan karte/katha balte...shunchhi/shunechhi.

Did you see him go ?

তাকে যাইতে-   -যেতে দেখছ/দেখেছ ?

Take jaite—jate—   dekhchha/dekhechha ?

I saw him climb the tree.   We heard him say it.

তাকে গাছে উঠতে দেখলাম ।   আমরা তাকে তা বলতে শুনছি/শুনেছি
[তা = এই কথা] ।

Take gachhe uthte dekhlam.   Amra take ta balte shunchhi/
shunechhi [ta = ei katha].

Lesson 93

INFINITIVE—XI—Begin, Start

Nomin. + INFIN. + লাগা l*aga*, আরম্ভ করা *a*rambha kar*a*.

Start/begin to eat/eating.

খাইতে—   খেতে শুরু/আরম্ভ কর ।
Kh*ai*te—   khete shuru/*a*rambha kara.

They began to laugh/think/cry…(usually past tense)
তারা হাসতে/চিন্তা করতে/কাঁদতে…লাগল ।
T*ara* h*a*shte/chint*a* karte/k*a*ndte…l*a*gla.

He began to insist on eating/talking in class.
সে ক্লাসে খাবার/কথা বলবার [জন্য] জিদ করতে লাগল ।
She kl*a*she kh*a*b*a*r/kath*a* balb*a*r [janna] jid karte l*a*gla.

Lesson 94

INFINITIVE—XII—Infinitives governed by nouns :

Power, time, joy, dare, trying, hope, delay, shame, fear, courage, teaching etc.

I have no power to force you.
তোমাকে বাধ্য করতে আমার শক্তি/ক্ষমতা নাই/নেই ।
Tom*a*ke b*a*dhdha karte *a*m*a*r shakti/ khamat*a* n*a*i/nei.

I've no time to play/talk…
আমার খেলতে [খেলবার] কথা বলবার সময় নাই/নেই ।
*A*m*a*r khelte [khelb*a*r]/kath*a* balb*a*r shamay n*a*i/nei.

I dare to say that. (courage…fear to
আমি এ কথা বলতে সাহস করি…ভয় করি ।
*A*mi e kath*a* balte sh*a*hash kari…bhay kari.

He tried to go/read...

সে যাইতে–   যেতে/পড়তে...চেষ্টা করছে/করেছে ।

She jaite–   jete/parte...chesta karchhe/karechhe.

I dare not stay here.   courage.

এখানে থাকতে সাহস পাইনা ।

Ekhane thakte shahash paina.

He taught me to read.

সে আমাকে পড়তে শিখাইছিল/শিখিয়েছিল ।

She amake parte shikhaichhila/shikhiyechhila.

Lesson 95

INFINITIVE—XIII—Double Infinitive—WHILE.

95 (a).   Two verbs **:**   SAME subject—Used as a participle.

While pulling/plucking flowers, he...

ফুল তুল তে তুল তে, সে...

Ful tulte tulte, she...

While [I was] going to school, I met Rahim.

স্কুলে যাইতে যাইতে/যেতে যেতে রহিমের সঙ্গে দেখা হইল/হল ।

Skule jaite jaite/jete jete Rahimer shange dekha haila/hala.

95 (b).   INFIN.—XIV—Used as a participle, shows Duration
translate as WHILE.

While there is life/time/light/day...

প্রাণ/সময়/বেলা/দিন...থাকতে ।

Pran/shamay/bela/din...tkakte.

95 (c). INFIN—XV—INFIN.+some form of আছে—achhe—
shows continuity of action.

He/she keeps on eating/sitting/looking...

সে খাইতে–খাতে–খেতে/বসতে/দেখতে...আছে ।

She khaite–khate–khete/bashte/dekhte...achhe.

95 (d). INFIN.—XVI—INFIN. + আছে *achhe* ; নাই n*ai*/নেই
nei [Fut. থাকা th*aka*] — Permission by Law, Religion or custom

Is it permissible to go/sit there ?···to go to your room···

সেখানে যাইতে-   যেতে/বসতে আছে ? ···আপনার কামরায় যাইতে···
Shekh*a*ne j*a*ite-   jete/bashte *a*chhe ?···*a*pn*a*r k*a*mr*a*y j*a*ite···

No, it is not.   ·· to marry again···.

না যাইতে-যেতে নাই   ···আবার বিয়া করতে···
N*a* j*a*ite–jete n*a*i.   ···*a*b*a*r biy*a* karte···

It is not permissible to act like this/to speak like this.

এ রকম করতে নাই/নেই ।   এমন কথা বলতে নাই ।
E rakam karte n*a*i/nei...   em*a*n kath*a* balte ñ*a*i.

95 (e).—INFIN.—XVII—Double INFIN.— Similar to 95 (a)

Continuous rubbing wears away the stone.   while playing···

ঘষতে ঘষতে পাথর ক্ষয় হয় ।   খেলতে খেলতে···
Ghashte ghashte p*a*thar kkhay hay.   khelte khelte...

while weeping...   while singing...

কাঁদতে কাঁদতে ···   গান করতে করতে···
k*a*ndte k*a*ndte...   g*a*n karte karte...

Lesson 96

INFINITIVE—XVIII—Governed by an *adjective* :
ready, willing eager, able, beautiful, sweet, nice

I am ready to die···willing to go···

আমি মরতে প্রস্তুত·· যাইতে/যেতে রাজি/ইচ্ছুক···
*A*mi marte prastut···j*a*ite/jete r*a*ji/ichchhuk···

This is good to eat/see/know/hear/read···

এটা খাইতে-খেতে/দেখতে/জানতে/শুনতে/পড়তে···ভাল/সুন্দর···
E*ta* kh*a*ite–khete/dekhte/j*a*nte/shunte/pa*r*te···bh*a*la/ sundar...

This mango/lichi/candy—is good to eat.

এই আম/লিচু/মিঠাই —খাইতে-খেতে ভাল ।

Ei am/lichu/mithai...khaite–khete bhala.

This orange is sweet (to eat).

এই কমলালেবু খাইতে-খেতে মিষ্টি ।

Ei kamla lebu khaite–khete mishti.

Your poem is nice to read.	I am ashamed to admit this.
তোমার কবিতা পড়তে বেশ ।	আমি এই কথা স্বীকার করতে লজ্জিত/ লজ্জা করি ।
Tomar kabita parte besh.	Ami ei katha sheekar karte lajjita/lajja kari.

Lesson 97

DEFINITIVE PARTICLES—ও, o—And, Also, Even, Too—
ও, o is added to any part of speech and gives a **conjunctive**
meaning such as *also, and, too, even*..

I take tea *and* puffed rice in the morning.

[আমি] সকালে মুড়ি ও চা খাই ।

[Ami] shakale muri o cha khai.

He/she *too* is sitting under the tree.	I *too* was happy...
সেও গাছের তলায় বসে ।	আমারও সুখ...ছিল ।
She-o gachher talay bashe.	Amar-o shukh...chhila.
He doesn't *even* have a paisa on hand.	My father *too* will go.
তার হাতে একটি পয়সাও নাই/নেই ।	আমার বাবাও যাবেন ।
Tar hate ekti paysha-o nai/nei.	Amar baba-o jaben.

Lesson 98

J. **PARTICIPLE in ইয়া iya—A CONJUNCTION**

This participle is never used as a noun. It can serve as a
conjunction. It is better to translate the sentence using two

independent verbs. (See L. 112. when this ppl, is used, both clauses ordinarily have the *same subject*).

He/she sat down and wrote a letter.
সে বসিয়া/বসে চিঠি লেখিছে/লেখেছে ।
She bashiy*a*/bashe chi*t*hi lekhchhe/lekhechhe.

May I go and get a drink of water ?   (Go and return)
জল খাইয়া/খেয়ে আসি ?
Jal kh*a*iy*a*/kheye *a*shi ?

Go and tell him/her...   Sit down and eat.
তাকে গিয়া বল...   বসিয়া/বসে খাও ।
T*a*ke giy*a* bala...   Bashiy*a*/bashe kh*a*o.

Let me stay and become your servant.
আমাকে তোমার দাস হইয়া/হয়ে থাকতে দাও/দেও ।
*A*m*a*ke tom*a*r d*a*sh hoiy*a*/hoye th*a*kte d*a*o/deo.

He climbed the tree and picked some fruit.
(climbing the tree he...)
সে গাছে উঠিয়া/উঠে কিছু ফল পাড়ল ।
She g*a*chhe u*t*hiy*a*/u*t*he kichhu fal p*a*rla.

He took leave and went home.
সে ছুটি নিয়া/নিয়ে বাড়ী গেল ।
She chhu*t*i niy*a*/niye b*a*ree gela,

Keep quiet and sit down.   Boil the eggs and bring them in.
চুপ করিয়া/করে বস ।   ডিম সিদ্ধ করিয়া/করে আন ।
Chup kariy*a*/kare basha.   *D*im shiddha kariy*a*/kare *a*na.

They were sitting in the house and telling stories.
ঘরে বসিয়া/বসে তারা গল্প করতেছিল/করছিল ।
Ghare bashiy*a*/bashe t*ara* galpa kartechhila/karchhila.

Lesson 99

A DIFFERENCE: II. PARTICIPLE—ইয়া iya and ইতে...ইতে, ite·
...ite— WHEN, AFTER

This participle qualifies the verb whereas the duplicated
participle in ইতে ite qualifies the subject.   q. v. L. 95.

Hearing what I said he flew into a rage.(He heard...and he flew...)
আমার কথা শুনিয়া/শুনে সে রাগিয়া/রেগে উঠল ।
Amar katha shuniya/shune she ragiya/rege uthla.
On reaching home I found dad ill.
বাড়ী পৌঁছিয়া/পৌঁছে দেখলাম বাবার অসুখ ।
Baree pounchhiya/pounchhe dekhlam babar ashukh.
Finishing my meal I went out.   (after I...)
খাওয়া শেষ করিয়া/করে বাইরে গেলাম ।
Khaoya shesh kariya/kare baire gelam.
He came and told us this.
সে আসিয়া/এসে আমাদের কাছে এ কথা বলল/জানাল ।
She ashiya/eshe amader kachhe e katha balla/janala.
Having finished her work, the woman went home.
তার কাজ শেষ করিয়া/করে স্ত্রীলোকটি বাড়ীতে ফিরল ।
Tar kaj shesh kariya/kare streelokti bareete firla.

Lesson 100

III.   PARTICIPLE—in ইয়া iya—shows   CAUSE.

Sometimes the participle gives the *reason* for the action
denoted by the finite verb. This participle is used as an
adverbial phrase expressing *Cause*.

Because I was awake all night I got sick.
রাত্রি/রাত জাগিয়া/জেগে আমার অসুখ হইছে/হয়েছে ।
Ratri/rat jagiya/jege amar ashukh haichhe/hayechhe.

On hearing this he got angry.

এ কথা শুনিয়া/শুনে সে রাগ করল ।

E katha shuniya/shune she rag karla.

Because we walked 5 miles, we became tired. Having walked...

পাঁচ মাইল হাঁটিয়া/হেঁটে আমরা ক্লান্ত হইলাম/হলাম ।

Panch mail hantiya/hente amra klanta hailam/halam.

Seeing the tiger he became afraid.

বাঘটি দেখিয়া/দেখে সে ভয় পাইছে/পেয়েছে ।

Baghti dekhiya/dekhe bhay paichhe/peyechhe.

He cried because he was/got punished.

শাস্তি পাইয়া/পেয়ে সে কাঁদছিল/কেঁদেছিল ।

Shasti paiya/peye she kandchhila/kendechhila.

On hearing the noise we went outside.   Because we heard...

শব্দ[টি] শুনিয়া/শুনে আমরা বাইরে গেলাম ।

Shabda[ti] shuniya/shune amra baire gelam.

Because he mixed with bad boys he went to the dogs.

দুষ্ট ছেলেদের সঙ্গে মিশিয়া/মিশে সে গোল্লায় গেছে/গিয়েছে ।

Dushta chheleder shange mishiya/mishe she gollay gechhe/
giyechhe,

Lesson 101

IV.   PARTICIPLE in ইয়া iya — ADVERBIAL USES

This participle is used to form adverbial phrases.   Some
writers also include what is considered the Instrumental Case
in দিয়া diya as simply the participle of the Verb দেওয়া deoya.
Page says :—This ppl. is used to form adverbial phrases
expressing *means*, instrument, route etc.

He worked with my tools.

সে আমার যন্ত্র নিয়া/দিয়া–দিয়ে কাজ করছে/করেছে ।

She amar jantra niya/diya diye—kaj karchhe/karechhe.

He/she came by boat.

সে নৌকা করিয়া/করে আসছে/এসেছে। [নৌকা দিয়া

She nouka kariya/kare ashchhe/eshechhe. [nouka diya/noukay

Speak plainly.	keep quiet
স্পষ্ট করিয়া/করে কথা বল।	চুপ করিয়া/করে থাক
Spashta kariya/kare katha bala.	Chup kariya/kare thaka
in a good way/well	in a hurry/quickly
ভাল করিয়া/করে	শীঘ্র করিয়া/করে
bhala kariya/kare	sheeghra kariya/kare
one by one	via/by way of Calcutta
একজন একজন করিয়া/করে	কলিকাতা হইয়া/হয়ে
ek jan ek jan kariya/kare	kalikata haiya/haye
How much are these apiece ?	Sit up straight.
এগুলি কত করিয়া/করে ?[প্রতিটি	সোজা হইয়া/হয়ে বস।
E guli kata kariya/kare ?]	Shoja haiya/haye basha.
What will you do with this book ?	Please/kindly...
এই বই নিয়া/নিয়ে কি করবে ?	দয়া করিয়া/করে...
Ei bai niya/niye ki karbe ?	Daya kariya/kare...

Lesson 102

V.   PARTICIPLE — in ইয়া iya — MANNER

This participle is used to form adverbial phrases expressing *manner.*

He came running.	Bite it off/cut it by biting.
সে দৌড়াইয়া/দৌড়ে আসল।	কামড়াইয়া/কামড়ে ছিঁড়িয়া/ছিঁড়ে ফেল।
She douraiya/doure ashla/	Kamraiya/kamre chhinriya/
আসছিল = ashchhila.	chhinre fela.

Horses sleep standing.

ঘোড়া দাঁড়াইয়া/দাঁড়িয়ে ঘুমায় ।

Ghora danraiya/danriye ghumay.

You didn't write this well.

তুমি এ কথা ভাল করিয়া/করে লেখ নাই/নি ।

Tumi e katha bhala kariya/kare lekha nai/ni.

Treacle/molasses is made by crushing sugarcane.

আখ মাড়িয়ে/ গুড় প্রস্তুত হয় ।

Akh mariye/ gur prastut hay.

Speak plainly/clearly.

স্পষ্ট করিয়া/করে কথা বল ।

Spashta kariya/kare katha bala.

The boys came to me in a group. (forming a group

দল বাঁধিয়া/বেঁধে ছেলেরা আমার কাছে আসছে/এসেছে ।

Dal bandhiya/bendhe chhelera amar kachhe ashchhe/eshechhe.

We/one must obey the law. (...obeying...proeeed)

আইন [মান্য করিয়া–করে] মানিয়া–মেনে চলতে হয় ।

Ain [manna kariya–kare] maniya–mene chalte hay.

What is the good of buying it ?

ইহা/তা কিনিয়া/কিনে লাভ কি ?

Iha/ta kiniya/kine labh ki ?

What is the point in/use of talking like this ?

এমন কথা বলিয়া/বলে কি লাভ ?

Eman katha baliya/bale ki labh ?

What is the use of quarreling ?   ...of arguing

ঝগড়া করিয়া/করে লাভ কি ?   ...তর্ক করিয়া

Jhagra kariya/kare labh ki ?   ...tarka kariya

6—

Lesson 103

VI. PARTICIPLE — in ইয়া *iya* — BY MEANS OF

He lives by farming/begging...

সে চাষ/ভিক্ষা...করিয়া/করে খায় ।

She ch*a*sh/bhikkh*a*...kariy*a*/k*a*re kh*a*y.

How can I say ?

আমি কি করিয়া/করে বলব ?

*A*mi ki kariy*a*/k*a*re balba ?

He reached Dacca in 3 hours by cycling.

সাইকেল চড়িয়া/চড়ে সে তিন ঘন্টায় ঢাকায় পৌঁছিল ।

Sh*a*ikel ch*a*riy*a*/ch*a*re she tin ghan*tay Dha*k*a*y pou*n*chhla.

By resting you'll get better.

বিশ্রাম করিয়া/করে আপনার/তোমার অসুখ সারবে ।

Bishr*a*m kariy*a*/k*a*re *a*pn*a*r/tom*a*r ashukh sh*a*rbe.

What are you going to do with this book ?

এই বই নিয়া/নিয়ে কি করবে ?

Ei bai niy*a*/niye ki k*a*rbe ?

We come by boat/bus/car/cycle...

আমরা নৌকা করিয়া/করে আসি ।...বাস/গাড়ী/সাইকেল

*A*mr*a* nouk*a* kariy*a*/k*a*re *a*shi...b*a*s /g*a*ri/ s*a*ikel...

This is similar to L. 101 q. v.

Lesson 104

VII. PARTICIPLE — with যাওয়া, *jaoya* — CONTINUED ACTION — Used to INTENSIFY, to FINISH SOMETHING

The wind has blown out the lamp/candle.

বাতাসে বাতি নিবিয়া/নিবে গেছে/গিয়েছে ।

B*a*t*a*she b*a*ti nibiy*a*/nibe gechhe/giyechhe.

The cow ran away/broke loose.

গরু[টা] ছুটিয়া/ছুটে গেল ।

Garu [*ta*] chhuti*ya*/chhu*ţe* gela.

The boat/ship/steamer/boy.,.sank.

নৌকা/জাহাজ/ছেলে[টি]···ডুবিয়া/ডুবে গেছে/গিয়েছে ।

Nauk*a*/j*a*h*a*j/chhele[*ţi*]···*ḍ*ubiy*a*/*ḍ*ube gechhe/giyechhe.

It's going to break.	The boys ran away.
ভাঙ্গিয়া/ভেঙ্গে যাবে ।	ছেলেরা পলায়া/পালিয়ে গেল।
Bh*a*ngiy*a*/bhenge j*a*be.	Chhele*ra* pa*ţaya*/pali*ye* gela.
He fell down.	My clothes got torn.
সে পড়িয়া/পড়ে গেছে/গিয়েছে ।	আমার কাপড় ছিঁড়িয়া/ছিঁড়ে গেছে/গিয়েছে ।
She pa*ŗiya*/pa*ŗe* gechhe/giyechhe.	A*ma*r kapa*r* chhin*ŗiya*/ chhin*ŗe* gechhe/giyechhe.

My hand/arm/foot···has/is broken.

আমার হাত/পা··· ভাঙ্গিয়া/ভেঙ্গে গেছে/গিয়েছে ।

A*ma*r h*a*t/p*a*···bh*a*ngiy*a*/bhenge gechhe/giyechhe,

lost	split	get spoiled
হারাইয়া গেল	ফাটিয়া গেল	নষ্ট হইয়া যাওয়া
h*a*r*a*iy*a* gela	f*a*ţiy*a* gela	nash*ţ*a haiy*a* j*a*oy*a*
stop	take away	
থামিয়া যাওয়া	নিয়া/নিয়ে যাওয়া	
th*a*miy*a* j*a*oy*a*	niy*a*/niye j*a*oy*a*	

For more **:**   Look up যাওয়া j*a*oy*a* in a big dictionary.

Lesson 105

VIII. (a).   PARTICIPLE—in ইয়া iy*a* with দেওয়া deoy*a*

(for another)

(b).   PARTICIPLE—in ইয়া iy*a* with নেওয়া neoy*a*

(for oneself)

Cut the thread (for me).

সূতা কাটিয়া/কেটে দেও/দেন ।

Shoota katiya/kete deo/den.

Will you write a letter for me ?

চিঠি লেখিয়া/লেখে দিবেন/দিবে ?

Chithi lekhiya/lekhe diben/dibe ?

He read the letter to us.

সে চিঠি পড়িয়া/পড়ে দিছে/দিয়েছে or, পড়িয়া শুনাইল ।

She chithi pariya/pare dichhe/diyechhe [or pariya shunaila

Won't you show us some/any pictures ?

ছবি দেখাইয়া/দেখিয়ে দিবেন না ?

Chhabi dekhaiya/dekhiye diben na ?

Let go.

ছাড়িয়া/ছেড়ে দেও ।

Chhariya/chhere dao.

Stop prompting.

কইয়া/কয়ে দিও না ।

Kaiya/kaye dio na.

I cut the thread (for myself).

সূতা কাটিয়া/কেটে নিলাম ।

Shoota katiya/kete nilam.

Examine the account for yourself.

হিসাবটা দেখিয়া/দেখে নেও/নেন ।

Hishabta dekhiya/dekhe neo/nen.

They bought some food (for themselves).

তারা খাবার কিনিয়া/কিনে নিছে/নিয়েছে ।

Tara khabar kiniya/kine nichhe/niyechhe.

MILNE—"In other cases দেওয়া deoya after the partieiple
in ইয়া iya seems to have an intensifying use only."

I sent the book.

বই পাঠাইয়া দিছি/পাঠিয়ে দিয়েছি ।

Bai pathaiya dichhi/pathiye diyechhi.

I told you...

তোমাকে বলিয়া/বলে দিলাম...

Tomake baliya/bale dilam···

Give it to me.

আমাকে দিয়া/দিয়ে দাও ।

amake diya/ dao.

Answer the letter.
চিঠির উত্তর লেখিয়া/লেখে দাও
Chithir uttar lekhiya/lekhe dao.

The storm is over.
ঝড় হইয়া/হয়ে গেল ।
Jhar haiya/haye gela.

Lesson 106

IX. PARTICIPLE—in ইয়া iya — with ফেলা fela — is used with the participle in ইয়া iya to convey the idea of *completeness*, *thoroughness*. (Its literal meaning is *to throw*.)

I pulled out his/her tooth.
আমি তার দাঁত তুলিয়া/তুলে ফেল্‌লাম ।
Ami tar dant tuliya/tule fellam.

The baby tore up the book.
শিশু[টি] কাগজ ছিঁড়িয়া/ছিঁড়ে ফেলল ।
Shishu[ti] kagaj chhinriya/chhinre fella.

He/she ate up his/her food.
সে তার খাবার খাইয়া/খেয়ে ফেলল ।
She/tar khabar khaiya/kheye fella.

He killed the lion.
সে সিংহ মারিয়া/মেরে ফেলল ।
She shingha mariya/mere fella.

Pull up the tree.
গাছটা তুলিয়া/তুলে ফেল ।
Gachhta tuliya/tule fela.

He will read the book in two days.
সে দুই দিনের মধ্যে বই পড়িয়া/পড়ে ফেলবে ।
She dui diner maddhe bai pariya/pare felbe.

Cut the tree down.
গাছটা কাটিয়া ফেল ।
Gachhta katiya fela.

Wipe it out/up.
মুছিয়া/মুছে ফেল ।
Muchhiya/muchhe fela.

Finish up the work.
কাজ শেষ করিয়া/করে ফেল ।
Kaj shesh kariya/kare fela.

Lesson 107

X.   PARTICIPLE in ইয়া iya With থাকা thaka – CONTINUITY

It shows continuity, habit, permanence and frequency. This added significance flows from the primary meaning of the Verb : stay, keep on, remain.

In its future form it is the future perfect tense (shown below).

I usually teach in this school.

এ স্কুলে আমি পড়াইয়া/পড়িয়ে থাকি ।

E skule *a*mi pa*r*aiy*a*/pa*r*iye th*a*ki.

We are in the habit of praying.

আমরা প্রার্থনা করিয়া/করে থাকি ।

*A*mr*a* pr*a*rthan*a* kariy*a*/kare th*a*ki.

He usually/habitually comes at 3 o'clock.

সে তিনটার সময় আসিয়া/এসে থাকে ।

She tin*ſ*a*r* shamay *a*shiy*a*/eshe th*a*ke.

The gardener works in the garden as a rule.

মালী বাগানে কাজ করিয়া/করে থাকে ।

M*a*lee b*a*gane k*a*j kariy*a*/kare th*a*ke.

FUTURE PERFECT TENSE

By then my lesson will be over.   (Study)

এর মধ্যে আমার পড়া হইয়া/হয়ে যাবে ।

Er maddhe *a*m*a*r pa*r*a haiy*a*/haye j*a*be.

Then the flowers will have bloomed.

তখন ফুলগুলি ফুটিয়া/ফুটে থাকবে ।

Takhan fulguli fu*ſ*iy*a*/fu*ſ*e th*a*kbe.

We shall have done our work before you come.

তোমার আসবার আগে আমাদের কাজ শেষ হইয়া/হয়ে যাবে ।

Tom*a*r *a*shb*a*r *a*ge *a*m*a*der k*a*j shesh haiy*a*/haye j*a*be.

(a) These denote actions which will be completed at a future time referred to in the context.

(b) To denote the probability of something taking place. You may have heard this.

তুমি এ কথা শুনিয়া/শুনে থাকবে।

Tumi e katha shuniya/shune thakbe.

Perhaps he has gone.

হয়ত সে গিয়া/গিয়ে থাকবে।

Hayta she giya/giye thakbe.

Lesson 108

XI. PARTICIPLE in ইয়া iya—UNTIL/WITHOUT/UNLESS

The participle in ইয়া iya preceded by না na is translated *until*, provided the main verb is also in the negative.

He/she won't come till he/she eats.

সে না খাইয়া/খেয়ে আসবে না।

She na khaiya/kheye ashbe na.

He won't speak till/unless he thinks.

সে চিন্তা না করিয়া/করে কথা বলবে না।

She chinta na kariya/kare katha balbe na.

Don't go without getting/until—unless you get permission.

অনুমতি না পাইয়া/পেয়ে যাইবেনা—যাইও/যেয়ো না।

Anumati na paiya/peye jaibe na—jaio/jeyo na.

I can't live/stay without eating/drinking...

না খাইয়া/খেয়ে—জল না খাইয়া/খেয়ে···থাকতে পারি না।

Na khaiya/kheye—jal na khaiya/kheye·· thakte pari na.

without finishing work...

কাজ শেষ না করিয়া/করে···

kaj shesh na kariya/kare···

without closing the door/opening the window···

দরজা বন্ধ না করিয়া–করে/জানালা না খুলিয়া/খুলে...

darja bandha na kariya–kare/janala na khuliya/khule...

without giving a bribe/preparing his lesson···

ঘুষ না দিয়া–দিয়ে/পড়া প্রস্তুত না করিয়া–করে···

ghush na diya–diye/para prastut na kariya–kare...

Lesson 109

XII. PARTICIPLE in ইয়া iya + ও, o—ALTHOUGH, EVEN IF.

With ও,o added to it, this participle conveys the idea of *although, even if*.

Although I went there, I could not see him.

আমি গিয়াও/গিয়েও তাকে দেখতে পাইলাম/পেলাম না ।

Ami giya–o/giye-o take dekhte pailam/pelam na.

Although he didn't go, he got to know about it.

সে না গিয়াও/গিয়েও জানতে পাইল/পেল ।

She na giya–o/giye-o jante paila/pela.

Even though he was punished, he didn't cry.

শাস্তি পাইয়াও/পেয়েও সে কাঁদে নাই/নি ।

Shashti paiya-o/peye-o she kande nai/ni.

Even if he is punished, he doesn't cry.

শাস্তি পাইয়াও/পেয়েও সে কাঁদে না ।

Shashti paiya-o/peye-o she kande na.

Although he begs, he gets nothing.

ভিক্ষা করিয়াও/করেও সে কিছু পায় না ।

Bhikkha kariya-o/kare-o she kichhu pay na.

With all forms, meanings and usages of this participle, the subject of the component clauses [or English clauses] must be *the same*. L. 112.

Lesson 110

XIII. PARTICIPLE in ইয়া iya+ই, i—AS SOON AS.

With ই, i added to it, this participle conveys the idea of *as soon as*. The subject of the component clauses must be the same (L. 112).

Tell your father this as soon as you come home.

বাড়ী গিয়াই/গিয়েই এ কথা বাবাকে বলবে/বলিয়া দিবে।

Baree giya-i/geye-i e katha babake balbe/baliya dibe.

As soon as I tell him, I'll return.

তাকে বলিয়াই/বলেই আমি ফিরিয়া/ফিরে আসব।

Take baliya-i/bale-i ami firiya/fire ashba.

As soon as you finish your work, come to do my work.

কাজ শেষ করিয়াই/করেই আমার কাজ করতে আস/এস।

Kaj shesh kariya-i/kare-i amar kaj karte asha/esha.

As soon as I lay on the bed I fell asleep.

আমি বিছানায় শুইয়াই/শুয়েই ঘুমাইয়া/ঘুমিয়ে পড়লাম। *

Ami bichhanay shuiya-i/shuhe-i ghumaiya/ghumiye parlam.

Lesson 111

XIV. PARTICIPLE in ইয়া iya—REPETITION, FREQUENCY

Repetition of this participle implies frequency or practice.

Constant/practise/singing makes the singer.

গাইয়া গাইয়া/গেয়ে গেয়ে গায়ক হয়

Gaiya gaiya/geye geye gayak hay.

Or, গাইতে গাইতে/গেতে গেতে গায়ক হয়।

Gaite gaite/gete gete gayak hay.

Or, গাইয়াই/গেয়েই গায়ক হয়।

Gaiya-i/geye-i gayak hay.

---

* PPL. with পড়া para a change to a worse or lessened activity.

He learned by constant listening.

শুনিয়া শুনিয়া/শুনে শুনে সে শিখত।

Shunia shunia/shune shune she shikhta.

Lesson 112

XV. PARTICIPLES in ইয়া iya and ইলে ile ঃ—

The perfect participle (in ইয়া) may only be used to qualify the subject of the sentence. (This rule allows of exceptions where the subject is the logical though not the grammatical subject of the sentence.) Dutt says, "1. Use ইয়া, iya in a sentence where the subject agrees with the finite verb. (e.g. He ate and went to work). 2. Use ইলে, ile in a sentence where there is one subject for the non–finite verb (ppl.) and another subject for the finite verb. (e.g. I'll go when he comes.)"

I shall go when he comes.

সে আসলে আমি যাইব।

She ashle ami jaibo.

The final verb (real or main, NOT the participle) is a consequence of the verb in the participle in ইলে, ile. The conditional participle qualifies a noun or a pronoun in the nominative absolute, expressed or understood. Occasionally however a genitive is substituted for the nominative.

Lesson 113

I. PARTICIPLE in ইলে, ile — when

With a noun this participle is used in a nominative construction.

The thief having gone wisdom increases.

Wisdom increases when the thief
has fled.

When you come I'll go.

চোর গেলে বুদ্ধি বাড়ে ।
Chor gele buddhi bare.

তুমি আসলে/এলে আমি যাব ।
Tumi ashle/ele ami jaba

I began to read when he lit the lamp.

সে বাতি জ্বালাইলে/জ্বালালে আমি পড়তে শুরু করছি/করলাম ।
She bati jjalaile/jjalale ami parte shuru karchhi/Karlam.

When you pump hold (the handle, it) like this.

পাম্প করলে এমনে ধর ।
Pamp karle emne dhara.

I'll play football when/if you do.   (too)

তুমি ফুটবল খেললে আমিও খেলব ।
Tumi futbal khelle ami-o khelbo.

Make some biscuits when he brings the eggs.

সে ডিম আনলে বিস্কুট বানাবে ।
She dim anle bishkut banabe.

When you go to the market/bazar buy some eggs.

বাজারে গেলে কয়েকটা ডিম কিনিয়া/কিনে আনিও ।
Bajare gele kayekta dim kiniya/kine anio...

Lesson 114

II. PARTICIPLE in ইলে, ile with পর par—AFTER.

With পর par, পরে pare the participle retains its adverbial
sense—it denotes a succession of events.

After you eat/after eating, come to me.

ভাত খাইলে/খেলে পর আমার কাছে আস/এস ।
Bhat khaile/khele par amar kachhe asha/esha.

After I come from school I eat.

স্কুল থেকে আসলে/এলে পর আমি খাই ।

Skul theke *a*shle/ele par *a*mi kh*a*i

After I got into the boat, the boatmam asked for my fare.

আমি নৌকায় উঠলে পর মাঝি ভাড়া চাইল ।

*A*mi nauk*a*y uthle par m*a*jhi bh*a*ra ch*a*ila.

Lesson 115

III. PARTICIPLE in ইলে, ile—IF.

This participle implies condition and is equivalent to a conditional clause. Its common use is to express a condition or hypothesis.

If I walk, he runs.

আমি চললে/হাঁটলে সে দৌড়ায় ।

*A*mi challe/h*a*ntle she daur*ay*.

He will do well to go there/if he goes there.

সেখানে গেলে তার ভাল হয় ।

Shekh*a*ne gele t*a*r bh*a*la hay.

If the mail comes, I shall inform you.

ডাক আসলে/এলে তোমাকে জানাব ।

*D*ak *a*shle/ele tom*a*ke j*a*n*a*bo.

If he is sick he cannot work.

অসুখ হইলে/হলে সে কাজ করতে পারে না ।

Ashukh haile/hale she k*a*j karte p*a*re n*a*.

If you are good/well you may go.

ভাল হইলে/হলে যাইতে/যেতে পারবে ।

Bh*a*la haile/hale j*a*ite/jete p*a*rbe.

It's a sin to steal.

চুরি করলে পাপ হয় ।

Churi karle p*a*p hay

If it's necessary, you may go.

দরকার হইলে/হলে যাইতে/যেতে পার ।

Dark*a*r haile/hale j*a*ite/jete p*a*ra.

If I see it. I can tell.

[টা] দেখলে, বলতে পারব ।

[Ta] dekhle, balte parba.

Lesson 116

IV.   PARTICIPLE   in ইলে, ile with না na, not.

NOTE **:**   The negative particle precedes the participle in ইলে, ile.

If he doesn't come, I shall go away.

সে না আসলে/এলে আমি চলিয়া/চলে যাব ।

She na ashle/ele ami chaliya/chale jaba.

If he hasn't come, I shall go away.

সে না আসিয়া-এসে থাকলে আমি চলিয়া/চলে যাব ।

She na ashiya-eshe thakle ami chaliya/chale jaba.

If you don't try you'll never be able (to do it)

চেষ্টা না করলে কখনও পারবে না ।

Chesta   na karle kakhano parbe na.

If you don't keep silence, you'll be punished.

চুপ করিয়া-করে না থাকলে শাস্তি পাবে ।

Chup kariya—kare na thakle shasti pabe.

If he hadn't come, I wouldn't have gone.

সে না আসলে/এলে আমি যাইতাম/যেতাম না ।

She na ashle/ele ami jaitam/jetam na.

Lesson 117

V.   PARTICIPLE in ইলে, ile with ই, i — AS SOON AS.

With ই, i this particle also conveys the idea of **:** *directly*, *only*, *if only*.

As soon as the sun came up, he went away.

সূর্য উঠলেই সে চলিয়া/চলে গেল । (তিনি···গেলেন।

Shoorja ut*h*le–i she chaliy*a*/chale gela. (tini···gelen.

I shall come as soon·as I can.

আমি আসতে পারলেই আসব ।

*A*mi *a*shte p*a*rle–i *a*shba.

I'll return the book as soon as I finish reading it.

আমি বই   পড়ে শেষ করলেই ফেরত দিব ।

*A*mi bai pare shesh karle–i ferat diba.

As soon as he ate that rice he took/got sick.

ঐ/সে ভাত খাইলেই/খেলেই তার অসুখ হইছে/হয়েছে ।

Oi/she bh*a*t kh*a*ile–i/khele–i t*a*r ashukh haichhe/hayechhe.

As soon as he saw me I ran down the path.

সে আমাকে দেখলেই আমি পথ দিয়া দৌড়িয়া/দৌড়ে গেলাম ।

She *a*m*a*ke dekhle–i *a*mi path diy*a* dau*r*iy*a*/dau*r*e gel*a*m.

I'll go as soon as the bell rings.

ঘন্টা পড়লেই যাব ।

Ghan*ta* p*a*r*h*le–i j*a*ba.

One has only to go there to be sure of meeting him.

সেখানে গেলেই তার সঙ্গে নিশ্চয় দেখা হবে ।

Shekh*a*ne gele–i t*a*r shange nishchay dekh*a* habe.

As soon as he comes, the song will begin.

তিনি আসলেই/এলেই গান শুরু/আরম্ভ হবে ।

Tini *a*shle–i/ele–i g*a*n shuru/*a*rambha habe.

As soon as one sees (it), one understands.

দেখলেই বুঝা যায় ।

Dekhle–i bujh*a* j*a*y.

Lesson 118

VI. PARTICIPLE in ইলে, ile with ও, o

With ও, o added to it, this participle means *although, even if, as well*.

Even if you go, he will not go.   I shall come even if it rains.

তুমি গেলেও সে যাবে না ।   বৃষ্টি পড়লেও/হলেও যাব ।

Tumi gele–o she jabe na.   Brishti parle–o/hale–o jaba.

Even if he had asked, no one would have given it to him

কারও কাছে চাইলেও/চেলেও, কেহ দিত না ।

Karo kachhe chaile–o/chale–o keha dita na.

Although (he is) good he is not a saint.

ভাল হলেও সে সাধু না/ নয় ।

Bhala hale–o she shadhu na / nay.

Even if I write a note, you won't get it.

আমি চিঠি লেখলেও তুমি তা/ওটা পাবে না ।

Ami chithi lekhle–o tumi ta/ota pabe na.

Even if I'm sick, I'll work.

আমার অসুখ হলেও কাজ করব ।

Amar ashukh hale–o kaj karba.

Although I was sick he didn't come.

আমার অসুখ হলেও, সে আসে নাই/নি ।

Amar ashukh hale–o she ashe nai/ni.

Lesson 119

VII. DEFINITIVE PARTICLES ই, i—an intensive.

ই, i IS ADDED TO ANY PART OF SPEECH AS AN INTENSIVE. It is equivalent to the emphasis obtained by underlining a word. It forms a separate syllable.

I shall go.   I shall *go*.   *Go* I will.

আমিই যাব ।   যাইবই/যাবই ।

*A*mi-i j*a*ba.   J*a*iba-i/j*a*ba-i.

Do it I *will*.   (hyphen only in transliteration)

আমি ইহা করবই করব ।

*A*mi ih*a* karba–i karba.

I have been at *home* all this time.

আমি এত ক্ষণ বাড়ীতেই আছি ।

*A*mi eta khan b*a*reete-i *a*chhi.

I shall be *very glad* if you come.

তুমি এলে বড়ই সুখী হইব/হব ।

Tumi ele. bara-i shukhee haiba/haba.

He felt *very* tired.   You *must*/*shall* do this work.

তার বড়ই ক্লান্তি লাগল ।   তোমার এই কাজ করতেই হবে ।

T*a*r bara–i kl*a*nti l*a*gla.   Tom*a*r ei k*a*j karte-i habe.

Both of them did it.   *No* one went out.

তারা উভয়ই [তা] করছে/করেছে ।   কেহই বাইরে যায় নাই/নি ।

T*a*ra ubhay-i [t*a*] karchhe/   Keha–i b*a*ire jay n*a*i/ni.
karechhe.

This will do.   Come *quickly*.

এতেই/তাই হবে/চলবে ।   শীঘ্রই আস/এস ।

Ete–i/t*a*–i habe/chalbe.   Sheeghra-i *a*sha/esha.

Lesson 120

DEFINITIVE PARTICLES—ত, ta ; তো, to—surely, of course

ত, ta is COMMONLY called the challenging particle, and is used when one states a conviction on a subjective truth, and challenges discussion or argument on the point. It has this sense when used with a *noun* or a *pronoun*. When used with a *verb* it indicates that the speaker or writer wishes to persuade someone. In English it is equivalent to : *surely, though, you know, if, of course, then*

There certainly is a God.

ঈশ্বর ত আছেন ।

Eeshshar ta *a*chhen ?

I trust you're well.

ভাল আছেন ত ?

Bh*a*la *a*chhen ta ?

He is but a babe in arms.

সে ত কোলের ছেলে ।

She ta koler chhele.

Go if you like.

যাবে ত যাও ।

J*a*be ta j*a*o.

All are well, aren't they ?

সবাই/সবলে ভাল ত ?

Shab*a*i/shakale bh*a*la ta ?

You're going now, I suppose.

এখন যাবে/যাবেন ত ?

Ekhan j*a*be/j*a*ben ta ?

I know you will do this.

জানি তুমি ত এ কাজ করবে ।

J*a*ni tumi ta e k*a*j karbe.

Say it (if you can).

বল ত ।

Bala ta.

This work is not at all important.

এ কাজ ত জরুরী ।

E k*a*j ta jaruree.

Your house is nearby, isn't it ?

বাড়ী কাছে ত ?   বাড়ী ত কাছে ?

B*a*ree k*a*chhe ta ?   B*a*ree ta k*a*chhe ?

Indeed he is not a fool.

সে ত বোকা না ।

She ta bok*a* n*a*.

Today is Sunday, isn't it ?

আজ ত রবিবার, না ?

*A*j ta Rabib*a*r, n*a* ?

Very well, go home.

বেশ ত, তুমি বাড়ী যাও ।

Besh ta, tumi b*a*ree j*a*o.

I suppose he studies at home.

সে বাড়ীতে পড়ে ত ?

She b*a*reete pa*r*e ta ?

Fine ! Swell ! Good ! O.K.

বেশ তো ।

Besh to.

That's right.

সে কথা ত ঠিক । [Or, ঠিকই ।

She kath*a* ta *th*ik. [*th*ik-i

98

Lesson 121

EXCLAMATORY SENTENCE

These sentences do not differ from the affirmative sentence in written Bengali. The words কত kata, কি ki precede the adjectives of quality in exclamatory sentences, but are not used in affirmative sentences. In speaking, however, exclamatory sentences begin with a rising tone.

Good ! Fine ! Swell !	How beautiful/lovely !
বেশ ত !	কি সুন্দর !
Besh ta !	Ki shundar !

What a fine idea/view scene...!	What do you say !
কি চমৎকার কথা/দৃশ্য......!	বল কি !
Ki chamatkar katha/drishsha...!	Bala ki !

How dreadful !	What wisdom	nonsense !	What do you say !
কি ভয়ানক !	কি বুদ্ধি !		বল কি !
Ki bhayanak !	Ki buddhi !		Bala ki !

How clever he/she is !	How smart he/she is !
সে কেমন চালাক ! [কত...	তার কেমন বুদ্ধি !
She keman chalak ! [kata...	Tar keman buddhi ?

What a lot of things they saw there !	How pretty !
সেখানে তারা কুত কি দেখল !	কি/কত সুন্দর !
Shekhane tara kata ki dekhla !	Ki/kata shundar !

What rain !	But it's raining !
কী বৃষ্টি !	বৃষ্টি আসল/এল যে !
kee brishti !	Brishti ashl/ela je !

Lesson 122

CAUSAL CLAUSES—INTRODUCED by BECAUSE.

He is absent because he has a cold.

সে অনুপস্থিত/সে আসে নাই/নি কারণ তার সর্দি হইছে/হয়েছে ।

She arupasthit/ she ashe nai/ni karan tar shardi haichhe hayechhe.

He is holy because he loves God and men.

সে পবিত্র কারণ সে ঈশ্বর ও মানুষকে ভালবাসে ।

S   pabitra karan she Eeshshar o manushke bhalabashe.

He is sick because he ate too many mangoes.

তার অসুখ কারণ সে অনেক বেশী আম খাইছিল/খেয়েছিল ।

Tar ashukh karan she anek beshee am khaichhila/kheyechhila.

He didn't come because he is busy (with work).

সে আসে নাই/নি কারণ সে কাজে ব্যস্ত ।

She ashe nai/ni karan she kaje baesta.

I am sorry that he is ill.

সে অসুস্থ বলিয়া/বলে আমি দুঃখিত ।

She ashustha balia/bale ami duikhita.

Lesson 123

THE SENTENCE—DEPENDENT CLAUSES

A dependent clause in Bengali almost always precedes the main clause. This is especially the case when the subordinate clause is introduced by যে, je. (A modifying phrase precedes the noun it modifies.)

In a complex sentence the subject of the main verb comes after the subordinate clause (i. e. nearest the main verb). If

the subject does come first, the subordinate clause should be
set off by commas.

I know that you are good.	He doesn't know your name.
তুমি যে ভাল [তা] আমি জানি ।	তোমার কি নাম তা সে জানে না ।
Tumi je bhala [ta] ami jani.	Tomar ki nam ta she jane na.

I can't say when he comes. ✳ time/day...

আমি বলতে পারি না সে ✳ কখন/কবে আসে ।

Ami balte pari na she ✳ kakhan/kabe ashe.

Do you know where Haider will live/stay ?

তুমি জান হায়দার কোথায়/কই থাকবে ?

Tumi jana Haydar kothay/kai thakbe ?

I can't say who you are.	They knew whom he wanted.
তুমি কে তা আমি বলতে পারি না ।	তারা জানত সে কাকে চায় ।
Tumi ke ta ami balte pari na.	Tara janta she kake chay.

I could not understand how you knew it.

আমি বুঝতে পারলাম না তুমি কেমনে জান ।

Ami bujhte parlam na tumi kemne jana.

What has been said is true.

যা বলা হইছে/হয়েছে তা সত্য ।	যা—তা
Ja bala haichhe/hayechhe ta shatta.	ja—ta

The boy who studies hard/well gets a prize.

যে বালক ভালমত পড়ে সে পুরস্কার পায় ।	যে—সে ।
Je balak bhala mata pare she purashkar pay.	je—she.

The man you saw is a teacher.

যে লোক তুমি দেখছ/দেখেছ সে/তিনি শিক্ষক ।	যে — সে ।
Je lok tumi dekhchha/dekhechha she/tini shikkhak.	je—she

Lesson 124

(MORE) DEPENDENT CLAUSES

It matters little whether you go or not.

তুমি যাও বা না যাও তাতে কিছু আসে যায় না ।

Tumi jao ba na jao tate kichhu ashe jay na,

What is it to you whether I go or stay?

আমি থাকি বা যাই তাতে তোমার কি?

Ami thaki ba jai tate tomar ki?

He comes so that he may see me.

সে আসে যেন আমাকে দেখতে পায়।   /দেখবার জন্য

She ashe jena amake dekhte pay.   /dekhbar janna.

I shall go where you live.

তুমি যেখানে থাক সেখানে যাব।   যেখানে...সেখানে

Tumi jekhane thaka shekane jaba.   jekhane...shekhan.

He said it to me while he lived there.

সেখানে থাকবার/থাকার সময় আমায় তা বলছিল/বলেছিল।

Shekhane thakbar/thakar shamay amay ta balchhila/balechhila.

I am surprised he hasn't come.

আমি আশ্চর্য হইলাম/হলাম সে আসে নাই/নি।

Ami ashcharja hailam/halam she ashe nai/ni.

He said as he saw me...   The more you read,
                                  the more you'll know.

সে আমাকে দেখিয়া/দেখে বলল···   যতই পড়বে ততই শিখবে।

She amake dekhiya/dekhe balla...Jata-i parbe;tatai shikhbe.

You can see me whenever you come here.

তুমি যখনই আসবে [তখনই] আমাকে এখানে দেখতে পাবে।

Tumi jakhan-i ashbe [takhan-i] amake ekhane dekhte pabe.

Whoever goes there will see the beauty of the place.

যে কেহই সেখানে যাবে, সে স্থানের সৌন্দর্য দেখতে পাবে।

Je keha-i shekhane jabe, she sthaner saundarja dekhte pabe.

Lesson 125

CONDITIONAL CLAUSES—IF — যদি, jodi

(a) The four most common types of English conditional sentences are represented in Bengali by three types only.

If he comes, I'll go away. (...should come...

সে যদি আসে, তবে আমি চলিয়া/চলে যাব।

She jodi ashe, tabe ami chaliya/chale jabo.

If he came, I' d go away.

সে যদি আসত, আমি চলে যেতাম ।

She jodi *a*shta, *a*mi ҫhale jet*a*m.

If he has come, I should go away.   (shall go...)

সে যদি আসিয়া–এসে থাকে, তবে আমি চলিয়া/চলে যাব ।

She jodi *a*shiy*a*–eshe th*a*ke, tabe *a*mi chaliy*a*/chale j*a*bo.

If he had come, I should have gone away.

সে যদি আস্‌ত, তবে আমি চলিয়া/চলে যাইতাম/যেতাম ।

She jodi *a*shta, tabe *a*mi chaliy*a*/chale j*a*it*a*m/jet*a*m.

    (b)   তবে, tabe, then, may be replaced by তা হ'লে t*a* hale.

    (c)   Instead of the যদি jodi clause the conditional clause in ইলে, ile (L. 115) may be used.

    (d)   To express concession (L. 118) ও, o is added to যদি–যদিও jodi–jodio, although, even, if.

    (e)   না n*a*—no, not—precedes the verb :—

If he doesn't come, I shall not go away.

সে যদি না আসে, আমি চলিয়া/চলে যাব না ।

She jodi n*a* *a*she, *a*mi chaliy*a*/chale j*a*ba n*a*.

    (f)   Go and see if he's there or not.

গিয়া দেখ সে আছে কি না ।   (গিয়ে

Giy*a* dekha she *a*chhe ki·n*a*.   (giye

    (g)   Alternate short form :

I shall go if I can.	I shall go if you tell me to.
পারি তো যাব ।	বলেন/বল তো যাই ।
P*a*ri to j*a*bo.	Balen/bala to j*a*i.

Lesson 126

REPORTED SPEECH—direct quotation.

    (a) In reported speech the person is changed as needed, but the same tense is kept as in the direct speech.

He said he would come tomorrow.

সে বল্‌ছিল/বলেছিল [যে] * সে কাল আসবে ।

She balchhila/balechhila [je] * she k*a*l *a*shbe. [* use is optional]

He asked who had come.

সে জিজ্ঞাসা করল কে আসছে/এসেছে ।

She jigg*a*sh*a* karla ke *a*shchhe/eshechhe.

He asked whom I wanted.

সে জিজ্ঞাসা করল কাকে চাই ।

She jigg*a*sh*a* karla k*a*ke ch*a*i.

He asked where I lived/how I knew...

সে জিজ্ঞাসা কর্‌ল কোথায় থাকি/কেমনে জানি···

She jigg*a*sh*a* karla koth*a*y th*a*ki/kemne j*a*ni...

(b)   Direct speech is often introduced by যে je, that :—

He said, "Yes, of course I'll come."

সে বলছিল/বলেছিল যে, "হাঁ আসব তো ।"

She balchhila/balechhila je, "H*a*n, *a*shba to."

Lesson   127

TENSE—PRESENT PROGRESSIVE/CONTINUOUS (root

কর্‌, kar for   করতেছি/করছি kartechhi/karchhi—I am doing

                 ;, ছ/   ছ „ chha/ „ chha—You are „

              „ ছে/ ছে „ chhe/ „ chhe—He is   „

for eat, go, get forms :

যাইতেছি/   যাচ্ছি   j*a*itechhi/   j*a*chchhi—I am going

    ছ/   চ্ছ   a/   a—You are „

    ছে/   চ্ছে   e/   e—He is   „

It is used—

(a)   To indicate that the action IS TAKING PLACE at the time of speaking—and is not yet completed.

I'm writing a letter/eating...

আমি চিঠি লেখতেছি–লিখছি/খাইতেছি–খাচ্ছি···

Ami chithi lekhtechhi–likhchhi/khaitechhi–khachchhi...

I can't understand what he's saying.

আমি বুঝতে পারি না সে কি বলতেছে/বলছে ।

Ami bujhte pari na she ki baltechhe/balchhe.

(b) To denote immediately future action.

Come on ! All right ! I'm coming.

আস/এস না ! আচ্ছা ! আসতেছি/আসছি ।

Asha/esha na ! achchha ! ashtechhi/ashchhi.

I'm on my way/I'm going.

যাইতেছি/যাচ্ছি ।

Jaitechhi/jachchhi.

Listen, I'll tell you everything.

শুন, আমি তোমাকে সব বলিয়া দিতেছি/বলে দিচ্ছি ।

Shuna, ami tomake shab baliya ditechhi/bale dichchhi.

(c) Where English uses the present perfect continuous.

He has been studying Bengali for a long time.

সে অনেক দিন থেকে/যাবৎ বাংলা পড়তেছে/পড়ছে ।

She anek din theke/jabat Bangla partechhe/parchhe.

(d) In a subordinate adverbial clause to describe some vivid action in the past.

He came/turned up while I was eating.

আমি ভাত খাইতেছি/খাচ্ছি, এমন সময় সে আসিয়া/এসে পড়ল ।

Ami bhat khaitechhi/khachchhi, eman shamay she ashiya/eshe parla.

As in English, these verbs are not usually used in the present continuous/progressive tense :   love, hope, like, choose, want, owe, cost, believe, know (person, thing), understand, realize, hear, see, smell, need, feel, look, seem, agree.

Lesson 128

TENSE— SIMPLE PAST

1. I/we did   2. You/you did   3. He/they did

করলাম, karlam   কর্লে, karle   কর্ল, karla

(a)   Used to describe a chain of events in the past.

He said...   brought...   asked...

সে বলল···   আন্ল···   জিজ্ঞাসা কর্ল···

She balla...   anla...   jiggasha karla...

(b)   Used to describe action which has just taken place and even action about to take place. ✳

Where have you come from ?

তুমি কই থেকে আসলে/এলে ?

Tumi kai theke ashle/ele ?

He arrived just now.   ...sat down to eat...

সে এই মাত্র আসিয়া/এসে পড়ল ।   ···খাইতে/খেতে বস্ল... ●

She ei matra ashiya/eshe parla   ...khaite/khete bashla...

Where are you going ?   I give you this book.

কোথায় চল্লে ?   তোমাকে এই বই দিলাম ।

Kothay challe ?   Tomake ei bai dilam.

(c)   The negative na না may be added.

I went but he did not go.

আমি গেলাম কিন্তু সে গেল না/যায় নাই-নি ।

Ami gelam kintu she gela na/jay nai-ni.

Lesson 129

TENSE—PAST FREQUENTIVE/HABITUAL—USED TO

I/we used to go	you/you used to do	he/they used to do
কর্তাম	কর্তে	কর্ত
kartam	karte	karta

(a) To describe customary/habitual action in the past.

I used to go/live/study…there.

সেখানে যাইতাম–যেতাম/থাকতাম/পড়তাম…

Shekhane jaitam–jetam/thaktam/partam…

The Aryans used to worship the sun.

আর্যরা সূর্য পূজা করত।

Arjjara shoorjja pooja karta.

(b) Often used where English uses the past imperfect or the simple past (indefinite).

I stayed in this building when I was studying in this college.

আমি যখন এই কলেজে পড়তাম তখন এই বাসায় থাকতাম।

Ami jakhan ei kaleje partam takhan ei bashay thaktam

(c) Used as a past conditional :

If I had gone there I should have met you.

যদি সেখানে যাইতাম–যেতাম তবে তোমার সঙ্গে দেখা হ'ত।

Jodi shekhane jaitam–jetam tabe tomar shange dekha hata.

I'd run away if a tiger came.

বাঘ যদি আসত [যদি…তা হলে] পলাইয়া/পলিয়ে যাইতাম/যেতাম।

Bagh jodi ashta [jodi…ta hale] palaiya/paliye jaitam/jetam.

Lesson 130

TENSE —PAST PROGRESSIVE/CONTINUOUS

I was/we were doing	you/you were doing	he/they were doing
করতেছিলাম/করছিলাম	—ছিলে/—ছিলে	—ছিল/—ছিল
kartechhilam/karchhi-lam	—chhile/—chhile	—chhila/—chhila.

I met him while/as I was going home.

আমি যখন বাড়ী যাইতেছিলাম/যাচ্ছিলাম তখন তার সঙ্গে দেখা হ'ল।

Ami jakhan baree jaitechhilam/jachchhilam takhan tar shange
dekha hala.

At that time I was sleeping.

সে সময় আমি ঘুমাইতেছিলাম/ঘুমাচ্ছিলাম।

She shamay ami ghumaitechhilam/ghumachchhilam.

Lesson 131
TENSE—PAST PERFECT

I/we did	you/you did.	he/they did
করছিলাম/করেছিলাম	—ছিলে/—ছিলে	—ছিল/—ছিল
karchhilam/karechhilam	—chhile/—chhile	—chhila/—chhila

To express past completed action. Equal to English simple past and past perfect.

Many years ago he went abroad.

অনেক বৎসর আগে সে বিদেশে গেছিল/গিয়েছিল।

Anek batshar age she bideshe gechhila/giyechhila.

I went there yesterday.

আমি কাল সেখানে গেছিলাম/গিয়েছিলাম।

Ami kal shekhane gechhilam/giyechhilam.

না na, not/no is not used after this tense. Use the simple present and নাই nai/নি ni.

It was he who went, not I.

তিনি গেছিলেন/গিয়েছিলেন, আমি যাই নাই/নি।

Tini gechhilen/giyechhilen, ami jai nai/ni.

Lesson 132
RELATIVE CLAUSES—Adverb, noun, Adjective

I know who he is.	I didn't know...
সে কে তা আমি জানি।	···তা আমি জানতাম না।
She ke ta ami jani.	...ta ami jantam na.

I heard that he would come,

সে যে আসবে তা আমি শুনলাম।

She je ashbe ta ami shunlam.

The man who came yesterday has come again.

কাল যে লোক আসছিল/এসেছিল সে আবার আসছে/এসেছে।

Kal je lok ashchhila/eshechhila she abar ashchhe/eshechhe.

I have brought the book that you told me to bring.

তুমি যে বই আনতে বললে তাই আনছি/এনেছি।

Tumi je bai ante balle ta-i anchhi/enechhi.

I'll go where you tell me to go.

তুমি যেখানে যাইতে/যেতে বল সেখানে যাব।

Tumi jekhane jaite/jete bala shekhane jaba.

We'll come when they go away.

তারা যখন চলিয়া–চলে যাবে তখন আমরা আসব।

Tara jakhan chaliya–chale jabe takhan amra ashba.

What's the name of the man who teaches you Bengali ?

যিনি তোমাকে বাংলা পড়ান তাঁর নাম কি ?

Jini tomake Bangla paran tanr nam ki ?

Tell me where you live.

তুমি কোথায় থাক তা আমাকে বলিয়া–বলে দেও/বল।

Tumi kothay thaka ta amake baliya-bale deo/bala.

Whoever wishes may come.   anyone who...

যে কেহ আসতে চায় সে আসতে পারে।

Je keha ashte chay she ashte pare.

I'll be satisfied with whatever you give me.

আপনি আমাকে যা কিছু দিবেন তাতে সন্তুষ্ট হ'ব।

Apani amake ja kichhu diben tate shantushṭa haba.

They went each to his own home.

তারা যে যার বাড়ীতে চলিয়া–চলে গেল।

Tara je jar bareete chaliya–chale gela.

Lesson 133
INTERROGATIVES

who—কে ? ke ; plural কারা kara ; what—কি, ki, কি কি, ki ki

whose—কার ? kar ; * কাদের—kader   কিসের—kisher

whom—কাকে ? kake ; কাদের kader

   —কারে—kare ;   [* used for pl. obj /accusative colloq.].

   from whom—কার কাছ-থেকে kar kachh theke.

which ?	কোন্ kon	pron.— কোন্টি konti
where	কই kai	কোথায়— kothay
when (day)	কবে kabe ?	when (time) কখন kakhan ?
why	কেন kena ?	(কি জন্য ki janna) ? কিসের জন্য kisher janna.

from where কই-/কোথা-থেকে, kai/kotha theke?

how many/much কত kata কয় kai ; pron. কতটা katata, কয়টা kaita?

how far	কত দূর kata door	
how long	কতদিন kata din ,	কতক্ষণ katakkhan
how often	কতবার kata bar ,	কয়বার kai bar.
how many	কয় kai ;	pron. কয়টা kaita
how	কেমন keman	কেমন আছ ? keman achha ?
	How are you ?	
how	কেমনে kemne : কি করিয়া ki kariya/kare করে	
	How did you do it ?	
	কেমনে/কি করিয়া–করে/করছ-করেছ ?	
	kemne/ki kariya–kare/karchha–karechha ?	

How many/much   water/time/days/people/mangoes/time... ?

কত   জল/সময়/ক্ষণ/লোক/আম/বার··· ?

Kata   jal/shamay/kkhan/lok/am/bar... ?

PRONOUNS

	I—আমি	we আমরা	you তুমি	you তোমরা	he, she, it	they
NOM.	*a*mi	*a*mr*a*	tumi	tomr*a*	সে, ও, এ, তা, হি। she, o, e, t*a* ih*a*	ওরা, এরা, তারা, তারা। or*a*, er*a*, tar*a*, tar*a*
GEN.	my আমার *a*m*a*r	our আমাদের *a*m*a*der	your তোমার tom*a*r	your তোমাদের tom*a*der	his, her, its তার, এর, ওর, হাহার। t*a*r, er, or, ih*a*r	their তাদের, ওদের, এদের, ইহাদের। t*a*der, oder, eder, ih*a*der
OBJ./ ACC./ IND. O.	me আমাকে *a*m*a*ke	us আমাদের *a*m*a*der	you তোমাকে tom*a*ke	you তোমাদের tom*a*der	him, her, it তাকে, একে, ওকে, হাহাকে। t*a*ke, eke, oke, ih*a*ke,	them তাদের, ওদের, এদের, ইহাদের। t*a*der, oder, eder, ih*a*der
LOC.	to/in me আমায় *a*m*a*y (i)	to/in us আমাদের —	to you তোমাকে তোমায় tom*a*y	to you —	to him/her/it তাতে, এতে, ওতে, ইহাতে। t*a*te, ete, ote, ih*a*te	—

(1.) Commonly used for accusative : আমার *a*m*a*re, etc is also used. from me ? আমার কাছ থেক *a*m*a*r k*a*chh-theke L. 64—from *a* person.

it—this—e, এ, also এটা et*a*, এটি eti.

That—সে, she; ও—o, also সেটা, she*t*a, ওটা, ot*a* with ending as in the CHART.

Polite form—

1. The person addressed is আপনি, *a*pn-i, আপনারা *apnara*. The rest is as in the chart ঃ আপ্ন *a*pn—is the root.

2. The 3rd person is তিনি, tini ; plural তাঁরা t*anra*. The rest is as in the chart following the 3*rd* person. *n*–a half n or nasal sound in the first syllable. উনি uni and ইনি ini are used like তিনি—meaning *that* person and *this* person (held in regard/esteem).

———

VOCABULARY WITH SENTENCES

Will you be able to go there alone ?　　　　| able
　তুমি [কি] একা সেখানে যাইতে/যেতে পারবে ?　| পারা
　　Tumi [ki] eka shekhane jaite/jete parbe ?　| para

What do you know about this ?　[Postpos.]　| about
　এ বিষয়ে তুমি কি জান ?　　　　　　　　| বিষয়ে
　　E bishaye tumi ki jana ?　　　　　　| bishaye

He went there about an hour ago.　　　　| about
　প্রায় এক ঘণ্টা হয় সেখানে গেছে/গিয়েছে　| প্রায়
　　Pray ek ghanta hay shekhane /giyechhe.　| pray

The mango is hanging just above his head.　| above
　আমটা ঠিক তার মাথার উপরে ঝুলতেছে/ঝুলছে ।　| উপরে
　　Amta thik tar mathar upare jhultechhe/　| upare
　　jhulchhe.

Work according to my instructions [words].　| according to
　আমার কথামত কাজ কর ।　　　　　　| মত
　　Amar katha mata kaj kara.　　　　| mata

There is a mistake in your account.　　| account
　তোমার হিসাবে ভুল আছে ।　　　　　| হিসাব
　　Tomar hishabe bhul achhe.　　　　| hishab

My head aches.　　　　　　　　　| ache
　আমার মাথা ব্যথা করে/ধরে ।　　　　| ব্যথা
　　Amar matha baetha kare/dhare.　　| baetha

Do you know my address ?　　　　| address
　তোমরা [কি] আমার ঠিকানা জান ?　　| ঠিকানা
　　Tomra [ki] amar thikana jana ?　　| thikana

There is nothing to be afraid of. He is afraid. | be afraid.
　ভয় করার কিছু নাই/নেই । সে ভয় করে ।　| ভয় করা
　　Bhay karar kichhu nai/nei. She bhay kare.　| bhay kara

Our dog has returned after three days. | after
Go after me.

তিন দিন পরে আমাদের কুকুরটা ফিরিয়া আসূছে/ফিরে
এসেছে ।   আমার পরে যাও । | পরে
    Tin din pare *am*ader kukur*ta* firi*ya* | pare
    *a*shchhe/fire eshechhe.   *A*m*a*r pare j*a*o.

We play football everyday in the afternoon. | afternoon
| in the

আমরা রোজ বিকালে ফুটবল খেলি । | বিকালে
    *A*mr*a* roj bik*a*le fu*t*bal kheli. | bik*a*le

I shall go to see him again. | again
আমি তাকে আবার দেখতে যাইব/যাব । | আবার
    *A*mi t*a*ke *a*bar dekhte j*a*ibo/j*a*bo. | *a*bar

Don't speak against me. | against
আমার বিরুদ্ধে কথা বলিও/বল না । | বিরুদ্ধে
    *A*m*a*r biruddhe kath*a* balio/balo n*a*. | biruddhe

What is his/her age ?   How old is she/he ? | age
তার বয়স কত ? | বয়স
    T*a*r bayash kata ? | bayash

I cannot agree with him. | agree
আমি তার সঙ্গে একমত হইতে/হতে পারি না । | একমত হওয়া
    *A*mi t*a*r shange ek mat haite/hate p*a*ri n*a*. | ek mat
| haw*a*

There is no air in this room. (breeze) | air
এই ঘরে বাতাস নাই/নেই । | বাতাস
    Ei ghare b*a*t*a*sh n*a*i/nei. | b*a*t*a*sh

Alas !   What happened ? | alas !
হায় ! কি হইল/হল ? | হায়
    H*a*y ! Ki haila/hala ? | h*a*y

Alas ! It broke again. | alas
হায়রে ! ইহা আবার ভাঙ্গিয়া গেছে/ভেঙ্গে গেল । | হায়রে
Hayre ! Iha abar bhangiya/ | hayre
gechhe/bhenge gela.

All farmers work. | all
সব কৃষক কাজ করে । | সব, সকল
Shab krishak kaj kare. | shab, shakal

All right, you may go now. | all right
আচ্ছা, এখন তুমি যাইতে/যেতে পার । | আচ্ছা
Achchha, ekhan tumi jaite/jete para. | achchha

The work is almost finished. | almost
কাজটা প্রায় শেষ । | প্রায়
Kajta pray shesh. | pray

Has he/she come alone ? | alone
সে [কি] একা আসৃছে/এসেছে ? | একা
She [ki] eka ashchhe/eshechhe ? | eka

Don't let the baby go alone. | alone
খোকাকে একলা যাইতে/যেতে দিও না । | একলা
Khokake ekla jaite/jete dio na. | ekla

I can't hear (you) ; speak aloud. | aloud
শুনতে পাই না, জোরে বল । | জোরে
Shunte pai na, jore bala. | jore

It is altogether bad (not good). | altogether
ইহা মোটেই ভাল না । | মোটেই
Iha mote–i bhala na. | mote–i

Who among you can play ? | among
তোমাদের মধ্যে কে কে খেলতে পারে ? | মধ্যে
Tomader madhdhe ke ke khelte pare ? | madhdhe

After raising the anchor the ship/steamer left. | anchor
নঙর তোলার পর জাহাজ/স্টীমার ছাড়ল । | নঙর
Nangar tolar par jahaj/steemar chharla. | nangar

No one is here except you and me.	and
এখানে তুমি ও/আর আমি ছাড়া কেহ নাই/নেই ।	ও/আর
Ekhane tumi o/ar ami chhara keha nai/nei.	o/ar
You and I are enough to do this work.	and
এ কাজ করতে তুমি আর আমি যথেষ্ট ।	আর
Ei kaj karte tumi ar ami jatheshta.	ar
I am angry with him.	be angry
আমি তার সঙ্গে রাগ করছি/করেছি ।	রাগ করা
Ami tar shange rag karchhi/karechhi.	rag kara
A wild animal does not like to stay in a cage.	animal
বন্য পশু খাঁচায় থাকতে চায় না ।	পশু
Banna pashu khanchay thakte chay na.	pashu
Is that animal still alive ?	animal
সেই জন্তুটা [কি] এখনও জীবিত আছে ?	জন্তু
Shei jantuta [ki] ekhano jeebita achhe ?	jantu
That sound annoys people.	annoy
সেই শব্দ লোকদের বিরক্ত করে ।	বিরক্ত
Shei shabda lokder birakta kare.	birakta
If he wants another one, give it to him.	another
সে আর একটা চাইলে তাকে দিও ।	আর একটা
She ar ekta chaile take dio.	ar ekta
Not this one, get another book.	another
এটা না, অন্য একটা বই আন ।	অন্য
Eta na anna ekta bai ana.	anna
Answer these questions.	answer
এই প্রশ্নগুলির উত্তর দাও ।	উত্তর
Ei prashna gulir uttar dao.	uttar deoya
I don't know what answer I shall give.	answer
কি উত্তর দিব, বুঝি না ।	উত্তর
Ki uttar diba, bujhi na.	uttar

Ants ate up the candy/sweets. | ant
পিঁপড়া মিঠাই খাইয়া/খেয়ে ফেল্ল। | পিঁপড়া
Pinpra mithai khaiya/keye fella. | pinpra

Anyone can do this. | any
যে কোন লোক এটা করতে পারে। | যে কোন
Je kona lok eta karte pare. | je kona

I don't see any paper. | any
আমি কোন কাগজ দেখি না। | কোন
Ami kona kagaj dekhi na. | kona

He/she appears to be sick. (looks, seems) | appear
তাকে অসুস্থ দেখায়। | দেখায়
Take ashusta dekhay. | dekhay

I have applied for leave. | apply for
আমি ছুটির জন্য দরখাস্ত করছি/করেছি। | দরখাস্ত করা
Ami chhutir janna darkhasta | darkhasta
karchhi/karechhi. | kara

Apply for the post/job. | apply for
চাকুরির জন্য দরখাস্ত দাও। | দরখাস্ত দেওয়া
Chakurir janna darkhasta dao. | darkhasta
 | dewa

Will you employ a cook ? | appoint
আপনি [কি] বাবুর্চি রাখবেন ?/নিযুক্ত করবেন ? | রাখা
Apni [ki] baburchi rakhben ? | rakha

He was in the army. | army
সে সেনাবাহিনীতে ছিল। | সেনাবাহিনী
She shenabahineete chilla. | shenabahinee

Arrange the books neatly. | arrange
বইগুলি সুন্দর করিয়া/করে সাজাও। | সাজান
Baiguli shundar kariya/kare shajao. | shajan

What arrangement(s) have you made ? | arrangement

তুমি কি বন্দোবস্ত করছ/করেছ ? | বন্দোবস্ত

    Tumi ki bandabasta karchha/karechha ? | bandabasta

What arrangements have you made to go to Dacca ? | arrangements

ঢাকা যাবার কি ব্যবস্থা করছ/করেছ ? | ব্যবস্থা

    *Dha*ka ja*ba*r ki baebasth*a* karchha/ karechha ? | baebasth*a*

The police (have) arrested the thief. | arrest

পুলিশ চোরকে গ্রেপ্তার করছে/করেছে (ধরেছে) | গ্রেপ্তার করা

    Pulish chorke grept*a*r karchhe/karechhe (dharechhe). | grept*a*r kar*a*

When will the boat arrive ? | arrive

নৌকা কখন আসিয়া/এসে পৌঁছবে ? | পৌঁছা

    Nauk*a* kakhan *a*shiy*a*/eshe pou*n*chhbe ? | pou*n*chha

Sit on that chair as if you were a king. | as if

ঐ চেয়ারে বস, তুমি যেন রাজা। | যেন

    Oi chey*a*re basha, tumi jena r*a*j*a*. | jena

A monkey can easily climb/ascend a tree. | ascend/climb

বানর সহজে গাছে চড়তে/উঠতে পারে। | চড়া/উঠা

    B*a*nar shabaje g*a*chhe charte/u*th*te p*a*re. | chara/u*tha*

Ask him/her if he/she will go. | ask

তাকে জিজ্ঞাসা কর সে যাবে কি না। | জিজ্ঞাসা করা

    T*a*ke j*i*ggash*a* kara she j*a*be ki n*a*. | j*i*ggash*a* kar*a*

I was astonished at the tumult/disturbance. | astonished

আমি গোলমাল শুনিয়া/শুনে অবাক হইছি/হয়েছি। | অবাক

    *A*mi golm*a*l shuniy*a*/shune ab*a*k haichhi/ hayechhi. | ab*a*k

I did not hear (of) him at all. (2 meanings) | at all

আমি তার কথা মোটেই শুনি নাই/নি! | মোটেই

    *A*mi t*a*r kath*a* mo*t*e-i shuni n*a*i/ni. | mo*t*e-i

This rice is not at all good. | at all
এ চাউল একেবারেই ভাল না । | একেবারেই
   E chaul ekebare-i bhala na. | ekebare-i

I need at least one blanket. | at least
আমার কমের পক্ষে একটা কম্বল লাগে । | কমের পক্ষে
   Amar kamer pakkhe ekta kambal lage. | kamer pakkhe

Attempt it once more. (try) | attempt
আর একবার চেষ্টা কর । | চেষ্টা করা
   Ar ekbar chesta kara. | chesta kara

Pay attention to your work.   attend to) | pay attention
তোমার কাজে মনোযোগ দাও । | মনোযোগ দেওয়া
   Tomar kaje manojog dao. | manojog dewa

Wicked boys do not pay attention | pay attention
to their studies. |
দুষ্ট ছেলেরা পড়ায় মন দেয় না । | মন দেওয়া
   Dushta chhelera paray man dey na. | man dewa

He/she has a great attraction toward music. | attraction
গান বাজনার দিকে তার খুব টান । | টান
   Gan bajnar dike tar khub tan. | tan

In autumn the days are fine. | autumn
শরৎকালে দিনের অবস্থা ভাল থাকে । | শরৎকাল
   Sharatkale diner abastha bhala thake. | sharatkal

On the average the price of each pair of | on the average
pants is taka thirty. |
গড়ে প্রত্যেকটি প্যান্টের দাম ত্রিশ টাকা । | গড়ে
   Gare prattekti penter dam trish taka. | gare

An axe is needed to cut a tree. | axe
গ্যছ কাটতে কুড়াল লাগে । | কুড়াল
   Gachh katte kural lage. | kural

The baby looks pretty.   (beautiful) | baby
শিশুকে সুন্দর লাগে/দেখায় । | শিশু
   Shishuke shundar lage/dekhay. | shishu

He has two babies/small children. | baby
তার দুইটা বাচ্চা আছে । | বাচ্চা
   Tar duita bachcha achhe. | bachcha

Don't say bad words. | bad, wicked
খারাপ কথা বলিও/ব'জ না । | খারাপ
   Kharap katha balio/bala na. | kharap

Only bad people act like this. | bad
দুষ্ট লোকেরাই এ রকম কাজ করে । | দুষ্ট
   Dushta lokera-i e rakam kaj kare. | dushta

What is in your bag ? | bag
তোমার থলির ভিতর কি [আছে] ? | থলি/ব্যাগ
   Tomar thalir bhitar ki [achhe] ? | thali

Did you bake the bread/meat well ? | bake
রুটি/মাংস ভাল করিয়া সেঁকছ/করে সেঁকেছ তো ? | সেঁকা
   Ruti/mangsha bhala kariyashen kchha/ | shenka
kare shenkechha to ?

He teaches me Bengali. | Bengali
তিনি আমাকে বাংলা শিখান । | বাংলা
   Tini amake Bangla shikhan. | Bangla

Throw the ball to me. | ball
বলটা আমার দিকে ছুঁড়িয়া/ছুঁড়ে দাও । | বল
   Balta amar dike churiya/chunre dao. | bal

There is a clump of bamboos behind our house. | bamboo
আমাদের বাড়ীর পাছে বাঁশের ঝোপ আছে । | বাঁশ
   Amader bareer pachhe bansher jhop achhe. | bansh

Everybody likes to eat bananas. | banana
সকলে কলা খাইতে/খেতে ভালবাসে । | কলা
   Shakale kala khaite/khete bhalobashe. | kala

The banian tree is the biggest tree in this country. | banian tree

বটগাছ এদেশে সবচেয়ে বড় গাছ । | বটগাছ

    Bat gachh e deshe shab cheye bara gachh. | bat gachh

I (shall) need a barber to cut my hair. | barber

চুল কাটতে আমার একজন নাপিত লাগবে । | নাপিত

    Chul katte amar ek jon napit lagbe. | napit

He is as bashful as a girl. | bashful

সে মেয়েদের মত লাজুক । | লাজুক

    She meyeder mata lajuk. | lajuk

Get a basket and put the waste paper in it. | basket

একটা টুকরি আনিয়া/এনে বাজে কাগজগুলি তাতে রাখ । | টুকরি

    Ekta tukri aniya/ene baje kagajguli tate rakha. | tukri

Are there mangoes in your basket ? | basket

তোমার ঝুড়িতে আম নাকি ? | ঝুড়ি

    Tomar jhurite am na ki ? | jhuri

You should bathe everyday. | bathe

রোজ তোমাদের স্নান করা উচিৎ/উচিত। | গোসল/ স্নান করা

    Roj tomader snan kara uchit. | gosal/ snan kara

The seeds of this tree are like beans. | bean

এ গাছের বীজ শিমের মত । | শিম

    E gachher beej shimer mata. | shim

Who can bear such pain ? | bear, endure

এমন ব্যাথা কে সহ্য করতে পারে ? | সহ্য করা

    Eman baetha ke shajja karte pare ? | shajja kara

I can't carry (bear) such a load. | carry (bear)

এমন বোঝা আমি বহন করতে পারি না । | বহন করা

    Eman bojha ami bahan karte pari na. | bahan kara

Many people grow/keep beards. | beard

অনেক লোকই দাঁড়ি রাখে । | দাঁড়ি

    Anek lok–i danri rakhe. | danri

Why do you beat the dog ?	beat
কুকুরটা মার কেন ?	মারা
Kukur*ta* m*a*ro keno ?	m*a*r*a*

The sky looks very beautiful today.	beautiful
আকাশ আজ ভারি সুন্দর দেখায় ।	সুন্দর
Ak*a*sh *a*j bh*a*ri shundar dekh*a*y.	shundar

He/she will not go to school today because he/she is ill.	because
সে আজ স্কুলে যাবে না, কারণ তার অসুখ ।	অসুখ
She *a*j skule j*a*be n*a*, k*a*ran t*a*r ashukh.	k*a*ran

Because of illness he/she did not go home today.	because of
অসুখের কারণে সে আজ বাড়ী যায় নাই/নি ।	কারণে
Ashukher k*a*rane she *a*j b*a*ree j*a*y n*a*i/ni.	k*a*rane

How are you ? I am well. Mother is well.	are, am (be)
কেমন আছ ? ভাল আছি । মা ভাল আছেন ।	আছ, আছে
Keman *a*chha ? Bh*a*la *a*chhi. M*a* bh*a*la *a*chhen.	*a*chha, *a*chhe

What (is) your name ? My name (is) John.	be
তোমার নাম কি ? আমার নাম জন ।	হওয়া
Tom*a*r n*a*m ki ? *A*m*a*r n*a*m Jan.	haw*a*

One day he/she will be/become a good student.	be, become
একদিন সে ভাল ছাত্র/ছাত্রী হবে ।	হওয়া
Ek din she bh*a*la chh*a*tra/chh*a*tree habe.	haw*a*

Let it become/get redder.	become
এটা আরও লাল হতে দাও । [হইয়া উঠা]	হওয়া/থাকা
E*t*a *a*ro l*a*l hate d*a*o. [haiy*a* u*th*a]	haw*a*, th*a*k*a*

Your bed is in that room.	bed
ঐ ঘরে তোমার বিছানা আছে ।	বিছানা
Oi ghare tom*a*r bichh*a*na *a*chhe.	bichh*a*n*a*

There are many bugs in my bedstead. (cot) | bedstead
আমার খাটে অনেক ছারপোকা [আছে] । | খাট
Amar khate anek chharpoka [achhe]. | khat

Bees make honey. | bee
মৌমাছিরা মধু তৈরী করে । | মৌমাছি
Mowmachhira madhu tairee kare. | mowmachhi

He will go before me. | before
সে আমার আগে যাবে । | আগে
She amar age jabe. | age

Who can stand before a tiger ? (in front of) | before
বাঘের সামনে কে দাঁড়াইতে/দাঁড়াতে পারে ? | সামনে
Bagher shamne ke danraite/danrate pare ? | shamne

Poor men beg from door to door. | beg
গরীব লোকেরা দরজায় দরজায় ভিক্ষা করে । | ভিক্ষা করা
Gareeb lokera doijay dorjay bhikkha | bhikkha kara
kare.

Aren't you ashamed to beg (alms) ? | beg (alms)
ভিক্ষা চাইতে/চেতে তোমার লজ্জা হয়/করে না ? | ভিক্ষা চাওয়া
Bhikkha chaite/chete tomar lajja | bhikkha chawa
hay/kare na ?

Give the beggar a taka. | beggar
ভিক্ষুককে একটা টাকা দাও । | ভিক্ষুক
Bhikkhuk ke ekta taka dao. | bhikkhuk

Now begin writing. | begin
এখন লেখা আরম্ভ/শুরু কর । | আরম্ভ করা
Ekhan lekha arambha/shuru kara. | arambha kara

Say/tell it from beginning to end. | beginning
আরম্ভ থেকে শেষ পর্যন্ত বল । | আরম্ভ
Arambha theke shesh parjanta bala. | arambha

Everybody was pleased with his behaviour.	behaviour
সকলেই তার ব্যবহারে সন্তুষ্ট হইছিল/হয়েছিল ।	আচরণ/ব্যবহার
Shakale-i tar baebahare shantushta haichhila/hayechhila.	acharan, baebahar
Stand behind me.	behind
আমার পাছে দাঁড়াও ।	পাছে/পিছে
Amar pachhe danrao.	pachhe/pichhe
I always believe him.	believe
আমি সব সময় তাকে বিশ্বাস করি	বিশ্বাস করা
Ami shab shamay take bishash kari.	bishash kara
I did not hear the 5 o'clock bell.	bell, hour
আমি পাচটার ঘন্টা শুনি নাই/নি ।	ঘন্টা
Ami panchtar ghanta shuni nai/ni.	ghanta
There is a star just below the moon.	below, under
চাঁদের ঠিক নীচে একটা তারা আছে । [GRAM.	নীচে
Chander thik neeche ekta tara achhe.	neeche
I shall do it for your benefit/good.	benefit
আমি তোমার মঙ্গলের জন্য এটা করব ।	লাভ/মঙ্গল
Ami tomar mangaler janna eta karba.	labh, mangal
Do you know Bengali /Bangla ? No, but I'm learning.	Bengali
আপনি [কি] বাংলা জানেন ? না, কিন্তু শিখতেছি ।	বাংলা
Apni [ki] Bangla janen ? Na, kintu shikhtechhi.	Bangla
Stand beside the house. (at the side of) [See GRAM.]	beside
ঘরের পাশে দাঁড়াও ।	পাশে
Gharer pashe danrao.	pashe
Besides all this you will get candy/sweets too. [GRAM.]	besides
এ সব ছাড়া তোমরা মিঠাইও পাবে ।	ছাড়া
E shab chhara tomra mithai-o pabe.	chhara

I have no one besides God/Allah. [POSTPOS. | besides

ঈশ্বর/আল্লা বিনা আমার কেহ নাই/নেই । | বিনা

Eeshshar/Allah bina amar keho nai/nei. | bina

Divide the mangoes between Jadu and | between
Madhu. [GRAM.

যদু আর মধুর মধ্যে আমগুলি ভাগ করিয়া/করে দাও । | মধ্যে

Jadu ar Madhur madhdhe am guli bhag | madhdhe

kariya/kare dao [GRAM.

He is a big man. Dacca is a big city, | big

সে একজন বড় লোক ।   ঢাকা একটা বড় শহর । | বড়

She ekjan bara lok. Dhaka ekta bara shahar. | bara

Bind the goat with a rope. | bind, tie

ছাগলটা দড়ি দিয়া/দিয়ে বাঁধ । | বাঁধা

Chagalta dari diya/diye bandha. | bandha

Some birds can sing. | bird

কোন কোন পাখী গান করতে পারে । | পাখী

Kono kono pakhee gan karte pare. | pakhee

Today is my birthday. | birth

আজ আমার জন্মদিন । | জন্ম

Aj amar janmadin. | janma

John was born in Dacca. | birth

ঢাকায় জনের জন্ম হইছে/হয়েছে । | জন্ম

Dhakay Janer janma haichhe/hayechhe. | janma

My dog will not bite you. | bite

আমার কুকুর তোমাকে কামড়াবে না । | কামড়ান

Amar kukur tomake kamrabe na. | kamran

This medicine tastes bitter. | bitter

এ ঔষধ তিতা লাগে । | তিতা

E oushadh tita lage. | tita

That black shirt is mine. | black
ঐ কাল সার্ট আমার । | কাল
   Oi kala shart amar. | kala

Why do you blame me ? | blame
আমার দোষ ধর কেন ? | দোষ ধরা
   Amar dosh dhara kena ? | dosh dhara

I need two blankets in winter. | blanket
শীতকালে আমার দু'টা কম্বল লাগে । | কম্বল
   Sheetkale amar duta kambal lage. | kambal

A blind man cannot walk without a stick. | blind
অন্ধলোক লাঠি ছাড়া চলতে পারে না । | অন্ধ
   Andha lok lathi chhara chalte pare na. | andha

Much blood flowed from his wound. | blood
তার ঘা থেকে অনেক রক্ত পড়ছিল/পড়েছিল । | রক্ত
   Tar gha theke anek rakta parchhila/
              parechhila. | rakta

Blot up the ink with a rag. (wipe) | blot
নেকড়া দিয়া/দিয়ে কালি মোছ । | মোছা
   Nekra diya/diye kali muchha. | muchha

A blot fell on my paper. (spot, mark) | blot
আমার কাগজে দাগ বসছে/বসেছে । | দাগ
   Amar kagaje dag bashchhe/bashechhe. | dag

The sky looks blue. | blue
আকাশ নীল দেখায় । | নীল
   Akash neel dekhay | neel

A cold wind blows in winter. | blow
শীতকালে ঠান্ডা বাতাস বয় । | (বাতাস) বহা
   Sheetkale thanda batash boy. | (batas)
                 baha

Yesterday we saw a boat race.	boat
গতকাল আমরা নৌকা বাইছ দেখছি/দেখেছি ।	নৌকা
Gata kal amra nauka baichh dekhchhi/ dekhechhi.	nauka
O boatman, row/ply the boat fast.	boatman
[ও] মাঝি, নৌকা জোরে চালাও ।	মাঝি
[O] majhi, nauka jore chalao.	majhi
He has no strength in his body.	body
তার শরীরে বল নাই/নেই ।	শরীর
Tar shareere bal nai/nei.	shareer
See, the water is boiling.	boil (v. i.)
দেখ, জল/পানি ফুটতেছে/ফুটছে	ফুটা
Dekho, jal/pani futtechhe/futchhe.	futa
Boil the water well.	boil (v. t.)
জল ভাল করিয়া/করে ফুটাও ।	ফুটান
Jal bhala kariya/kare futao.	futan
Boil an egg for me.	boil
আমার জন্য একটা ডিম সিদ্ধ কর ।	সিদ্ধ করা
Amar janna ekta dim shiddha kara.	shiddha
	kara
I eat rice.	(boiled) rice
আমি ভাত খাই ।	ভাত
Ami bhat khai.	bhat
What is the price/cost of this book ?	book
এ বই'র/বইয়ের দাম কত ?	বই
E boir/boi-er dam kata ?	boi
I borrowed five taka from Mati.	borrow
আমি মতির কাছ থেকে পাঁচ টাকা ধার করছি/করেছি ।	ধার করা
Ami Matir kachh theke panch taka dhar karchhi/karechhi.	dhar kara

9—

Both of them will come tomorrow.	both
তারা উভয়ই কাল আসবে ।	উভয়
Tara ubhay-i kal ashbe.	ubhay
Both the fish are rotten.	both
মাছ দু'টাই পঁচা ।	দু'টাই
Machh duta-i pancha.	duta-i
Don't bother me. (vex)	bother
আমাকে বিরক্ত কর না ।	বিরক্ত করা
Amake birakta kara na.	birakta kara
What is at the bottom of the glass ?	bottom, at
গেলাসের তলায় কি [আছে] ?	তলায়, তলে
Gelasher talay ki [achhe] ?	talay, tale
This is the boundary of our land.	boundary
এটা আমাদের জমির সীমা/সীমানা ।	সীমা
Eta amader jamir sheema/sheemana.	sheema
Fasten the box with nails.	box
পেরেক দিয়া/দিয়ে বাক্সটা বন্ধ কর ।	বাক্স
Perek diya/diye bakshata bandha kara.	baksha
This boy is very intelligent.	boy
এ বালক/ছেলে ভারি বুদ্ধিমান ।	বালক/ছেলে
E balak/chhele bhari buddhiman.	balak/ chhele
I have known him from his boyhood.	boyhood
আমি তাকে ছেলেবেলা থেকে চিনি ।	ছেলেবেলা
Ami take chhelebela theke chini.	chhelebela
Women like to wear bracelets.	bracelet
স্ত্রীলোকেরা চুড়ি পরতে ভালবাসে ।	চুড়ি
Streelokera churi parte bhalabashe.	churi
A bird is sitting on the branch.	branch
ডালে একটা পাখী বসিয়া/বসে আছে,	ডাল
Dale ekta pakhee bashiya/bashe achhe,	dal

This is made of brass. | brass
এটা পিতলের তৈরী । | পিতল
   Eta pitaler tairee. | pital

Boil this in a brass pot. | brass
এটা পিতলের হাড়িতে জ্বাল দেও । | পিতল
   Eta pitaler harite jjal deo. | pital

The man seems brave. | brave
লোকটাকে সাহসী বলিয়া/বলে মনে হয় । | সাহসী
   Loktake shahasee baliya/bale mane hay. | shahashee

Be careful ! don't break the plate. | break
সাবধান ! প্লেট/থাল ভাঙ্গিও/ভেঙ্গ না । | ভাঙ্গা
   Shabdhan ! plet/thal bhangio/bhengo na. | bhanga

What shall I do with this broken plate ! | broken
এ ভাঙ্গা প্লেট দিয়া/দিয়ে আমি কি করব ? | ভাঙ্গা
   E bhanga plet diya/diye ami ki karba ? | bhanga (ad.)

Is this breakfast time ? Serve tea for
breakfast | breakfast.

এটা [কি] নাস্তার সময় ? নাস্তার জন্য চা
দিবে । | নাস্তা/চা
   Eta [ki] Nastar shamay ?
   Nastar janna cha dibe. | nasta/cha

Every night their cow breaks loose. | break loose
প্রত্যেক রাত্রে তাদের গরু ছুটিয়া/ছুটে যায় । | ছুটিয়া যাওয়া
   Prattek ratre tader garu chhutiya/
                 chhute jay | chhutiya
                     | jawa

Breathe slowly. | breathe (in)
ধীরে ধীরে নিশ্বাস টান । | নিশ্বাস টানা
   Dheere dheere nisshash tana. | nisshash
                 | tana

English	Bengali	Transliteration

How much of a bribe does he want ? | bribe

সে কত টাকা ঘুষ চায় ? | ঘুষ

    She kata *taka* ghush ch*a*y ? | ghush

Why do you bribe him ? He takes bribes. | bribe

তোমরা তাকে ঘুষ দেও কেন ? সে ঘুষ খায় । | ঘুষ দেওয়া

    Tomr*a* t*a*ke ghush deo keno ? She

ghush kh*a*y. | ghush dew*a*

Ask the mason how many bricks will be

needed. | brick

রাজমিস্ত্রীকে জিজ্ঞাসা কর কত ইট লাগবে । | ইট

    R*a*jmistreeke jigg*a*sh*a* kara kata i*t* l*a*gbe. | i*t*

The new bride is very bashful. | bride

নূতন বৌ খুব লাজুক । | বৌ

    Nootan bau khub l*a*juk. | bau

The bridegroom has not arrived yet. | bridegroom

বর এখনও আসিয়া/এসে পৌঁছে নাই/নি । | বর

    Bar ekhano *a*shiya/eshe poun*ch*he n*a*i/ni. | bar

There is an iron bridge in Dacca. | bridge

ঢাকায় একটা লোহার পুল আছে । | পুল

    *Dh*ak*a*y ek*ta* loh*a*r pul *a*chhe. | pul

The bright light hurts * my eyes. (* hits, strikes) bright

উজ্জ্বল আলোটা আমার চোখে লাগে * । | উজ্জ্বল

    Ujjal *a*lo*ta a*ma*r chokhe l*a*ge * | ujjal

Bring the chair here. Bring the boy here. | bring

চেয়ারটা এখানে আন । ছেলেকে এখানে নিয়া আস/

নিয়ে এস । | আনা

    Chey*a*rta ekh*a*ne *a*na. Chheleke

ekh*a*ne niy*a a*sha/niye esha. | *a*n*a*

He cannot walk with his broken leg. | broken

ভাঙ্গা পা দিয়া/দিয়ে সে চলতে পারে না । | ভাঙ্গা

    Bh*a*ng*a* p*a* diy*a*/diye she chalte

        p*a*re n*a*. | bh*a*ng*a*

Clean the yard with a broom. | broom

ঝাড় দিয়া/দিয়ে উঠান পরিস্কার কর । | ঝাড়

Jharu diya/diye uthan parishkar kara. | jharu

Who is your brother ? | brother

কে তোমার ভাই ? | ভাই

Ke tomar bhai ? | bhai

I like brown. | brown

আমি বাদামী রং পছন্দ করি । | বাদামী

Ami badamee rang pachhanda kari. | badamee

Give me a bucket of water. | bucket

আমাকে এক বাল্তি জল দাও । | বাল্তি

Amake ek balti jal dao. | balti

Peter will build a house. | build

পিটার একখানা ঘর তৈরী করবে/উঠাইবে । | তৈরী করা

Pitar ek khana ghar tairee karbe/uthaibe. | tairi kara

Bullocks pull carts. | bullock

বলদে গাড়ী টানে । | বলদ

Balade garee tane. | balad

This bullet is needed for tiger hunting. | bullet

এ গুলি বাঘ শিকার করতে লাগে । | গুলি

E guli bagh shikar karte lage | guli

I burn waste paper. | burn (v. tr.)

আমি বাজে কাগজ পোড়াই । | পোড়া

Ami baje kagaj porai. | pora

The lamp is burning. | burn (v. in.)

বাতি জ্বলতেছে/জ্বলছে । | জ্বলা

Bati jjaltechhe/jjalchhe. | jjala

Jackals live in the bushes. | bush

ঝোপে শিয়াল থাকে । | ঝোপ

Jhope shiyal thake. | jope

He/she is always busy working. | busy
তিনি/সে সব সময় কাজে ব্যস্ত থাকেন/থাকে। | ব্যস্ত
    Tini/she shab shamay kaje baesta thaken/ thake. | baesta

I shall go there, but (I) won't eat anything. | but
আমি সেখানে যাব কিন্তু, কিছু খাব না। | কিন্তু
    Ami shekhane jaba kintu, kichhu khaba na. | kintu

I want bread and butter every morning. | butter
রোজ সকালে আমি মাখন রুটী চাই। | মাখন
    Roj shakale ami makhan rutee chai. | makhan

Can you catch the butterfly ? | butterfly
প্রজাপতিটা ধরতে পার ? | প্রজাপতি
    Prajapatita dharte para ? | prajapati

There is no button on my shirt. | button
আমার সার্টে বোতাম নাই/নেই। | বোতাম
    Amar sharte botam nai/nei. | botam

I shall buy a coat for you. | buy
আমি তোমার জন্য একটা কোট কিনব। | কিনা
    Ami tomar janna ekta kot kinba. | kina

Go home by rickshaw/bus. [see POSTP.] | by
রিক্সা/বাস দিয়া/দিয়ে বাড়ী যাও। | দিয়া/দিয়ে
    Riksha/bas diya/diye baree jao. | diya/diye

What will you gain by that ? | by that
তাতে তোমার কি লাভ হবে ? | তাতে
    Tate tomar ki labh habe ? | tate

There are many cabbages in our garden. | cabbage
আমাদের বাগানে অনেক বাঁধা কপি আছে। | বাঁধা কপি
    Amader bagane anek bandha kopi achhe. | bandha
 | kopi

Keep/put the bird in a cage. | cage
পাখীটাকে খাঁচায় রাখ । | খাঁচা
Pakheetake khanchay rakho. | khancha

Mother made/prepared many cakes. | cake
মা অনেক পিঠা বানাইছে/বানিয়েছে । | পিঠা
Ma anek pitha banaichhe/baniyechhe. | pitha

Ask the baker to make a cake. | cake
রুটীওয়ালাকে একটা কেক্ তৈরী করতে বল । | কেক্/কেইক
Ruteewalake ekta kek tairee karte bala. | kek/keik

Fix a date after looking at the calendar. | calendar
পঞ্জিকা দেখিয়া/দেখে একটা দিন ঠিক কর । | পঞ্জিকা
Panjika dekhiya/dekhe ekta din thik kara. | panjika

Call the boy. | call
ছেলেকে ডাক । বালকটিকে ডাকিয়া/ডেকে আন । | ডাকা
Chheleke daka. Balaktike dakiya/deke ano. | daka

Didn't you hear my call/me ? | call (N.)
আমার ডাক শুন নাই/নি ? | ডাক
Amar dak shuna nai/ni ? | dak (N)

Can the sick man walk now ? [INFIN. L. 84 | can, be able
রোগা লোকটি [কি] এখন হাঁটতে পারে ? | পারা
Roga lokti [ki] ekhan hantte pare ? | para

In summer this canal dries up. | canal
গ্রীষ্মকালে এ খাল শুকাইয়া/শুকিয়ে যায় । | খাল
(Grishmakale) Grisshakale e khal
shukaiya/shukiye jay. | khal

Light the lamp/candle. | candle, lamp
বাতি জ্বালাও । | বাতি
Bati jjalao. | bati

Dacca is the capital of Bangladesh. | capital
ঢাকা বাংলাদেশের রাজধানী । | রাজধানী
Dhaka Bangladesher rajdhanee. | rajdhanee

The patient needs good care. (has need of) | eare (N)
রোগীটির ভাল যত্নের দরকার । | যত্ন
Rogeetir bhala jatner darkar. | jatna

Why don't you take care of the baby ? | take care
শিশুটির যত্ন নেও/নাও না কেন ? | যত্ন নেওয়া
Shishutir jatna neo/nao na keno ? | jatna newa

Be careful from now on. | careful
এখন থেকে সাবধান হও । | সাবধান হওয়া
Ekhan theke shabdhan hao. | shabdhan
| hawa

I need a carpenter to repair my chair. | carpenter
আমার চেয়ার মেরামত করতে ছুতার মিস্ত্রি লাগবে । | ছুতার মিস্ত্রি
Amar cheyar meramat karte chhutar | chhutar
mistri lagbe. | mistri

Rich people put carpets on the floors of houses. | carpet
ধনীলোকেরা ঘরের মেঝেতে গালিচা রাখে । | গালিচা
Dhanee lokera gharer mejhete galicha rakhe. | galicha

Whose motor car is this ? | car, carriage
এই মোটর গাড়ী কার ? | গাড়ী
Ei motar garee kar ? | garee

A camel can carry a heavy load. | carry, (bear)
উট ভারী বোঝা বইতে পারে । | বহা
Ut bharee bojha baite pare. | baha

He will carry/bring my luggage. | carry, bring
সে আমার মালপত্র নিয়া/নিয়ে আসবে । | নিয়া আসা
She amar malpatra niya/niye ashbe. | niya asha

Carry/take this bundle with you. | carry, take
এ পুটলিটা তোমার সঙ্গে নিয়া/নিয়ে যাও । | নিয়া যাওয়া
E putlita tomar shange niya/niye jao. | niya jawa

When you go out, take some cash with you.	cash
বাইরে যাবার/যাওয়ার সময় কিছু নগদ টাকা সঙ্গে নিও।	নগদ টাকা
Baire jabar/jawar shamay kichhu nagad taka shange nio.	nagad taka
Cats can see even in the dark of night.	cat
বিড়ালেরা অন্ধকার রাত্রেও দেখতে পায়।	বিড়াল
Biralera andhkar ratre–o dekhte pay.	biral
I shall catch the bird.	catch
আমি পাখীটা ধরব।	ধরা
Ami pakheeta dharba.	dhara
He/she caught hold of my hand.	catch
সে আমার হাত ধরল।	ধরা
She amar hat dharla.	dhara
Cauliflowers grow/mature earlier than cabbages.	cauliflower
ফুল কপি বাঁধাকপির আগে জন্মে।	ফুলকপি
Ful kopi bandha kopir age janme.	ful kopi
What is the cause of this disturbance/uproar ? [see Caus. v.]	cause, n.
এ গোলমালের কারণ কি ?	কারণ
E golmaler karan ki ?	karan
I got the work done by him.	get done (caus. of do)
আমি তাকে দিয়া/দিয়ে কাজটা করালাম।	করান
Ami take diya/deye kajta karalam. (caus. v.)	karan
A certain person will come to see you.	a certain....
অমুক লোক তোমাকে দেখতে আসবে।	অমুক/কোন এক
Amuk lok tomake dekhte ashbe.	amuk
Certainly I shall go to your home/house some day.	certainly
অবশ্য একদিন আমি তোমাদের বাড়ী যাব।	অবশ্য
Abassha ekdin ami tomader baree jaba.	abassha

Certainly that wicked boy has done this. | certainly
নিশ্চয় সেই দুষ্ট ছেলেটা এ কাজ করছে/করেছে । | নিশ্চয়
    Nishchay shei dusta chheleta e kaj | nishchay
    karchhe/karechhe.

Sit on that chair. | chair
ঐ চেয়ারে বস । | চেয়ার
    Oi cheyare basha. | cheyar

Don't lose/miss this chance/opportunity | chance
এ সুযোগটা হারাইও না । | সুযোগ
    E shujogta haraio na. | shujog

Can you give me a taka's change ? | change (coin)
আমাকে এক টাকার ভাঙতি দিতে পার ? [রেজ্‌গি, খুচরা] | ভাঙতি
    Amake ek takar bhangti dite para ? [rejgi,
    khuchra] | bhangti

Change the note (taka). (Give me change.) | change
নোটখানা ভাঙাও । | ভাঙান
    Notkhana bhangao. | bhangan

I have to change my (dress) clothes. | change
আমার কাপড় বদলাতে হবে । | বদলান
    Amar kapor badlate habe. | badlan

Aziz is a boy of good character. | character
আজিজ ভাল স্বভাবের ছেলে । | স্বভাব
    Aziz bhala shabhaber chhele. | shabhab

Chase the goat from the garden. | chase (away)
ছাগলটাকে বাগান থেকে তাড়াও/খেদাও । | তাড়ান
    Chhagaltake bagan theke tarao/khedao. | taran

Fish is not cheap today. | cheap
আজ মাছ সস্তা না । | সস্তা
    Aj machh shasta na. | shasta

I don't cheat anyone. | cheat
আমি কাকেও ঠকাই না। | ঠকান
Ami kake-o *thakai* na. | *thaka*n

Check your tongue and speak. (anger, boy...) | check (tongue)
মুখ সামলাইয়া/সামলিয়ে কথা বল। | (মুখ) সামলান
Mukh sham*laiva*/shamliye katha bala. | (mukh) shamlan

He has a sore/bruise on his cheek. | cheek
তার গালে একটা ঘা হইছে/হয়েছে। | গাল
Tar gale ek*ta* gha haichhe/hayechhe. | g*a*l

We get cheese from milk. | cheese
আমরা দুধ থেকে পনীর পাই। | পনীর
Amra dudh theke paneer p*a*i. | paneer

He has a very weak chest. | chest
তার বুক খুব দুর্বল। | বুক
Tar buk khub durbal. | buk

Keep this money in a strong chest/iron box. | chest
এ টাকাগুলি মজবুত সিন্দুকে রাখ/রেখ। | সিন্দুক
E *taka*guli majbut shinduke r*a*kha/rekha. | shinduk

Chew your food well. | chew
তোমরা খাবার ভালমত চিবাও। | চিবান
Tomra kh*a*b*a*r bh*a*la mata chib*a*o. | chib*a*n

Who is the chief guest at this feast? | chief
এ ভোজে প্রধান অতিথি কে? | প্রধান/বড়
E bhoje pradh*a*n atithi ke? | pradh*a*n, bara

He has no children. Call your children. | children
তার কোন সন্তান নাই/নেই। তোমার ছেলেমেয়েকে ডাক। | সন্তান
Tar kono shant*a*n n*a*i/nei. Tom*a*r chhelemeyeke d*a*k. | shant*a*n, chhelemeye

It is not good to use many chilies in the curry. | chilies

তরকারীতে বেশী লঙ্কা /মরিচ ব্যবহার করা ভাল না । লঙ্কা/মরিচ

Tarkareete beshee lanka/marich baebahar

kara bhalo na.

lahka/

| marich

Choose what you want. choose

যেটা ইচ্ছা বাছিয়া/বেছে নেও/নাও । বাছিয়া নেওয়া

Jeta ichchha bachhiya/bechhe neo/nao. bachhiya

newa

Let's go to church. now. | church

চল এখন গির্জায় যাই । গির্জা

Chalo ekhan girjjay jai. girja

Will you smoke a cigar ? | cigar

আপনি কি চুরুট খাবেন ? চুরুট

Apani ki churut khaben ? churut

His present circumstances are not good. | circumstances

তার বর্তমান অবস্থা ভাল না । অবস্থা

Tar bartaman abastha bhalo na. abastha

We cannot work under these conditions. | conditions

এ অবস্থায় আমরা কাজ করতে পারি না । অবস্থা

E abasthay amra kaj karte pari na. abastha

What is the name of this city/town ? | city

এ সহরের নাম কি ? সহর, নগর

E shaharer nam ki ? shahar,

nagar

What class are you in ? What class do you | class

read in ?

তুমি কোন্ শ্রেণীতে/ক্লাসে পড় ? শ্রেণী/ক্লাস

Tumi kon sreineete/klase para ? sreinee/

klas

Your clothes are clean. Clean it.

তোমার কাপড় পরিষ্কার। ইহা পরিষ্কার কর।

Tomar kapar parishkar. Iha parishkar kara.

	clean
	পরিষ্কার
	parishkar

The sound/word is clear now.

শব্দটা এখন স্পষ্ট হইছে/হয়েছে।

Shabdata ekhan spashta haichhe/hayechhe.

clear
স্পষ্ট
spashta

My father is an office clerk.

আমার বাবা আফিসের কেরানী।

Amar baba afisher keranee.

clerk
কেরানী
keranee

The boy appears/seems to be clever.

ছেলেকে চতুর/চালাক মনে হয়।

Chheleke chatur/chalak mane hay.

clever
চতুর/চালাক
chatur,
chalak

The climate of this place is good.

এ জায়গার আবহাওয়া/জলবায়ু ভাল।

E jaygar abhawa/jalbayu bhala [abhawa].

climate
[আবহাওয়া]
জলবায়ু
jalbayu

The clock is very big.

ঘড়িটা খুব বড়।

Gharita khub bara.

clock,watch
ঘড়ি
ghari

He told me to close the door.

সে আমাকে দরজা বন্ধ করতে বলছে/বলেছে।

She amake darja bandha karte balchhe/balechhe.

close/shut
বন্ধ করা
bandha
kara

I want two yards of cloth for my pants.

আমার প্যান্টের জন্য দু'গজ কাপড় চাই।

Amar penter janna du'gaj kapar chai.

cloth
কাপড়
kapar

Put on dry clothes.

শুকনা কাপড় পর।

shukna kapar para

clothes
কাপড়
kapar

Are there clouds in the sky ? (Is there a...?) | cloud
আকাশে [কি] মেঘ আছে ? | মেঘ
   *A*kashe [ki] megh *a*chhe ? | megh

We burn coal in this stove. | coal
আমরা এ চুলায় কয়লা পোড়াই । | কয়লা
   *A*mra e chu*la*y kay*la* po*ra*i/pu*ra*i. | kay*la*

Cobras are very dangerous. | cobra
গোক্ষুর সাপ বড় ভয়ানক । | গোক্ষুর সাপ
   Gokkhur sh*a*p ba*r*a bhay*a*nak. | gokkhur
   | sh*a*p

He/she is afraid of a cockroach. when he sees... | cockroach
সে তেলাপোকা দেখিয়া/দেখে ভয় পায় । | তেলাপোকা
   She tel*a*pok*a* dekhiya/dekhe bhay p*a*y. | tel*a*pok*a*

Everyone loves to eat coconut. | coconut
সকলে নারিকেল খাইতে/খেতে ভালবাসে । | নারিকেল
   Shakale n*a*rikel kh*a*ite/khete bh*a*la*ba*she. | n*a*rikel

The water of a green coconut is very useful/ | coconut
   beneficial | (green)
ডাবের জল/পানি খুব উপকারী । | ডাব
   *Da*ber jal/p*a*ni khub upak*a*ree. | *da*b

It was very cold last night. | cold
গত রাতে খুব ঠাণ্ডা ছিল । | ঠাণ্ডা
   Gata r*a*te khub **tha**n*da* chhila. | *tha*n*da*

I have caught a cold. (I have a cold.) | cold (N)
আমার সর্দি হইছে/হয়েছে । | সর্দি
   *A*m*a*r shardi haichhe/hayechhe. | shardi

Get some cold water for me. | cold (adj.)
আমার জন্য কিছু ঠাণ্ডা পানি/জল আন । | ঠাণ্ডা
   *A*m*a*r janna kichhu *tha*nda p*a*ni/jal *a*na | *tha*n*da*

Do you really feel cold ?   I feel cold | feel cold
তোমার শীত করে না কি ? শীত লাগে | শীত করা
   Tomar sheet kare na ki ? Sheet lage. | sheet kara

Collect/gather up the dry leaves. | collect
শুকনা পাতাগুলি জমা কর । | জমা করা
   Shukna pataguli jama kara. | jama kara

Collect the necessary thing. | collect
দরকারী জিনিসগুলি যোগাড় কর । | যোগাড় করা
   Darkaree jinishguli jogar kara. | jogar kara

What colour do you like ? | colour/dye
কোন্ রং তুমি পছন্দ কর ? | রং
   Kon rang tumi pachhanda kara ? | rang

Where is your comb ? | comb
তোমার চিরুণী কই ? | চিরুণী
   Tomar chirunee kai ? | chirunee

Comb your hair. | comb
তোমার চুল আঁচড়াও । | আঁচড়ান
   Tomar chul anchrao. | anchran

Come here everyday. When will he/she come ? | come
এখানে রোজ আসবে । সে কবে আসবে ? | আসা
   Ekhane roj ashbe. She kabe ashbe ? | asha

I am in comfort (happy) here. | comfort
আমি এখানে আরামে/সুখে আছি । | আরাম/সুখ
   Ami ekhane arame/shukhe achhi. | aram/
| shukh

Where will you stay/be this coming/next month ? | coming, next
আগামী মাসে তুমি কই/কোথায় থাকবে ? | আগামী
   Agamee mashe tumi kai/kothay thakbe ? | agamee

Obey the commands/orders of (your) elders. | command
গুরুজনের আদেশ পালন করিও/করো । | আদেশ
   Gurujaner adesh palan kario/karo. | adesh

This is our common/ordinary food. | common
ইহা আমাদের সাধারণ খাবার । | সাধারণ
Iha amader shadharan khabar. | shadharan

My companion will not return/come back. | companion
আমার সঙ্গী/সাথী ফিরিয়া/ফিরে আসবে না । | সঙ্গী/সাথী
Amar shangee/shathee firiya/fire ashbe na. | shangee/
| shathee

Compare these two things. | comparison
এ দু'টা জিনিস তুলনা কর । | তুলনা করা
E duta jinish tulana kara. | tulana
| kara

I shall complain to your father. | complain
আমি তোমার বাবার কাছে নালিশ করব । | নালিশ করা
Ami tomar babar kachhe nalish karba. | nalish
| kara

He/she may go when he/she completes the work. | complete
কাজ শেষ করলে সে যাইতে/যেতে পারে । | শেষ করা
Kaj shesh karle, she jaite/jete pare. | shesh
| kara

This is completely rotten. | completely
এটা একেবারে/একদম পঁচা । | একেবারে,
| একদম
Eta ekebare/ekdam pancha. | ekebare

I like the servant because his conduct is good. | conduct
চাকরটাকে আমি পছন্দ করি, কারণ তার ব্যবহার ভাল । | ব্যবহার/
Chakartake ami pachhanda kari, karan | আচরণ
tar baebahar/acharan bhala. | baebahar

Confess your guilt. [admit. | confess
তোমার দোষ স্বীকার কর । | স্বীকার করা
Tomar dosh sheekar kara. | sheekar
| kara

Your conscience will tell you what to do. | conscience
তোমার বিবেক বলিয়া/বলে দিবে কি করতে হবে। | বিবেক
Tomar bibek baliya/bale dibe ki karte habe. | bibek

It requires your father's consent/permission. | consent
এতে তোমার বাবার অনুমতি দরকার। | অনুমতি
Ete tomar babar anumati darkar. | anumati

His father gave his consent. | give consent
তার বাবা অনুমতি দিচ্ছে/দিয়েছে। | অনুমতি দেওয়া
Tar baba anumati dichhe/diyechhe. | anumati
| dewa

We considered the matter together. | consider
আমরা বিষয়টা একসঙ্গে বিবেচনা করলাম। | বিবেচনা করা
Amra bishayta ek shange bibechana | bibechana
karlam. | kara

He/she constantly wears/uses glasses. | constantly
তিনি সব সময়ে চশমা ব্যবহার করেন। | সব সময়ে
Tini shab shamaye chasma baebahar karen. | shab
| shamaye

He/she is contented now. | contented
সে এখন সন্তুষ্ট। | সন্তুষ্ট
She ekhan shantushta. | shantushta

I have contracted to buy wood from him. | contract, v.
তার কাছ থেকে কাঠ কিনতে চুক্তি করলাম। | চুক্তি করা
Tar kachh theke kath kinte chukti karlam. | chukti
| kara

I cannot control this wicked boy. | control
এ দুষ্ট ছেলেকে আমি সামলাইতে/সামলাতে পারি না। | সামলান
É dusta chheleke ami shamlaite/shamlate
pari na. | shamlau

10—

Control your son/tongue/anger. | control
তোমার ছেলেকে/মুখ/রাগ সামলাও । | সামলান
Tomar chheleke/mukh/rag shamlao. | shamlan

Come here at your convenience. | convenience
তোমার সুবিধামত এখানে আসিও/এস । [সুযোগ] | সুবিধা
Tomar shubidha mata ekhane ashio/
esha. [shujog] | shubidha

Moti is conversing with his friend. | converse
মতি তার বন্ধুর সঙ্গে আলাপ করতেছে/ করছে । | আলাপ করা
Moti tar bandhur shange alap kartechhe/
karchhe. | alap kara

The name of our cook is John. | cook (N)
আমাদের বাবুর্চির নাম জন । | বাবুর্চি
Amader baburchir nam Jon. | baburchi

My mother can cook well. | cook
আমার মা ভাল পাক করতে পারে । | পাক করা
Amar ma bhala pak karte pare. | pak kara

I want a copy of this deed. | copy (N)
এ দলিলের একটা নকল/কপি চাই । | নকল/কপি
E daliler ekta nakal/kapi chai. | nakal/kapi

Don't copy from someone else's paper. | copy (V.)
অপরের কাগজ নকল করিও/কর না । | নকল করা
Aparer kagaj nakal kario/kara na. | nakal kara

I like to eat corn. | corn
আমি ভুট্টা খাইতে/খেতে ভালবাসি । | ভুট্টা
Ami bhutta khaite/khete bhalabashi. | bhutta

Put the almirah in a corner of the room. | corner
আলমারিটা ঘরের এক কোণে/কোণায় রাখ । | কোণ/কোণা
Almarita gharer ek kone/konay rakha. | kon/kona

What I am saying is correct. | correct
আমি যা বলতেছি/বলছি তা ঠিক/শুদ্ধ । | ঠিক/শুদ্ধ
   *A*mi j*a* baltechhi/balchhi t*a* t*h*ik/shuddha. | *th*ik,
  | shuddha

Correct your errors/mistakes. | correct (V.)
তোমার ভুলগুলো শুদ্ধ কর । | শুদ্ধ করা
   Tom*a*r bhulgulo shuddha kara | shuddha
  | kar*a*

Cloth is made from cotton. | cotton
তুলায় কাপড় তৈরী হয় । | তুলা
   Tul*a*y k*a*pa*r* tairee hay. | tul*a*

He has a cough. | cough
তার কাশ/কাশি আছে । | কাশ/কাশি
   T*a*r k*a*sh/k*a*shi *a*chhe. | k*a*sh

He/she always coughs. | cough
সে সব সময় কাশে । | কাশা
   She shab shamay k*a*she. | k*a*sh*a*

A child too can count from one to ten. | count
একটি শিশুও এক হ'তে/হইতে দশ পর্যন্ত গুণতে পারে । | গণা
   Ek*t*i shishu–o ek hate/haite dash parjanta
   gunte p*a*re. | gan*a*

Countless beggars were seen in the
streets of Dacca. | countless
ঢাকার রাস্তায় অসংখ্য ভিক্ষুক দেখা গেল । | অসংখ্য
   *Dha*ka*r* r*a*sta*y* ashankhkha bhikkhuk dekh*a*
   gela. | ashankhkha

We shall be glad if you come to see our
country. | country
আপনি আমাদের দেশ দেখতে আসলে সুখী হইব/হব । | দেশ
   *A*pni *a*m*a*der desh dekhte *a*shle shukhee | desh
   haiba/haba.

Country–made cigarettes are not bad. | country–made

দেশী সিগারেট খারাপ না । | দেশী

Deshee sigaret kharap na. | deshee

I shall stay in the country a few days. | the country

আমি কয়েক দিন মফঃস্বলে/গ্রামে থাকব । | মফঃস্বল/গ্রাম

Ami kayek din mafashale/grame thakba. | mafashal/ gram

Who has courage to speak against him ? | courage

তার বিরুদ্ধে কথা বলবার/বলার সাহস কার আছে ? | সাহস

Tar biruddhe katha balbar/balar shahash kar achhe ? | shahash

The dogs are barking in the courtyard | courtyard, yard

উঠানে কুকুরগুলি ঘেউ ঘেউ করতেছে/করছে । | উঠান

Uthane kukur guli gheu gheu kartechhe/ karchhe. | uthan

Why don't you cover the sweets ? | cover

মিষ্টিগুলি ঢাক না কেন ? | ঢাকা

Mishtiguli dhaka na kena ? | dhaka

Cows are grazing in the field. | cow

মাঠে গরুগুলি চরতেছে/চরছে । | গরু

Mathe garuguli chartechhe/charchhe. | garu

We keep/rear cows to get milk. | cow

আমরা দুধের জন্য গাভী পুষি | গাভী, গাই

Amra dudher janna gabhee pushi. | gabhee, gai

Crazy men talk like this. | crazy man

পাগলে এরকম কথা বলে । | পাগল

Pagale erakam katha bale. | pagal

Why don't I see cream in this milk ? | cream

এ দুধে সর দেখি না কেন ? | সর

E dudhe shar dekhi na kena ? | shar

Make the crooked iron rod straight. | crooked/bent
বাঁকা শিক সোজা কর । | বাঁকা/বেঁকা
Banka shik shoja kara. | banka/benka

Heavy rain destroys crops. | crop
বেশী বৃষ্টি শস্য নষ্ট করে । | শস্য/ফসল
Beshee brishti shassha nashta kare. | shassha/fashal

I shall cross the river by boat. | cross, (I.V.)
নৌকা দিয়া/দিয়ে নদী পার হব । | পার হওয়া
Nauka diya/diye nodee par haba. | par hawa

How much do you want to carry me across the river ? | carry across t.v.
নদী পার করতে কত চাও ? | পার করা
Nodee par karte kata chao ? | par kara

I could not pick him out in the crowd. | crowd
তাকে ভীড়ের মধ্যে বার/বের করতে পারলাম না । | ভীড়
Take bheerer maddhey bar/ber karte parlam na. | bheer

A cruel dog has killed my cat. | cruel
একটা নিষ্ঠুর কুকুর আমার বিড়ালটা মারিয়া ফেলেছে/মেরে ফেলেছে । | নিষ্ঠুর
Ekta nishthur kukur amar biralta mariya felchhe/mere felechhe. | nishthur

Why does the child cry so much ? | cry
শিশুটা এত কাঁদে কেন ? | কাঁদা/কান্না
Shishuta eta kande kena ? | kanda

Children cry out every now and then. | cry out (to)
শিশুরা যখন তখন চীৎকার করে । | চীৎকার করা
Shishura jakhan takhan chitkar kare. | chitkar kara

Cucumbers are available in the rainy season. | cucumber
বর্ষাকালে শসা পাওয়া যায় । | শসা
  Barshakale shasha pawa jay. | shasha

Cultivators work in the field. | cultivator
কৃষকরা ক্ষেতে কাজ করে । | কৃষক/চাষী
  Krishakra kkhete kaj kare. | krishak/
 | chashi

Don't trust this clever boy. (cunning) | clever
এ চালাক ছেলেকে বিশ্বাস করিও/করো না । | চালাক
  E chalak chheleke bisshash kario/karo na. | chalak

Give me a cup of tea. | cup
আমাকে এক কাপ চা দেও/দাও । | 'কাপ'/পেয়ালা
  Amake ek kap cha deo/dao. | kap/peyala

The current of a/the river becomes very | current
strong in the rainy season. |
বর্ষাকালে নদীর স্রোত খুব প্রবল হয় । , | স্রোত
  Barshakale nodeer srot khub prabal hay. | srot

We shall receive our current month's salary. | current, adj
চলতি মাসের বেতন আমরা আস্‌ছে মাসের পয়লা পাব । | চলতি
  Chalti masher betan amra ashchhe | chalti
  masher payla paba. |

The curry was not bad today | curry
তরকারিটা আজ মন্দ ছিল না । | তরকারি/কারি
  Tarkarita aj manda chhila na | tarkari/
 | kari

There is someone behind the curtain. | curtain
পরদার পিছনে কেহ আছে । | পরদা/পর্দা
  Pardar pichhane keha achhe. | parda

Give the patient a mosquito curtain and a cushion.	mosquito curtain
রোগীটাকে একটা মশারী ও গদি দাও।	মশারী
Rogee*ta*ke ek*ta* mash*a*ree o gadi d*a*o.	mash*a*ree
I don't know the custom(s) of this place.	custom
এ স্থানের নিয়ম/রীতি আমি জানি না।	নিয়ম, রীতি
E sth*a*ner niyam/reeti *a*mi j*a*ni n*a*.	niyam, reeti
Cut the old branches of the tree.	cut
গাছের পুরাতন/পুরান ডালগুলো কাট।	কাটা
G*a*chher pur*a*tan/pur*a*n d*a*lgulo k*a*ta.	k*a*ta
He/she comes here daily.	daily
সে রোজ এখানে আসে।	রোজ
She roj ekh*a*ne *a*she.	roj
Don't sleep in a wet place.	wet/damp
ভিজা জায়গায় ঘুমাইও/ঘুমিও না।	ভিজা
Bhij*a* j*a*yg*a*y ghum*a*i–o/ghumio n*a*.	bhij*a*
I saw the dance by Mrs. Bulbul.	dance, v.
মিসেস্ বুলবুলের নাচ আমি দেখছি/দেখেছি।	নাচ
Misses Bulbuler n*a*ch *a*mi dekhchhi/dekhechhi.	n*a*ch
He/she dances very well.	dance
সে খুব ভাল নাচে।	নাচা
She khub bh*a*la n*a*che.	n*a*ch*a*
Paul is now in great danger.	danger
পল এখন খুব বিপদের মধ্যে আছে।	বিপদ
Pal ekh*a*n khub bip*a*der maddhe *a*chhe.	bip*a*d
A jackal can move in the dark.	dark (-ness)
শিয়াল অন্ধকারে চলতে পারে।	অন্ধকার/ আঁধার
Shiy*a*l andhak*a*re chalte p*a*re.	andhak*a*r
	*an*dh*a*r

Do you know the date of his/her arrival ?	date
তার পৌঁছার তারিখ জান [কি] ?	তারিখ
Tar pounchhar tarikh jana [ki] ?	tarikh
Whose daughter is she ?	daughter
সে কার মেয়ে ?	মেয়ে
She kar meye ?	meye
We shall start/set out at dawn.	dawn
আমরা ভোরে রওনা হব ।	ভোর
Amra bhore raona haba.	bhor
It will take one day to finish the work.	day
কাজটা শেষ করতে একদিন লাগবে ।	দিন
Kajta shesh karte ek din lagbe.	din
Who can give the address of the dead man ?	dead
মৃত লোকটার ঠিকানা কে দিতে পারে ?	মৃত/মরা
Mrita loktar thikana ke dite pare ?	mrita/mara
Peter is my dear friend.	dear
পিটার একজন আমার প্রিয় বন্ধু ।	প্রিয়
Pitar ekjan amar priya bandhu.	priya
Rice is not so dear nowadays.	dear/expensive
আজকাল চাল এত দামি/দামী না ।	দামী
Ajkal chal eta damee na.	damee
Nobody knows when death will come.	death
মৃত্যু কখন আসবে কেহ জানে না ।	মৃত্যু/মরণ
Mrittu kakhan ashbe keha jane na.	mrittu/
	maran
I shall soon pay back my debt.	a debt, pay
শীঘ্রই আমার ঋণ শোধ করব । [কর্জ, ধার]	ঋণ শোধ করা
Sheegra-i amar reen shodh karba.	reen shodh
[karjja dhar]	kara

By no means can you deceive/fool me. | deceive/fool
কিছুতেই আমাকে ভুলাইতে/ভুলাতে পারবে না । [ঠকান] ভুলান
   Kichhute-i amake bhulaite/bhulate
   parbe na. [thakan] | bhulan

Deduct five taka from his salary/pay. | deduct, cut
তার বেতন থেকে পাঁচ টাকা কাটা দেও/দাও । | বাদ দেওয়া
   Tar betan theke panch taka kata deo/ dao. | bad dewa

The hilsha fish lives/stays in deep water. | deep
ইলিশ মাছ গভীর জলে থাকে । | গভীর
   Ilish machh gabheer jale thake. | gabheer

Don't delay on the way. | delay
পথে দেরি করিও/করো না । | দেরি না করা
   Phathe deri kario/karo na. | deri na kara

Fazlee mangoes are very delicious. | delicious
ফজলী আম বড় মজা । | মজা
   Fazlee am bara maja/shushadu. | maja

You should not demand any more. | demand/claim
আর বেশী দাবী করা তোমার উচিৎ না । | দাবী করা
   Ar beshee dabee kara tomar uchit na. | dabee kara

How much is your demand ? | demand (N)
তোমার দাবী কত ? | দাবী
   Tomar dabee kata ? | dabee

He denies his offence/fault. | deny (to)
সে তার দোষ অস্বীকার করে । ['না' বলা] | অস্বীকার করা
   She tar dosh asheekar kare. [na bala] | asheekar
  | kara

Deposit the money in your account. | deposit
টাকাটা তোমার হিসাবে জমা দাও । | জমা করা
   Takata tomar hishabe jama dao. | jama kara

My old father desires to see you.	desire, wish
আমার বুড়া বাবা তোমাকে দেখতে ইচ্ছা করেন।	ইচ্ছা করা
Amar bura baba tomake dekhte ichchha karen.	ichchha kara
The sudden flood destroyed the crops.	destroy
হঠাৎ বন্যায় শস্য নষ্ট করছে/করেছে।	নষ্ট করা
Hathat bannay shassha nashta karchhe/ karechhe.	nashta kara
Cold weather starts in the dewy season/ autumn.	dewy season
হেমন্তকালে শীত আরম্ভ হয়।	হেমন্তকাল
Hemanta kale sheet arambha hay.	hemanta kal
Consult a dictionary and correct the mistake.	dictionary
অভিধান দেখিয়া/দেখে ভুলটা শুদ্ধ/ঠিক কর।	অভিধান
Abhidhan dekhiya/dekhe bhulta shuddha/thik kara.	abhidhan
All will die.	die
সকলে মরবে।	মরা
Shakale marbe.	mara
There is a great difference between these two boys.	difference
এ দু'টা ছেলের মধ্যে অনেক তফাৎ আছে।	তফাৎ
E duta chheler maddhe anek tafat achhe.	tafat
We arrived there by a different way/path.	different
আমরা একটা ভিন্ন পথ দিয়া/দিয়ে সেখানে পৌঁছিলাম।	ভিন্ন/আলাদা
Amra ekta bhinna path diya/diye shekhane pounchhlam.	bhinna alada

It is difficult to pass the examination. | difficult
পরীক্ষায় পাশ করা কঠিন । | কঠিন/শক্ত
    Pareekkh*a*y p*a*sh kar*a* k*a*th*i*n. | k*a*th*i*n/
        shakta

I can't digest anything. Rice is digested easily. | digest
আমি কিছুই হজম করতে পারি না । ভাত সহজে হজম
                     হয় । | হজম করা
     *A*mi kichhu–i hajam karte p*a*ri n*a*. | hajam
     Bh*a*t shahaje hajam hay. | kar*a*

Now we shall have our dinner/meal. | dinner, meal
এখন আমরা খানা খাব । | খানা
     Ekhan *a*mr*a* kh*a*n*a* kh*a*ba. | kh*a*n*a*

Your hands are dirty. Don't wear dirty clothes. | dirty
তোমার হাত ময়লা । ময়লা কাপড় পর না । | ময়লা
     Tom*a*r h*a*t mayl*a*. Mayl*a* k*a*par para n*a*. | mayl*a*

Don't make it dirty. | make dirty
এটা ময়লা কর না । | ময়লা করা
     E*ta* mayl*a* kara n*a*. | mayl*a*
                  kar*a*

I disagreed with him in this matter. | disagree
এ বিষয়ে আমি তার সঙ্গে অমত হইছি/হয়েছি । | অমত হওয়া
     E bishaye *a*mi t*a*r shange amat haichhi/
     hayechhi. | amat haw*a*

The discipline in this school is good. | discipline
এ স্কুলের শাসন ভাল । | শাসন
     E skuler sh*a*shan bh*a*la. | sh*a*shan

Parents want to discipline their children
according to their wishes. | discipline
পিতা মাতা সন্তানদের নিজেদের ইচ্ছামত শাসন করতে
চায় । | শাসন করা
     Pit*a*mat*a* shant*a*nder nijeder | sh*a*shan
     ichchha mata sh*a*shan karte ch*a*y. | kar*a*

Discuss this matter with your teacher. | discuss
এ বিষয়টা তোমার শিক্ষকের সঙ্গে আলোচনা কর। | আলোচনা করা
E bishay*ta* tom*a*r shikkhaker shange | *a*lochan*a*
*a*lochan*a* kara. | kar*a*

He has been suffering from various diseases/illnesses. | disease
সে নানা রকম রোগে ভুগ্‌তেছে/ভুগ্‌ছে। | রোগ/অসুখ
She n*a*n*a* rakam roge bhugtechhe/ | rog/
bhugchhe. | ashukh

Put the sweets in this dish/plate. | dish, plate
মিষ্টিগুলো এ থালায়/প্লেটে রাখ। | থাল, থালা
Mish*ti*gulo e th*a*l*a*y/ple*te* r*a*kha. | th*a*l, th*a*l*a*

You must not disobey your teacher. | disobey
শিক্ষকের অবাধ্য হইবে/হবে না। | অবাধ্য হওয়া
Shikkhaker ab*a*ddha haibe/habe n*a*. | ab*a*ddha haw*a*

Go to the dispensary and get some medicine. | dispensary
ডাক্তারখানায় গিয়া/গিয়ে ঔষধ আন। [ঔষধালয়] | ডাক্তারখানা
D*a*kt*a*rkh*a*nay giya/giye aushadh *a*na. [aushadh*a*lay] | *da*ktar-kh*a*na

He/she is displeased with me. | displeased
তিনি আমার উপর অসন্তুষ্ট হইছেন/হয়েছেন। | অসন্তুষ্ট
Tini *a*m*a*r upar ashantush*ta* haichhen/hayechhen. | ashan-tush*ta*

There is disquiet/unrest among the students. | disquiet
ছাত্রদের মধ্যে অশান্তি হইছে/হয়েছে। | অশান্তি
Chh*a*trader maddhe ashanti haichhe/hayechhe. | ashanti

What is the distance from here to Tejgaon? | distance
এখান হইতে/হতে তেজগাঁও কত তফাৎ/দূর? | তফাৎ
Ekhan haite/hate Tejg*a*on kata taf*a*t/door? | taf*a*t

My house is quite distant.　Go away ! | distant
　আমার বাড়ী অনেক দূর ।　দূর হও । | দূর
　　*A*mar b*a*ree anek door. Door hao ! | door

A thing yet to come , far away , from a
distance. | distant
　দূরের কথা ; অনেক দূরে , দূর হতে । | দূর
　　Doorer kath*a* ; an*e*k doore , door ha te. | door

I live in the district of Dacca. | district
　আমি চাকা জেলায়/জিলায় বাস করি । | জিলা/জেলা
　　*A*mi *Dha*ka jel*a*y/jil*a*y b*a*sh kari. | jil*a*/jel*a*

What zone/region of Dacca city do
you live in ? | region, zone
　ঢাকা শহরের কোন্ অঞ্চলে তুমি থাক ? | অঞ্চল, পাড়া
　　*Dha*ka shaharer kon anchale | anchal,
　　tumi th*a*ka ? | p*a*ra

Divide the 12 mangoes among the two boys. | divide
　বারটা আম দুইজন ছেলের মধ্যে ভাগ কর । | ভাগ করা
　　B*a*ra*t*a *a*m dui jan chheler maddhe
　　bh*a*g kara. | bh*a*g kar*a*

What do you do ? I work. I have a job.
I make a house. | do, make
　কি কর ? কাজ করি । চাকরি করি । বাড়ি করি । | করা
　　Ki kara ? k*a*j kari. Ch*a*kri kari. B*a*ri kari. | kar*a*

Call a doctor. | doctor
　একজন ডাক্তার ডাকিয়া/ডেকে আন । | ডাক্তার
　　Ekjan *dak*tar *da*kiya/deke *a*na. | *dak*tar

My dog always barks. | dog
　আমার কুকুর সব সময় ডাকে । | কুকুর
　　*A*ma*r* kukur shab shamay *da*ke. | kukur

Don't close the door. | door
দরজা বন্ধ করিও/করো না । | দরজা
    Darja bandha kario/karo na. | darja

I never doubt him/his word. | doubt
আমি কখনও তার কথায় সন্দেহ করি না । | সন্দেহ করা
    Ami kakhano tar kathay shandeha | shandeha
    kari na. | kara

Get down from the bus (tree, roof). | get down
বাস থেকে নাম । | নামা
    Bas theke nama. | nama

Take the child down. | take down
শিশু [টাকে] নামাও । | নামান
    Shishu[take] namao. | naman

I like to draw pictures. | draw
আমি ছবি আঁকতে ভালবাসি । | আঁকা
    Ami chhabi ankte bhalabashi. | anka

Show me your drawing/plan. | drawing, plan
তোমার নক্সাটা আমাকে দেখাও । | নক্সা
    Tomar nakshata amake dekhao. | naksha

I saw him/her in a dream. | dream
আমি তাকে স্বপ্নে দেখছি/দেখেছি । | স্বপ্ন
    Ami take shapne dekhchhi/dekhechhi. | shapna

Dress quickly./Put your clothes on... | dress, v.
শীঘ্র কাপড় পর । | পরা
    Sheeghra kapar para. | para

I want to drink a glass of water. | drink, v.
আমি এক গেলাস/গ্লাস জল খাইতে/খেতে চাই । | খাওয়া
    Ami ek gelash/glass jal khaite/khete chai. | khawa

Can you drive a motor car ? (lead, manage) | drive, v.

তুমি মোটর গাড়ী চালাইতে/চালাতে পার ? | চালান

   Tumi motar garee chalaite/chalate para ? | chalan

Here is a drop of water. | drop

এখানে এক ফোঁটা জল আছে। | ফোঁটা

   Ekhane ek fonta jal achhe. | fonta

His words/speeches are dry. | dry (not juicy)

তার কথা নিরস। ফলটা নিরস। | নিরস

   Tar katha nirash. Falta nirash. | nirash

Dry dates can be had here. | dry

এখানে শুকনা খেজুর পাওয়া যায়। | শুকনা

   Ekhane shukna khejur pawa jay. | shukna

Dry the wet clothes. | dry, adj.

ভিজা কাপড় শুকাও। | শুকান

   Bhija kapar shukao. | shukan

The ducks are swimming in the tank. | duck

হাঁসগুলি পুকুরে সাঁতার কাটিতেছে/কাটছে। | হাঁস

   Hansh guli pukure shantar kattechhe/

   katchhe. | hansh

Pay the money due to me. | due

আমার পাওনা টাকা দেও/দাও। [বাকী, দেয়] | পাওনা

   Amar paona taka deo/dao. [bakee, deya] | paona

A dumb man cannot hear. | dumb

বোবা লোক শুনতে পায় না। | বোবা

   Boba lok shunte pay na. | boba

I never saw such a fool/a dumb person. | dunce, fool

আমি কখনও এমন বোকা দেখি নাই। | বোকা

   Ami kakhano eman boka dekhi nai. | boka

I don't see any dust here. | dust

এখানে তো কোন ধুলা দেখি না। | ধুলা

   Ekhane to kona dhoola dekhi na. | dhoola

Who lives in this house ? Stay here. | dwell, live, stay
এই বাড়ীতে কে থাকে ? এখানে থাক। | থাকা
Ei bareete ke thake ? Ekhane thaka. | thaka

He/she has dysentery. | dysentery
তার আমাশয় হইছে/হয়েছে। | আমাশয়
Tar amashay haichhe/hayechhe. | amashay

Give each boy/girl an orange. | each, every
প্রত্যেক ছেলেকে/মেয়েকে একটা কমলা দেও। | প্রত্যেক
Prattek chheleke/meyeke ekta kamala deo. | prattek

He/she comes here everyday. | everyday
সে এখানে প্রতিদিন আসে। | প্রতিদিন
She ekhane pratidin ashe. | pratidin

I cannot hear in my left ear. | ear
আমার বাম কান দিয়া/দিয়ে শুনতে পাই না। | কান
Amar bam kan diya/diye shunte pai na. | kan

Come early. | early
সকাল সকাল আসিও/এস। | সকাল সকাল
Shakal shakal ashio/esha. | shakal shakal

cannot earn much. | earn
আমি বেশী রোজগার করতে পারি না। | রোজগার করা
Ami beshee rojgar karte pari na. | rojgar kara

Jute does not grow well in this soil/earth. | earth, soil
এ মাটিতে পাট ভাল জন্মে না। | মাটি
E matite pat bhala janme na. | mati

The earth is round. | earth (world)
পৃথিবী গোল। | পৃথিবী/জগত
Preethibee gol. | preethibee, jagat

The sun rises in the east. | east
সূর্য পূব দিকে উঠে। | পূব দিক
Shoorja poob dike uthe. | poob dik

It is an easy task. This lesson is easy.	easy
এটা সোজা কাজ । এই পড়া শিক্ষা সহজ ।	সোজা, সহজ
E*ta* shoja *ka*j. Ei Pa*ra* shikkh*a* shahaj.	shoj*a*, shahaj
A baby cannot eat rice.	eat
শিশু ভাত খাইতে/খেতে পারে না ।	খাওয়া
Shishu bh*a*t kh*a*ite/khete p*a*re n*a*.	kh*awa*
Do not sit on the edge of the boat.	edge, side
নৌকার কিনারে বসিও/বসো না ।	কিনার, ধার
Nauk*a*r kin*a*re bashio/basho n*a*.	kin*a*r, dhar
What will be the effect of this ? (result)	effect, fruit
এটার ফল কি হবে ?	ফল
E*ta*r fal ki habe ?	fal
I take eggs every morning.	egg
আমি প্রত্যেকদিন সকালে ডিম খাই ।	ডিম, আণ্ডা
*A*mi prattek din shak*a*le *d*im kh*a*i.	*d*im, *a*nd*a*
Elevate the box a little.	elevate, raise
বাক্সটা আর একটু তোল/উঠাও ।	তোলা, উঠান
B*a*ksha*ta a*r ek*t*u tola/u*t*hao.	tol*a*, u*tha*n
The house is empty. Don't go empty-handed.	empty
ঘর খালি । খালি হাতে যাইও না/যেইও না ।	খালি
Ghar kh*a*li. kh*a*li h*a*te jaio n*a*/jeyo n*a*.	kh*a*li
There is no end to the sky. The game	
is ended. My last word.	end, last
আকাশের শেষ নাই/নেই । খেলা শেষ ।	
আমার শেষ কথা ।	শেষ
A*ka*sher shesh n*a*i/nei. Khel*a* shesh.	
*A*m*a*r shesh *k*ath*a*.	shesh
You must endure/bear it.	endure, bear
এটা তোমাকে সহ্য করতে/সইতে হবে ।	সহ্য করা, সহা
E*ta* tom*a*ke shajja karte/shaite habe.	shajja kar*a*,
	shah*a*

Dogs are the enemies of jackals. | enemy
কুকুর শিয়ালের শত্রু ।
Kukur shiyaler shatru. | shatru

I don't know good English. | English
আমি ভাল ইংরেজী জানি না । | ইংরেজী/ইংলীশ
Ami bhala Ingreji jani na. | Ingreji/Ingleesh

I shall engage/appoint a gardener. | engage
আমি একজন মালি রাখব । | রাখা (নিযুক্ত
করা)
Ami ekjan mali rakhba. | rakha (nijukta
kara)

Enough, no more. I have enough. | enough
বস্ আর না । আমার যথেষ্ট হইছে । | বস্, যথেষ্ট
Bas. ar na. Amar jatheshta haichhe. | bas, jatheshta

Did you enquire about him/her ? | enquire
তুমি [কি] তার খোঁজ করছ/করেছ ? | খোঁজ করা
Tumi [ki] tar khonj karchha/karechha ? | khonj kara

Why don't you enter the room ? | enter
ঘরে ঢুক না কেন ? | ঢুকা
Ghare dhuka na kena ? | dhuka

I am entirely satisfied. | entirely
আমি একেবারে সন্তুষ্ট হইছি/হয়েছি । | একেবারে
Ami ekebare shantushta haichhi/hayechhi. | ekebare

Get an envelope for me. | envelope
আমার জন্য একখানা খাম আন । | খাম
Amar janna ek khana kham ana. | kham

Don't envy anyone. | envy, v.
কাকেও হিংসা করিও/কর না । | হিংসা করা
Kake-o hingsha kario/kara na. | hingsha kara

My share and your share are equal. | equal
আমার অংশ ও তোমার অংশ সমান । | সমান
Amar angsha o tom*a*r angsha sham*a*n. | sham*a*n

Erase the word. Wipe the table. | erase, wipe
শব্দটা মুছিয়া/মুছে ফেল ।   টেবিলটা মুছ । | মুছিয়া ফেলা
Shabda*ta* muchhiya/muchhe fela. *Tebilta* |
muchha. | muchhiy*a* fel*a*

Stand erect/straight. | erect
খাড়া হইয়া/হয়ে দাঁড়াও । | খাড়া
Kh*ara* haiya/haye d*anra*o. | kh*ara*

This is my error/mistake. | error, mistake
এটা আমার ভুল । | ভুল
E*ta* am*a*r bhul. | bhul

I won't let you escape/run away. | escape
আমি তোমাকে পালাইতে/পালাতে দিব না । | পালান
*A*mi tom*a*ke p*ala*ite/p*ala*te diba n*a*. | p*ala*n

I did not even see him. (see defin. part.) | even
আমি তাকে দেখিও নাই/নি । | ও
*A*mi t*a*ke dekhi-o n*a*i/ni. |
[GRAM–DEF. PARTIC] | O

The place seems even to me. | even
জায়গাটা আমার কাছে সমান লাগে । | সমান
G*ayga*ta am*a*r k*a*chhe sham*a*n l*a*ge. | sham*a*n

We are even in height. | even (equal)
আমরা লম্বায় (উচ্চতায়) সমান । | সমান
Amr*a* lamb*a*y (uchchat*a*y) sham*a*n. | sham*a*n

It is good to walk in the evening.

I shall come in the evening. | evening

সন্ধ্যাবেলায় বেড়ান ভাল । আমি সন্ধ্যায় আসব । | সন্ধ্যা (বেলা)

Shandha belay beran bhala. | shandha

Ami shandhay ashba. | (bela)

Have you ever seen such a strange thing ? | ever

আপনি কখনও এমন আশ্চর্য্য জিনিস দেখছেন/

দেখেছেন ? | কখনও

Apni kakhan–o eman ashcharjja

jinish dekhchhen/dekhechhen ? | kakhan–o

Everybody knows it. Everybody did not

come. | everybody

সকলে এটা জানে । সবাই আসে নাই/নি । | সকল, সবাই

Shakale eta jane. Shabai ashe nai/nei. | shakal,

shabai

Do you work everyday ? | everyday

তুমি প্রতিদিন/রোজ রোজ কাজ কর ? | প্রতিদিন, রোজ রোজ

Tumi pratidin/roj roj kaj kara ? | pratidin,

roj roj

I shall examine the boy/girl. | examine

আমি ছেলেটিকে/মেয়েটিকে পরীক্ষা করব । | পরীক্ষা করা

Ami chheletike/meyetike | pareekkha

pareekkha karba. | kara

His/her singing is excellent. | excellent

তার গান চমৎকার/খুব সুন্দর । [খুবই ভাল] | চমৎকার/খুব সুন্দর

Tar gan chamatkar/khub shundar. | chamatkar/

                              [khub-i bhala] | khub shundar

Will you exchange your house for mine ?

[in exchange] | exchange

আমার বাড়ীর সঙ্গে তোমার বাড়ী বদলাইবে/
বদলাবে ? [বদলে] | বদলান

*A*m*a*r b*a*ree*r* shange tom*a*r b*a*ree
badl*a*ibe/badl*a*be ? [badale] | badl*a*n

Why, I did not say that ! Shame ! What do
you say ? Ah ! I can no longer bear this
burden. | (exclamations)

ইস্ ! তা বলি নাই/নি । ছি ছি । কি বল ?
ইস্ ! এ বোঝা আর বইতে পারি না । | ইস্ ! ছি !

Ish ! t*a* bali n*a*i/ni. Chhi chhi ! ki
bala ? Ish ! e bhoj*a* *a*r baite p*a*ri n*a*. | ish ! chhi !

Please excuse him this time. Excuse me. | excuse

এবার তাকে ক্ষমা করুন । আমাকে মাফ কর । | ক্ষমা করা,
মাফ করা

E b*a*i t*a*ke kkham*a* karun. *A*m*a*ke | kkham*a*/
m*a*f kara. | m*a*f kar*a*

What are your daily expenses ? Month's
expenses. | expenses

রোজ রোজ তোমার খরচ কত ? মাসের ব্যয় । | খরচ, ব্যয়

Roj roj tom*a*r kharach kata ? M*a*sher bae. | kharach, bae

This kind of cloth is very expensive/dear. | expensive

এ রকম কাপড় খুব দামী । | দামী

E rakam k*a*pa*r* khub d*a*mee. | d*a*mee

No one can explain anything to a
stupid person. | explain

বোকাকে কেহ বুঝাইতে/বুঝাতে পারে না । | বুঝান

Bok*a*ke keha bujh*a*ite/bujh*a*te p*a*re n*a*. | bujh*a*n

People could extinguish the fire quickly. | extinguish, put out
লোকেরা তাড়াতাড়ি আগুনটা নিবাইতে/নিবাতে পারল ।   নিবান
    Lokera taratari agunta nibaite/
    nibate parla.   niban

You may get extra paper if necessary. | extra
দরকার হলে অতিরিক্ত কাগজ পাইতে/পেতে পার ।   অতিরিক্ত, আরও
    Darkar hale atirikta kagaj paite/
    pete para.   atirikta, aro

I am extremely happy. | extremely
আমি যারপর নাই সুখী হইলাম/হলাম ।   যারপর নাই
    Ami jarpar nai shukhee hailam/halam.   jarpar nai

The elephant's eyes are very small. | eye
হাতীর চোখ খুব ছোট ।   চোখ
    Hateer chokh khub chhota.   chokh

Everyone likes to see the smiling
face of a child. | face, mouth
শিশুর হাসি মুখ দেখতে সকলে ভালবাসে ।   মুখ
    Shishur hashi mukh dekhte shakale
    bhalabashe.   mukh

The girl has a fair complexion. | fair
মেয়েটির রং ফর্সা/সাদা ।   ফর্সা
    Meyetir rang farsha/shada.   farsha

At times there are fairs in the village. | fair (N)
সময় সময় গ্রামে মেলা বসে ।   মেলা
    Shamay shamay grame mela bashe.   mela

I have no faith in him. | faith
তার উপর আমার বিশ্বাস নাই/নেই ।   বিশ্বাস
    Tar upar amar bisshash nai/nei.   bisshash

My servant is very faithful/trustworthy.	faithful
আমার চাকরটি খুব বিশ্বস্ত/বিশ্বাসী ।	বিশ্বস্ত
Amar chakarti khub bisshashta/bisshashee.	bisshasta

When the wind blows, leaves fall.	fall
বাতাস হলে, পাতা পড়ে । [পড়িয়া যাওয়া]	পড়া
Batash hale, pata pare. [pariya jawa]	para

A good boy never says anything false/ tells lies.	false
ভাল ছেলে কখনও মিথ্যা কথা বলে না ।	মিথ্যা
Bhala chhele kakhano miththa katha	
bale na.	miththa

He has no family.	family
তার পরিবার নাই/নেই ।	পরিবার
Tar paribar nai/nei.	paribar

I shall buy a fan.	fan
আমি একটি পাখা কিনব ।	পাখা
Ami ekti pakha kinba.	pakha

How far is your home?	far, distant
তোমাদের বাড়ী কত দূর ?	দূর
Tomader baree kata door?	door

I gave one taka as boat fare. House rent.	fare, rent
এক টাকা নৌকা ভাড়া দিলাম । ঘর ভাড়া ।	ভাড়া
Ek taka nauka bhara dilam. Ghar	
bhara.	bhara

Farmers/the farmer work in the field.	farmer
কৃষক ক্ষেতে কাজ করে ।	কৃষক, চাষী
Kreeshak kkhete kaj kare.	kreeshak
	chashee

I fastened the cow with a rope. | fasten, bind
আমি গরুটা দড়ি দিয়া/দিয়ে বাঁধলাম। | বাঁধা
*A*mi garu*ta* da*r*i diy*a*/diye b*a*ndhl*a*m. | b*a*ndh*a*

Nobody likes fasting/to fast. [fast, v.] | fasting
কেহ না খাইয়া থাকতে ভালবাসে না।[উপবাস] | না খাইয়া
Keha n*a* kh*a*iya th*a*kte bh*a*lab*a*she n*a*. [upab*a*sh] | n*a* kh*a*iya

This man is fat. This cloth is too coarse/thick | fat, coarse
লোকটা মোটা। এ কাপড় বেশী মোটা। | মোটা
Lok*ta* mo*ta*. E k*a*pa*r* beshee mo*ta*. | mo*ta*

The boy's father lives in Dacca. | father
বালকটির বাবা/পিতা ঢাকায় থাকেন। | বাবা/পিতা
B*a*lak*t*ir b*a*ba/pi*ta* *Dh*akay th*a*ken. | pit*a*/b*a*ba

Only babies do not commit any faults. | fault
কেবল শিশুরা দোষ করে না। | দোষ
kebal shishur*a* dosh kare n*a*. | dosh

Kindly do me a favour. | favour
দয়া করিয়া/করে আমার একটা উপকার কর। | উপকার
Day*a* kariy*a*/kare *a*m*a*r ek*ta* upak*a*r kara. | upak*a*r

He fears only God. | fear
সে কেবল ঈশ্বরকে ভয় করে। | ভয় করা
She kebal Eeshsharke bhay kare. | bhay kar*a*

I was not present at that big feast. | feast
সেই বড় খানায় আমি উপস্থিত ছিলাম না। | বড় খানা/ভোজ
Shei ba*r*a kh*a*nay *a*mi upasthit chhil*a*m n*a*. | ba*r*a kha-n*a*/bhoj

The mother feeds her son/daughter. | feed
মা ছেলেকে/মেয়েকে খাওয়ায়। | খাওয়ান
*M*a chheleke/meyeke kh*a*oyay. (kh*a*w*a*n) | kh*a*o*a*n

I feel he will not come. I feel hot | feel
বোধ করি/হয় সে আসবে না। আমার গরম | বোধ করা
   Bodh kari/hay she ashbe na. লাগে | bodh kara

How do you feel ? I feel well/good. | feel
তোমার কেমন লাগে ? আমার ভাল লাগে। | লাগা
   Tomar keman lage? Amar bhala lage. | laga

He repaired the fence | fence
সে বেড়াটা মেরামত করল। | বেড়া
   She berata meramat karla. | bera

Does the baby have a fever ? | fever
শিশুর জ্বর আছে ? | জ্বর
   Shishur jjar achhe ? | jjar

There was rice in the field. | field
ক্ষেতে ধান ছিল। | ক্ষেত/খেত
   Kkhete dhan chhila. | kkhet/khet

Boys are playing football in the field. | field
মাঠে ছেলেরা ফুটবল খেলতেছ/খেলছে। | মাঠ
   Mathe chhelera futbal kheltechhe/
khelchhe. | math

There was a fight between the two boys. | fight
ছেলে দু'টার মধ্যে মারামারি হইছে/হয়েছে। | মারামারি
   Chhele du'tar maddhe maramari
haichhe/hayechhe. | maramari

God has no form. Make it in another figure. | figure, form
ঈশ্বরের/আল্লাহর আকার নাই/নেই। অন্য
আকারে বানাও। | আকার
   Eeshsharer/Allahr akar nai/nei. Anna
akare banao. | akar

I filled up my pen with ink. | fill up
আমি কলমে কালি ভরলাম। | ভরা,পূরা
   Ami kalame kali bharlam. | bhara, poora

This is the final bell. Finish the work | final, end
এই শেষ ঘন্টা। কাজ শেষ কর। শেষ
Ei shesh ghan*ta*. K*a*j shesh kara. shesh

You have finally come. (at last) | finally, last
তুমি অবশেষে আস্ছ/এসেছ। অবশেষে
Tumi sheshe *a*shchha/eshechha. abasheshe

He found the big red ball | find
সে বড় লাল বলটা খুঁজিয়া পাইল/খুঁজে পেল। খুঁজিয়া পাওয়া
She b*a*ra l*a*l bal*ta* khu*n*jiy*a* p*a*ila/ khu*n*jiy*a*
khu*n*je pela. p*awa*

It is fine ! Very fine/good ! | fine (adj.)
বেশ হইয়াছে/হয়েছে। বেশ ভাল। [চমৎকার] বেশ
Besh haiy*a*chhe/hayechhe. Besh bh*a*la.
[chamatk*a*r] besh

He caught my fingers. | finger
সে আমার আঙুল ধরল। আঙুল
She *a*m*a*r *a*ngul dharla *a*ngul

I finished the work. | finish
আমি কাজটা শেষ করলাম। শেষ করা
*A*mi k*a*j*ta* shesh karl*a*m. shesh kar*a*

That house caught fire. | fire
ঐ বাড়ীতে আগুন লাগ্ল। আগুন
Oi b*a*reete *a*gun l*a*gla. *a*gun

The first house on the right is mine. | first
ডান দিকের প্রথম বাড়ীটা আমার। প্রথম
D*a*n diker pratham b*a*ree*ta* *a*m*a*r. pratham

I like to eat fish. | fish
আমি মাছ খাইতে/খেতে ভালবাসি। মাছ
*A*mi m*a*chh kh*a*ite/khete bh*a*labashi. m*a*che

The men went fishing/to fish.

লোকেরা মাছ মারতে/ধরতে গেল ।

Lokera machh marte/dharte gela.

fish, v.

মাছ মারা/ধরা

machh

mara/dhara

Fishermen need fishing nets.

জেলেদের জাল দরকার ।

Jeleder jal darkar.

fisherman

জেলে

Jele

That is a fit punishment.

You should keep quiet. [V. N.]

উচিত শাস্তি ! তোমার চুপ করা উচিত ।

Uchit shashti ! Tomar chup kara uchit.

fit, proper

উচিত /যোগ্য

uchit,jogga

His/her conduct is proper/correct.

তার ব্যবহার ঠিক ।

Tar baebahar thik.

fit, proper

ঠিক

thik

The pipe does not fit. The shoe does not fit right.

পাইপটা লাগে না । জুতাটা ঠিকমত লাগে না ।

Paipta lage na. Jutata thik mata lage na.

fit

লাগা

laga

Fix the machine.

কলটা ঠিক কর/মেরামত কর ।

Kalta thik kara/meramat kara.

fix

ঠিক করা

thik kara

Afix a stamp on the envelope.

খামে টিকেট লাগাও ।

Khame tiket lagao.

fix, stick

লাগান

lagan

Fly the flag.

নিশান/পতাকা উড়াও ।

Nishan/pataka urao.

flag

নিশান, পতাকা

nishan, pataka

Our field is quite flat/even. These sweets are flat.

আমাদের মাঠ বেশ সমান ।

Amader math besh chepta/shaman.

এই মিষ্টিগুলি চেপ্টা । Ei mishtiguli chepta.

flat, even

চেপ্টা, সমান

chepta

sham

We do not always eat meat.	flesh, meat
আমরা সব সময় মাংস খাই না ।	মাংস
*A*mr*a* shab shamay m*a*ngsha kh*a*i n*a*.	mangsha
Wood/timber floats on water.	float
কাঠ জলে ভাসে ।	ভাসা
K*a*th jale bh*a*she.	bh*a*sha
The boy is cleaning the floor of the room.	floor
ছেলেটা ঘরের মেঝে পরিষ্কার করতেছে/করছে ।	মেঝে
Chhele*ta* gharer mejhe **parishk*a*r kartechhe/**	
karchhe.	mejhe
Cakes are made of flour.	flour
ময়দা দিয়া/দিয়ে কেক্ তৈরী হয় ।	ময়দা
Mayd*a* diy*a*/diye kek tairee hay.	mayd*a*
I like bread made of good coarse flour	flour (coarse)
আমি ভাল আটার রুটী ভালবাসি ।	আটা
*A*mi bh*a*la *ata*r ru*t*ee bh*a*lab*a*shi	*ata*
The wind blows. The river flows by.	flow, blow
বাতাস বহে/বয় । নদী বইয়া/বয়ে যায় ।	বহা
B*a*t*a*sh bahe/bay. Nodee baiy*a*/baye	
jay.	bah*a*
Don't let flies sit on the food.	fly (N)
খাবারে মাছি বসতে দিও না ।	মাছি
Kh*a*ba*re* m*a*chhi bashte dio n*a*.	m*a*chhi
The bird flies in the sky. (birds fly)	fly
পাখী আকাশে উড়ে/উড়িয়া যায় ।	উড়া
Pakhee *aka*she u*re*/u*r*iy*a* jay.	u*ra*
Fold the clothes.	fold
কাপড়গুলি ভাঁজ কর । [পাট করা]	ভাঁজ করা
K*a*parguli bh*a*nj kara. [p*a*t kar*a*]	bh*a*nj kar*a*

The cook is supplied with food.
বাবুচিকে খোরাক দেওয়া হয় ।
Baburchike khorak dewa hay.

food (for work)
খোরাক
khorak

We spend a lot on food.
আমাদের খাবারের জন্য অনেক খরচ হয় ।
Amader khabarer janna anek kharach
hay.

food
খাবার
khabar

The man is a fool/is stupid.
লোকটা বোকা ।
Lokta boka.

fool, dunce
বোকা
boka

He suffered much for his foolishness.
তার বোকামির জন্য সে অনেক কষ্ট পাইল/গেল ।
Tar bokamir janna she anek kashta
pala/pela.

foolishness
বোকামি
bokami

We kick with our feet.
আমরা পা দিয়া/দিয়ে লাথি মারি ।
Amra pa diya/diye lathi mari.

foot, leg
পা
pa

Bring paper for writing.   This is for you.
লেখার জন্য কাগজ আন ।   এটা তোমার জন্য ।
Lekhar janna kagaj ana. Eta tomar
janna.

for
জন্য
janna

I have been waiting for three hours.{POSTP.
আমি তিন ঘন্টা যাবৎ দেরি করছি/করেছি ।
Ami tin ghanta jabat deri karchhi/
karechhi.

for (duration)
যাবৎ/জন্য
jabat/janna

Forbid the boys to play here.
ছেলেদের এখানে খেলতে মানা কর । [না করা]
Chheleder ekhane khelte mana kara.
        [na kara]

forbid
মানা/নিষেধ করা
mana/nishedh
kara

The wind is blowing with great force.	force
বাতাস জোরে বইতেছে/বইছে।	জোর
Batash jore baitechhe/baichhe.	jor
He took the pen from me by force.	by force
সে আমার কাছ থেকে কলমটা জোর করিয়া/	
করে নিল।	জোর করিয়া/করে
She amar kachh theke kalamta jor	jor kariya/
kariya/kare nila.	kare
He does not buy foreign goods.	foreign
সে বিদেশী জিনিস কিনে না।	বিদেশী
She bideshee jinish kine na.	bideshee
European/English/foreign medicines	
are good.	European, English
বিলাতী ঔষধ ভাল।	বিলাতী
Bilatee aushadh bhala.	bilatee
Many foreigners live in Dacca.	foreigner
ঢাকায় অনেক বিদেশী লোক বাস্ করে/থাকে।	বিদেশী লোক, সাহেব
Dhakay anek bideshee lok bash kare/thake.	bideshee lok,
	shaheb
Tigers live in the forest.	forest
বাঘ বনে বাস করে/থাকে।	বন, জঙ্গল
Bagh bane bash kare/thake.	ban, jangal
Don't forget to shut the door.	forget
দরজা বন্ধ করতে ভুলিয়া যাইও/ভুলে যেও না।	ভুলিয়া যাওয়া
Darja bandha karte bhuliya jaio/	
bhule jeyo na.	bhuliya jaoya
I forgive him.	forgive
আমি তাকে ক্ষমা করি।	ক্ষমা করা
Ami take kkhama kari.	kkhama kara

I shall buy a dozen spoons and forks.	fork, thorn
আমি এক ডজন কাঁটা চামচ কিনব ।	কাঁটা
*A*mi ek dajan k*a*nta ch*a*mach kinba.	k*a*nta
The form (shape) of the earth is round.	form, figure
পৃথিবীর আকার গোল ।	আকার
Preethibeer *a*k*a*r gol.	*a*k*a*r
The former boy is taller.	former
আগের ছেলেটা আরও লম্বা ।	আগের
*A*ger chhel*eta a*ro lamb*a*.	*a*ger
He has had good fortune/luck. He is lucky.	fortune, luck
তার ভাগ্য ভাল । [কপাল]	ভাগ্য
T*a*r bh*a*gga bh*a*la. [kap*a*l]	bh*a*gga
The price of four bananas is one taka.	four
এক হালি কলার দাম এক টাকা ।	হালি
Ek h*a*li kal*a*r d*a*m ek *taka*.	h*a*li
There is fragrance in the rose.	fragrance
গোলাপ ফুলের সুগন্ধ আছে ।	সুগন্ধ, সুবাস
Gol*a*p fuler shugandha *a*chhe,	shugandha, shub*a*sh
I got these clothes free.	free, gratis
এ কাপড়গুলো এমনি পাইছি/পেয়েছি ।	এমনি
E k*a*pa*r* gulo emne p*a*ichhi/peyechhi.	emne
All want freedom.	freedom, release
সবাই মুক্তি চায় ।	মুক্তি
Shab*a*i mukti ch*a*y.	mukti
It is good to eat fresh vegetables.	fresh
টাটকা সবজি খাওয়া ভাল ।	টাটকা/তাজা
Tatka shabji kh*a*oya bh*a*la.	*tatka, taja*

He will come next Friday. | Friday
সে আগামী শুক্রবারে আসবে। | শুক্রবার
Sne *aga*mee shukrab*a*re *a*shbe. | shukrab*a*r

I have no friend(s)/I haven't
any friend(s). | friend
আমার কোন বন্ধু নাই/নেই। | বন্ধু
*A*m*a*r kona bandhu n*a*i/nei. | bandhu

Do not frighten the little children/
babies. [take fright] | frighten
শিশুদের ভয় দেখাইও/দেখিও না। [ভয় পাওয়া] | ভয় দেখান
Shishuder bhay dekh*a*io/
dekhiyo n*a*. [bhay p*awa*] | bhay dekh*a*n

I brought books from school. | from
স্কুল থেকে বই আনলাম। | থেকে/হইতে
Skul theke bai *a*nl*a*m | theke/haite

From where have you come? | from where
কোথা থেকে আসলে? | কোথা থেকে
Kotha theke *a*shle? | kotha theke

There is a river in front of our house.
[postpos.] | in front of
আমাদের বাড়ীর সামনে নদী। | সামনে
*A*m*a*der b*a*reer sh*a*mne nodee. | sh*a*mne

This fruit is sweet. | fruit, result
এ ফল মিঠা/মিষ্ট/মিষ্টি। ফলটা | ফল
E fal mi*tha*/mista/mishti. fal*a* | fal

Fried fish are good to eat. [L. 96] | fry
ভাজা মাছ খাইতে/খেতে ভাল। | ভাজা
Bh*aja* m*a*chh kh*a*ite/khete bh*a*la. | bh*aja*

The pitcher is full of water. [L.68] | full
কলসীটা জলে ভরা/ভরতি। | ভরা
Kalshee*ta* jale bhar*a*/bharti. | bhar*a*

What fun ! What a fine/funny story ! | fun

কি মজা ! কি মজার গল্প । [তামাসা, কায়দা] | মজা

Ki maj*a* ! Ki maj*a*r galpa ! [t*a*mash*a*, k*a*yd*a*] | maj*a*

The bear has long fur. | fur

ভালুকের লম্বা লোম আছে । | লোম

Bh*a*luker lamb*a* lom *a*chhe. | lom

There are many furniture shops in Dacca. | furniture

ঢাকায় অনেক আসবাবপত্রের দোকান আছে । [জিনিসগপ্ত] আসবাবপত্র

Dh*a*k*a*y an*e*k *a*shb*a*bpatrer dok*a*n *a*chhe. | *a*shb*a*bpatra

Empty the full pitcher. | full

ভরা কলসীটা খালি কর । | ভরা, পূর্ণ/পুরা

Bhar*a* kalshee*ta* kh*a*li kara. | Bhara, poorna/pur*a*

He was there a full month. | full

সে পুরা একমাস সেখানে ছিল । | পুরা

She pur*a* ek m*a*sh shekh*a*ne chhila. | pur*a*

He gained five taka by selling a pen. | gain

সে কলম বেচিয়া/বেচে পাঁচ টাকা লাভ করল । | লাভ করা

She kalam bechiy*a*/beche p*a*nch *ta*ka |

labh karla. | l*a*bh kar*a*

Where is my 'gamchha' ?   [short, male

garment] | gamchha (towel)

আমার গামছা কোথায় ? | গামছা

*A*mar g*a*mchha koth*a*y ? | g*a*mchh*a*

I like football games. (the game of football) | game, play

আমি ফুটবল খেলা পছন্দ করি । | খেলা

*A*mi fu*t*bal khel*a* pachhanda kari. | khel*a*

We have a vegetable garden. [L.16] | garden

আমাদের সব্জির বাগান আছে । | বাগান

*A*m*a*der shabjir b*a*g*a*n *a*chhe. | b*a*g*a*n

12—

The gardener is working in the garden.

মালি বাগানে কাজ করতেছে/করছে ।

Mali bagane koj kartechhe/karchhe.

| gardener
| মালি
| mali

He was garlanded. What a nice garland !

তাঁর গলায় ফুলের মালা দেওয়া হল । কি সুন্দর মালা !

Tanr galay fuler mala dewa hala.

Ki shundar mala !

| garland
| মালা
| mala

Gather the papers together.

কাগজগুলো একত্র কর/রাখা ।

Kagajgulo ekatra kara/rakha.

| gather
| একত্র করা/রাখা
| ekatra kara/rakha

It rains here almost every day.

প্রায় রোজ এখানে বৃষ্টি হয় ।

Pray roj ekhane brishti hay.

| generally, almost
| প্রায়
| pray

He is a gentleman

তিনি ভদ্রলোক [ ] ।

Tini bhadralok [ ].

| gentleman
| ভদ্রলোক
| bhadralok

This taka is genuine,. not spurious/ counterfeit,

এ টাকাটা আসল, মেকি না ।

E takata ashal; meki na.

| genuine,
| আসল, খাঁটি
| ashal, khanti

I got your letter.

আমি তোমার চিঠি পাইছি/পেয়েছি ।

Ami tomar chithi paichhi/peyechhi.

| get
| পাওয়া
| pawa

You will get well, don't worry.

তোমার শরীর ভাল হইয়া/হয়ে যাবে, চিন্তা করিও/কর না ।

Tomar shareer bhala haiya/haye jabe,

chinta kario/kara na.

| get well
| [ভাল হওয়া
| bhala hawa

O Lord, this food is your gift.

হে প্রভু, এ খাবার তোমার-ই দান ।

Hey prabhu, e khabar tomar-i dan.

| gift
| দান, উপকার
| dan, upakar

	girl
The girls are dancing. No girls are here.	বালিকা, মেয়ে
বালিকারা নাচ্‌তেছে/নাচ্‌ছে। এখানে মেয়েরা নাই/নেই।	
Balikara nachtechhe/nachchhe.	
Ekhane meyera nai/nei.	

	give, allow
Give him five taka. Let him go.	দেওয়া
তাকে পাঁচটি টাকা দাও। তাকে যাতে/যেতে দাও।	dewa
Take panchti taka dao. Take jate/jete dao.	

	glad
Getting the paisa, the boy was glad. [L.100]	সন্তুষ্ট
পয়সা পাইয়া/পেয়ে ছেলেটি সন্তুষ্ট হল।	shantushta
Paisa paiya/peye chheleti shantushta hala.	

	glass
Bring a glass of water. Glass breaks easily.	গ্লাস, কাঁচ
এক গ্লাস জল আন। কাঁচ সহজে ভাঙ্গে। [গেলাস]।	glash, kanch
Ek glash jal ana. Kanch shahaje bhange.	

	glue
I need some glue.	আঠা
আমার কিছু আঠা দরকার।	atha
Amar kichhu atha darkar.	

	go
Go, go away. Let me go.	যাওয়া
যাও, চলিয়া/চলে যাও। আমাকে যাইতে/যেতে দাও।	jawa
Jao, chaliya/chale jao. Amake jaite/jete dao.	

	go out
Suddenly the lamp went out.	নিবা
বাতিটা হঠাৎ নিবিয়া/নিবে গেল।	niba
Batita hathat nibiya/nibe gela.	

	goat
What doesn't a goat eat ! [...don't goats...]	ছাগল
ছাগলে কি না খায় !	chhagal
Chhagale ki na khay !	

	God
God loves us.	ঈশ্বর, খোদা, আল্লাহ
আল্লাহ/ঈশ্বর আমাদের ভালবাসেন।	Eeshshar
Allah/Eeshshar amader bhalabashen.	Khoda, Allah

Goods are kept in godowns. (shed, barn) | godown

গুদামে মাল রাখা হয় ।   গুদাম

    Gudame mal rakha hay.   gudam

I have no gold or silver. | gold

সোনা-রুপা আমার কিছুই নাই/নেই ।   সোনা

    Shona–rupa amar kichhui nai/nei.   shona

Be good. This tea is good. I want good bread. | good

ভাল থাক । এ চা ভাল । ভাল রুটী চাই ।   ভাল

    Bhala thaka. E cha bhala. Bhala rutee chai.   bhala

We are alive by the grace of God. | grace

আল্লাহর/ঈশ্বরের কৃপায় আমরা বাঁচিয়া/বেঁচে আছি ।   কৃপা/অনুগ্রহ

    Allahr/Eeshsharer kreepay amra   kreepa
          banchia/benche achhi.

Gradually the school improved. | gradually

ক্রমে ক্রমে স্কুলের উন্নতি হল ।   ক্রমে ক্রমে

    Krame krame skuler unnati hala.   krame krame

Keet/put the grain in the barn. | grain

শস্য গোলায় রাখ ।   শস্য

    Shassha golay rakha.   shassha

The cows are grazing in the field. | graze

গরুগুলো মাঠে চরছে ।   চরা

    Garugulo mathe charchhe.   chara

Dacca is a big city. | great, big, large

ঢাকা একটা বড় শহর ।   বড়

    Dhaka ekta bara shahar.   bara

Leaves of trees are green. see raw, | green

গাছের পাতা সবুজ ।   সবুজ

    Gachher pata shabuj.   shabuj

The boy/girl is lying on the ground.
ছেলেটা/মেয়েটা মাটিতে শুইয়া আছে ।
Chhele*ta*/meye*ta* m*a*tite shuiy*a* *a*chhe.

ground, earth
মাটি
m*a*ti

Boys/girls play in groups.
ছেলেরা/মেয়েরা দল বাঁধিয়া/বেঁধে খেলা করে ।
Chheler*a*/meyer*a* dal b*a*ndhiy*a*/ben̐dhe
khel*a* kare.

group, party
দল
dal

Trees grow quickly if they get water.
জল পাইলে/পেলে গাছ তাড়াতাড়ি বাড়ে [বড় হয়] ।
Jal p*a*ile/pele g*a*chh t*a*rat*a*ri b*a*re.

grow (v. i.)
বাড়া
b*a*ra

When I grow up I'll be a doctor.
আমি বড় হইয়া/হয়ে ডাক্তার হব ।
*A*mi bara haiy*a*/haye d*a*kt*a*r haba.

grow up
বড় হওয়া
bara haw*a*

I guessed it.
আমি এটা অনুমান করছি/করেছি । [আন্দাজ]
*A*mi e*ta* anum*a*n karchhi/karechhi.
[*a*nd*a*j k.]

guess
অনুমান করা
anum*a*n kar*a*

Guests came/have come.   (The/a guest...)
অতিথি আসছে/এসেছে ।
Atithi *a*shchhe/eshechhe.

guest
অতিথি
atithi

I am guilty.   I admit I am guilty.
আমি দোষী ।   আমি দোষী স্বীকার করি ।
*A*mi doshee. *A*mi doshee sheek*a*r kari.

guilty
দোষী
doshee

The hunter is going with (his) gun.
শিকারী বন্দুক নিয়া যাইতেছে/নিয়ে যাচ্ছে ।
Shik*a*ree banduk niy*a* j*a*itechhe/niye j*a*chchhe.

gun
বন্দুক
banduk

Rising early is a good habit.
ভোরবেলা উঠা ভাল অভ্যাস ।
Bhor bel*a* u*tha* bh*a*la abb*a*sh.

habit
অভ্যাস
abb*a*sh

His hair is black. She braids/ties her hair. | hai

তার চুল কাল ।   সে তার চুল বাঁধে ।   চুল

    Tar chul kala. She tar chul bandhe.   chul

Buy half a seer of ghee. Give me half. | half

আধা সের ঘি কিনিয়া/কিনে আন । আমাকে

         অর্ধেক দাও ।   আধা/অর্ধেক

    Adha sher ghee kiniya/kine ana.

         Amake ardhek dao.   adha/ardhek

It is ten-thirty. It is 1:30(= $1\frac{1}{2}$). | half

সাড়ে দশটা বাজল । দেড়টা বাজছে/বেজেছে । সাড়ে, দেড়টা

    Share dashta bajla. Derta bajchhe/

         bejechhe.   share, derta

Hit the nail with the hammer. [Means] | hammer

হাতুড়ী দিয়া/দিয়ে পেরেক মার ।   হাতুড়/হাতুড়ী

    Haturee diya/diye perek mara.   haturee

We work with our hands. (forearm) | hand

আমরা হাত দিয়া/দিয়ে কাজ করি ।   হাত

    Amra hat diya/diye kaj kari.   hat

Give (me) a handful of rice. | handful

এক মুষ্ঠি/মুঠো চাউল দাও ।   মুষ্ঠি/মুঠো

    Ek mushthi/mutho chaul dao.   mushthi/mutho

I shall buy a dozen handkerchiefs. | handkerchief

আমি এক ডজন রুমাল কিনব ।   রুমাল

    Ami ek dajan rumal kinba.   rumal

Hang the picture on the wall. CAUS. L. 30 | hang

ছবিটা দেওয়ালে ঝুলাও ।   ঝুলান

    Chhabita deoale jhulao.   jhulan

The monkey is hanging from the branch. | hang

বানরটা ডাল ধরিয়া ঝুলতেছে/ধরে ঝুলছে ।   ঝুলা

    Banarta dal dhariya jhulteehhe/dhare jhulchhe.   jhula

What has happened ? Nothing has happened. | happen
কি হইছে/হয়েছে ? কিছু হয় নাই/নি । | হওয়া
   Ki haichhe/hayechhe ? Kiehhu hay nai/ni. | howa

Everyone wants happiness. I am happy. | happiness
সকলে সুখ চায় । সুখে আছি । | সুখ
   Shakale shukh chay. Shukhe achhi. | shukh

Seeing me he became happy. | happy
...happy to see me.) [PARTIC.] L. 100
আমাকে দেখিয়া/দেখে সে সুখী হল । | সুখী
   Amake dekhiya/dekhe she shukhee hala. | shukhee

Iron is very hard. This work is very hard. | hard
লোহা খুব শক্ত । কাজটা খুব কঠিন । | শক্ত/কঠিন
   Loha khub shakta. Kajta khub kathin. | shakta, kathin

Bats can hardly see during the day. | hardly
দিনে বাদুর প্রায়ই দেখতে পারে না । | প্রায়ই না
   Dine badur pray-i dekhte pare na. | pray-i...na

What do you gain by my harm ? | harm, loss
আমার ক্ষতিতে তোমার কি লাভ ? | ক্ষতি
   Amar kkhatite tomar ki labh ? | kkhati

The headmaster is strict, Don't use harsh words. | harsh, strict
হেড মাস্টার কড়া । কড়া কথা বলিও/বল না । | কড়া
   Hedmastar kara. Kara katha balio/bala na. | kara

He went home hastily. Come quickly. | hastily, quickly
সে তাড়াতাড়ি বাড়ী গেল । তাড়াতাড়ি আস । | তাড়াতাড়ি
   She taratari baree gela. Taratari asha. | taratari

I have a pencil. You have two. | have
আমার একটা পেন্সিল আছে । তোমার দুটা । | আছে
   Amar ekta pensil achhe. Tomar duta. | achhe

My head aches. Babies have big heads.   head

আমার মাথা ব্যথা করে । শিশুর মাথা বড় ।   মাথা

    Amar matha baetha kare.   matha

       Shishur matha bara.

I have a headache.   have headache

আমার মাথা ধরছে/ধরেছে ।   মাথা ধরা

    Amar matha dharchhe/dharechhe.   matha dhara

He takes care of his health. How is your health ?   health

সে তার স্বাস্থ্যের যত্ন নেয় । তোমার স্বাস্থ্য কেমন ?   স্বাস্থ্য

    She tar shasthther jatna ney.   shasththa

       Tomar shastbtha keman ?

Hear my words/listen to me. [heed]   hear

আমার কথা শুন ।   শুনা

    Amar katha shuna.   shuna

His heart is hard/tender.   heart

তার হৃদয় কঠিন/কোমল ।   হৃদয়

    Tar hriday kathin/komal.   hriday

There is heat in fire.   V. heat/warm.   heat

আগুনে তাপ আছে । গরম করা   তাপ

    Agune tap achhe. garam kara   tap

Heaven is a place of joy.   heaven

স্বর্গ সুখের স্থান ।   স্বর্গ

    Sharga shukher sthan.   sharga

This box/trunk is very heavy.   heavy

এ বাক্সটা খুব ভারী   ভারী

    E bakshata khub bharee.   bharee

Hell is a place of suffering.   hell

নরক বড় কষ্টের জায়গা ।   নরক

    Narak bara kashter jayga.   narak

Help poor people/the poor. | help

গরীব লোকদের সাহায্য কর ।   সাহায্য করা

Gareeb lokder sh*a*h*a*jja kara.   sh*a*h*a*jja kar*a*

Hens lay eggs. Buy a hen/chicken. | hen, chicken

মুরগী ডিম পাড়ে ।   একটা মুরগী কিন ।   মুরগী

Murgee *d*im p*a*re. Ek*ta* murgee kina.   murg*ee*

There is no one here. | here

এখানে কেউ/কেহ নাই/নেই ।   এখানে

Ekh*a*ne keu/keha n*a*i/nei   ekh*a*ne

Who has hidden my pen ? CAUS. L. 30. | hide, v

কে আমার কলম লুকাইছে/লুকিয়েছে ? [গোপনে থাকা]   লুকান

Ke *a*m*a*r kalam luk*a*ichhe/lukiyechhe ?

           [gopane th*a*k*a*, int. v.]   luk*a*n, t.v

This house is very high. How high ? | high

এ বাড়ীটা খুব উঁচু । কত উচ্চ ?   উঁচা/উঁচু

E b*a*re*cta* khub u*n*chu. Kata uchcha ?   u*n*ch*a*/u*n*chu

Now the price of flour is very high. | high (price

এখন ময়দার দাম খুব চড়া ।   চড়া (দাম)

Ekhan mayd*a*r d*a*m khub ch*a*r*a*.   ch*a*r*a* (d*a*m)

I hired a boat. | hire

আমি নৌকা ভাড়া করলাম ।   ভাড়া করা

*A*mi nauk*a* bh*a*r*a* karl*a*m.   bh*a*r*a* kar*a*

The owner of the house rented it out. | rent

বাড়ীওয়ালা বাড়ী ভাড়া দিল ।   ভাড়া দেওয়া

B*a*reew*a*l*a* b*a*ree bh*a*r*a* dila.   bh*a*r*a* dew*a*

like history. | history

আমি ইতিহাস ভালবাসি ।   ইতিহাস

*A*mi itih*a*sh bh*a*lab*a*shi.   itih*a*sh

Don't hit the dog.   He/she hit me. | hit, beat

কুকুরটাকে মারিও/মের না । সে আমাকে মারল । | মারা

Kukur*take* mario/mera n*a*. She *a*make m*a*rla. | m*a*ra

She/he held my hand. Seize/hold him. | hold, catch

সে আমার হাত ধরল ।   তাকে ধর । | ধরা

She *a*mar h*a*t dharla. T*a*ke dhara. | dhar*a*

There is a hole in this bucket. | hole

এ বালতিতে একটা ছিদ্র আছে । | ছিদ্র

E bal*ti*te ek*ta* chhidra *a*chhe. | chhidra

A snake entered this hole. (in the ground) | hole

এ গর্তে একটা সাপ ঢুকল । | গর্ত

E garte ek*ta* sh*a*p *dh*ukla. | garta

Our home is at Ramna. No one is at home. | home

আমাদের বাড়ী রমনায় । বাড়ীতে কেহ নাই/নেই । | বাড়ী/ঘর

*A*m*a*der b*a*ree Ramn*a*y. B*a*reete keha n*a*i/nei. | [b*a*ree/ghar

I do not know whether or not he is honest. | honest

সে সৎ কিনা তা আমি জানি না । | সৎ

She shat ki n*a* ta *a*mi j*a*ni n*a*. | shat

We ought to honour our parents. [L. 76] | honour

পিতামাতাকে সম্মান করা উচিত । | সম্মান করা

Pit*a*m*a*t*a*ke shamm*a*n kar*a* uchit. | shamm*a*n kar*a*

Everyone wants honour/respect. | honour (N)

সকলে সম্মান চায় । | সম্মান

Shakale shamm*a*n ch*a*y. | shamm*a*n

I have no hope of getting work. [See GER.] | hope (N)

আমার কাজ পাইবার/পাবার আশা নাই/নেই । | আশা

*A*m*a*r k*a*j p*a*ibar/p*a*bar *a*sha n*a*i/nei. | *a*sha

I hope he will return. | hope, v.

আমি আশা করি সে ফিরিয়া/ফিরে আসবে । | আশা করা

*A*mi *a*sha kari she firiy*a*/fire *a*shbe. | *a*sha kar*a*

It is very hot/warm today. Bring hot spices. | hot/warm

আজ খুব গরম । গরম মসলা আন । | গরম

Aj khub garam. Garam mashla ana. | garam

When the bell rings we go to class. After 3 hours. | bell, hour

ঘন্টা বাজলে আমরা ক্লাসে যাই । তিন ঘন্টা পরে । | ঘণ্টা

Ghanta bajle amra klase jai. Tin | ghanta
ghanta pare. [PARTIC.]

I shall build a house. | house, home

আমি একটা বাড়ী/ঘর তৈরী করব । | বাড়ী

Ami ekta baree ghar tairee karba. | baree

How do you do this ? How shall I do this ? | how

এটা কিভাবে কর ? এ কাজ কেমনে করব ? | কিভাবে, কেমনে

Eta ki bhabe kara ? E kaj kemne karba ? | ki bhabe, kemne

How are you ? How pretty ! | how

তুমি কেমন আছ ? কেমন সুন্দর ! | কেমন

Tumi keman achha ? Keman shundar ! | keman

How long will you deceive me ? (days) | how long

আর কতদিন তুমি আমাকে ঠকাবে ? | কতাদিন

Ar kata din tumi amake thakabe ? | kata din

How long will you study/read ? (time) | how long

তুমি কতক্ষণ পড়বে ? | কতক্ষণ

Tumi kata kkhan parbe. | kata kkhan

How many eggs did the gardener bring ? | how many

মালি কতগুলি ডিম / আনছে/এনেছে ? | কতগুলি

Mali kataguli dim anchhe/enechhe ? | kataguli

What time is it ? How many are there ? | how···, what

কয়টা বাজে ? কয়টা আছে ? | কয়টা

Kayta baje ? Kayta achhe ?   [PRON.] | kayta

How many eggs did you bring ? | how many ?

তুমি কতটা ডিম আনছ/এনেছ ? | কতটা

Tumi katata dim anchha/enechha ? | katata

How deep is this tank ? (pond)	how (much)
এ পুকুর কত গভীর ?	কত
E pukur kata gabheer ? INTERROG.	kata
There are one hundred students in this class.	hundred
এ ক্লাসে একশ' ছাত্র আছে ।	একশ'
E klase ek sha chhatra achhe.	(ek) sha
He is suffering from hunger.	hunger
সে ক্ষুধায় কষ্ট পাইতেছে/পাচ্ছে ।	ক্ষুধা
She kkhudhay kashta paitechhe/pachchhe.	kkhudha
I am/feel hungry.	be/feel hungry
আমার ক্ষুধা লাগে ।	ক্ষুধা লাগা
Amar kkhudha lage.	kkhudha laga
Don't hurt me.	hurt
আমাকে ব্যথা দিও না ।	ব্যথা দেওয়া
Amake baetha dio na.	baetha dewa
If you hurt (someone), you will be hurt.	hurt
কষ্ট দিলে কষ্ট পাইবে/পাবে ।	কষ্ট দেওয়া
Kashta dile kashta paibe/pabe. (PARTIC.)	kashta dewa
My wound (sore) hurts.	hurt (v. i.)
আমার ঘা ব্যথা করে ।	ব্যথা করা
Amar gha baetha kare.	baetha kara
Hush ! he/she is coming.	hush, v
চুপ কর ! সে আসতেছে/আসছে ।	চুপ করা
Chup kara ! she ashtechhe/ashchhe.	chup kara
She husks rice and sings. (husk, N.)	husk (rice), v.
সে ধান ভানে ও গান গায় । [তুষ]	ধান ভানা
She dhan bhane o gan gay. [toosh]	dhan bhana
Let us make ice.	ice
চল বরফ বানাই ।	বরফ
Chala baraf banai.	ba-af

Your idea is right/correct. | idea
তোমার ধারণা ঠিক । | ধারণা
   Tomar dharana thik. | dharana

These two boys appear identical/the same/ | identical, same
এই দুই ছেলেকে এক রকম দেখায় ।   alike. | একই, একরকম
   Ei dui chheleke ek rakam dekhay. | eki, ek rakam

These two boys are equal/identical in height. | identical, equal
এই দুই ছেলে লম্বায় এক সমান । | এক সমান
   Ei dui chhele lambay ek shaman. | ek shaman

Idle/lazy people suffer in life. | idle, lazy
অলস লোকেরা জীবনে কষ্ট পায় । | কুঁড়ে, অলস
   Alash lokera jeebane kashta pay. | kure, alash

If you tell me (to go), I shall go. [L. 115, 125] | if
যদি তুমি বল তবে আমি যাইব/যাব । | যদি
   Jodi tumi bala tabe ami jaibo/jabo. | jodi

Ift you tell (me to go). I shall go. [L.115,125] verb
| in ile, ইলে
তুমি বল্লে আমি যাইব/যাব । | ইলে
   Tumi balle, ami jaibo/jabo. | ile

Don't come if you are ill. | ill
অসুখ হইলে/হলে আসিও/এস্যো না । | অসুখ/অসুস্থ
   Ashukh haile/hale ashio/esho na. | ashukh/ashustha

Go immediately. (now) | immediately
[তুমি] এখনই যাও । | এখনই
   [Tumi] ekhan-i jao. | ekhan-i

He went immediately. (then/at once) | immediately
সে তখনই গেল । | তখনই
   She takhan-i gela. | takhan-i

This lesson is important. | important
এই পড়া দরকারী / জরুরী । | জরুরী, দরকারী
Ei para darkaree jaruree. | jaruree, darkaree

This is an important matter. | important/serious
এটা একটা গুরুতর ব্যাপার । | গুরুতর
Eta ekta gurutar baepar. | gurutar

It is impossible to do this work in 2 days. | impossible
এই কাজ দুই দিনে করা অসম্ভব | অসম্ভব
Ek kaj dui dine kara ashambhab. [V.N.] | ashambhab

Who is inside the house ? Come in. | in/into/inside
[LOC., Postp.]
ঘরের ভিতরে কে ? ভিতরে আস/এসো । | ভিতরে/মধ্যে
Gharer bhitare ke? Bhitare asha/esho | [bhitare/maddhe

Going in the rain will be inconvenient. | inconvenient
বৃষ্টিতে যাওয়া অসুবিধা হবে । | অসুবিধা
Brishtite jaoya ashubidha habe | ashubidha

Your answer is incorrect/a mistake | incorrect
তোমার উত্তর অশুদ্ধ/ঠিক না । [ভুল] | অশুদ্ধ, ঠিক না
Tomar uttar ashuddha/thik na. [bhool]. |ashuddha, thik na

The price of rice will /increase. | grow, increase
The tree will grow more.
চাউলের দাম বাড়বে । গাছ আরও বড় হবে । | বাড়া, বড় হওয়
Chauler dam barbe. Gachh aro bara habe. | bara, bara hawa

Indeed/surely It is true. | indeed
তাইতো । এটা সত্য । | তাইতো
Taito. Eta shatta. | taito

The infant is lying down. | infant
শিশুটা শুইয়া/ শুয়ে আছে । | শিশু
Shishuta shuiya/shuye achhe. | shishu

Boy/girl, what's your name ? (v.small) | boy/girl
খোকা/খোকী, তোমার নাম কি ? | খোকা/খোকী
   Knoka/khokee, tomar nam ki ? | khoka/ khokee

He did not inform me before going. [CAUS. V] | inform
সে যাবার আগে আমাকে জানায় নাই/নি । | জানান
   She jabar age amake janay nai/ni. | janan

You have done us an injustice. | injustice
তোমরা আমাদের প্রতি অন্যায় করছ/করেছ । | অন্যায়
   Tomra amader prati annay karchha/karechha. | annay

Bring a bottlo of ink. | ink
এক বোতল কালি আন । | কালি
   Ek botal kali ana. | kali

The man is insane   He acts crazy. | insane, crazy
লোকটা পাগল ।   সে পাগলের মত চলে । | পাগল
   Lokta pagal.   She pagaler mata chale. | pagal.

This insect bites. | insect
এই পোকা কামড়ায় । | পোকা
   Ei poka kamray. | poka

Instead of Ram I choose John. [postpos.] | instead of
রামের বদলে আমি জনকে বাছিয়া/বেছে নেই । | বদলে
   Ramer badale ami Janke   bachhiya/ | badale
   bechhe nei.

What musical instrument can you play ?(musical)instrument
আপনি কি বাজনা বাজাইতে/বাজাতে পারেন ? | বাজনা
   Apni ki bajna bajaite/bajate paren ? | bajna

The carpenter hasn't many instruments/tools. | instrument
ছুতার মিস্ত্রির বেশী যন্ত্র নাই/নেই । | যন্ত্র
   Chhutar mistrir beshee jantra nai/nei. | jantra

He has felt this insult very much. | insult
এ অপমান তার খুব লাগছে/লেগেছে । | অপমান
   E apaman tar khub lagchhe/legechhe. | apaman

Gopal has little intelligence.	intelligence
গোপালের বুদ্ধি অল্প/কম।	বুদ্ধি
Gopaler buddhi alpa/kam	buddhi
I came for this purpose/intention. [POSTP.]	intention, purpose
এই উদ্দেশ্যে আমি আসলাম।	উদ্দেশ্য
Ei uddeshe ami ashlam.	uddeshe
I have no interest in sports.	interest
আমার খেলার দিকে টান/ঝোঁক নাই/নেই।	টান, ঝোঁক
Amar khelar dike tan/jhonk nai/nei.	tan, jhonk
This story is very interesting.	interesting
ঐ গল্পটা খুব মজার।	মজার
E galpata khub majar.	majar
I sought an interview with the minister.	interview
আমি মন্ত্রীর সঙ্গে সাক্ষাৎ/দেখা করতে চাইলাম।	সাক্ষাৎ/দেখা করা
Ami mantreer shange shakkhat/	shakkhat(N),
dekha karte chailam.	dekha kara (V)
He invited me to his house.	invitation
সে আমাকে তার বাড়ীতে নিমন্ত্রণ করল।	নিমন্ত্রণ
She amake tar bareete nimantran karla.	nimantran
Iron is a useful metal.	iron (N)
লোহা একটা উপকারী ধাতু।	লোহা
Loha ekta upakaree dhatu.	loha
I am well. You are. He/she is.	am, are, is
আমি ভাল আছি। তুমি আছ। সে আছে।	আছি, আছ, আছে
Ami bhala achhi. Tumi achha.	achhi, achha.
She achhe.	achhe
How are you ? I am well	are
তুমি কেমন আছ ? ভাল আছি।	আছ
Tumi keman achha ? Bhala achhi.	achha

He is in the house.   is

    সে বাড়ীতে আছে ।   আছে,

      She b*a*reete *a*chhe.   *a*chhe

It is true. It is mine. Whose is this ?   it, this

    এটা/ইহা সত্য ।   এটা/ইহা আমার । এটা কার ?   এটা, ইহা

      E*ta*/iha shatta. E*ta*/iha *a*m*a*r. E*ta* k*a*r ?   eta/iha

Jackals live in the jungle.   jackal

    শিয়াল জঙ্গলে থাকে/বাস করে ।   শিয়াল

      Shiy*a*l jangale th*a*ke/b*a*sh kare.   shiy*a*l

A jackfruit is good to eat. [GRAM. INFIN.]   jackfruit

    কাঁঠাল খাইতে/খেতে ভাল ।   কাঁঠাল

      K*a*nth*a*l kh*a*ite/khete bh*a*la. [INF.]   k*a*nth*a*l

He has been jailed.   jail

    তার জেল হইছে/হয়েছে ।   জেল

      T*a*r jel haichhe/hayechhe.   jel

He envies me. Jealousy is a sin.   jealousy, envy

    সে আমাকে হিংসা করে । হিংসা পাপ [   ] ।   হিংসা

      She *a*make hingsh*a* kare. Hingsh*a* p*a*p [   ].   hingsh*a*

Broken bones too are joined.   join

    ভাঙ্গা হাড়ও জোড়া লাগে ।   জোড়া লাগা

      Bh*a*ng*a* h*a*r-o jo*ra* l*a*ge.   jo*ra* l*a*ga

Combine/join class 4 and class 5 today.   join, combine

    আজ ক্লাস ফোর ও ফাইভ মিলাও/একত্র কর ।   মিলান, একত্র করা

      Aj kl*a*s for o f*a*iv mil*a*o/ekatra kara.   mil*a*n, ekatra kar*a*

Don't joke with me.   joke

    আমার সঙ্গে ঠাট্টা করিও/কর না ।   ঠাট্টা করা

      *A*m*a*r shange *thatta* kario/kar*a* n*a*.   *thatta* kar*a*

His joy doesn't make me envious.   joy

    তার আনন্দ দেখিয়া/দেখে আমার হিংসা হয় না ।   আনন্দ

      T*a*r *a*nanda dekhiy*a*/dekhe *a*m*a*r

      hingsh*a* hay n*a*.   *a*nanda

13—

I was present at the judgement/case.	judgement, trial
বিচারে আমি উপস্থিত ছিলাম ।	বিচার
Bich*a*re *a*mi upasthit chhil*a*m.	bich*a*r
The juice (sap) of the date palm is sweet.	juice
খেজুর গাছের রস মিষ্টি ।	রস
Khejur g*a*chher rash mish*t*i.	rash
This pineapple is very juicy.	juicy, tasty
এ আনারস খুব রসাল ।	রসাল/সরস
E *a*na*ı*ash khub rash*a*l.	rash*a*l/ sharash
The monkey is jumping from tree to tree.	jump
বানরটা গাছে গাছে লাফাইতেছে/লাফাচ্ছে ।	লাফ দেওয়া/লাফান
B*a*nar*ta* g*a*chhe g*a*chhe l*a*f*a*itechhe/	l*a*f dewa/l*a*f*a*n
l*a*f*a*chchhe.	
He came just at 5 o'clock. Exactly 3 seers.	just, exactly, ⋯
⋯[orderly, arranged]	
সে ঠিক পাঁচটায় আসল । ঠিক তিন সের । [ঠিক ঠাক]	ঠিক
She *th*ik p*a*ncht*a*y *a*shla. *Th*ik tin sher. [*th*ik*th*ak]	*th*ik
He gave (me) just/only three rupees.	just, only
সে খালি/মাত্র তিনটা টাকা দিল ।	খালি, শুধু, মাত্র, কেবল
She kh*a*li/m*a*tra tin*ta* *taka* dila.	kh*a*li, shudhu,
	m*a*tra, kebal
He went just now.	just, now
সে এই মাত্র গেছে/গিয়েছে ।	এই মাত্র
She ei m*a*tra gechhe/giyechhe.	ei m*a*tra
We rely on jute. [Jute bag.]	jute
আমরা পাটের উপর নির্ভর করি । [পাটের ব্যাগ]	পাট
*A*mra p*a*ter upar nirbhar kari. [p*a*ter beg]	p*a*t
Keep an eye on the luggage. [watch]	keep an eye on
মালের উপর নজর রাখ ।	নজর রাখা
M*a*ler upar najar r*a*kha.	najar r*a*kha

Keep your hat there.	keep, put
আপনার টুপিটা ওখানে রাখেন/রাখুন।	রাখা
Apnar tupita okhane rakhen/rakhun.	rakha
Take the key out of the lock.	key
তালা থেকে চাবি বাইর/বের কর।	চাবি
Tala theke chabi bair/ber kara.	chabi
To kill anyone * is a sin. [=* someone]	kill
কাকেও মারিয়া/মেরে ফেলা পাপ।	মারিয়া ফেলা
Kake-o mariya/mere fela pap.	mariya fela
What kind of pudding will you make ?	kind, sort
কি রকম পুডিং বানাবে ?	রকম
Ki rakam puding banabe ?	rakam
Kindly tell (me). (polite form)	kindly, please
দয়া করিয়া/করে বলুন।	দয়া করিয়া/করে
Daya kariya/kare balun.	daya kariya/kare
The kind man helped him.	kind, merciful
দয়াল্ লোকটি তাকে সাহায্য করল।	দয়ালু
Dayalu lokti take shahajja karla.	dayalu
Kindness is a virtue. Show kindness to the poor.	kindness
দয়া এটা গুণ। দুঃখীদের প্রতি দয়া দেখাও।	দয়া
Daya ekta gun. Dukkheeder prati daya dekhao.	daya
Light the lamp. Kindle a fire in the oven.	kindle
বাতি জ্বালাও। চুলা জ্বালাও।	জ্বালান
Bati jjalao. Chula jjalao.	jjalan
The king of Monaco has come.	king
মনাকোর রাজা আস্ছেন/এসেছেন।	রাজা
Manakor raja ashchhen/eshechhen.	raja
The mother kisses her daughter. n. v.	kiss, v.
মা মেয়েকে চুমা দেয়।	চুমা দেওয়া
Ma meyeke chuma dey.	chuma dewa

Who is in the kitchen ? Clean the kitchen. | kitchen

রান্না ঘরে কে ?রান্না ঘর সাফ কর । | রান্না ঘর

Ranna ghare ke ? Ranna ghar shaf kara. | ranna ghar

The cook works in the kitchen. | kitchen

বাবুচি বাবুচিখানায় কাজ করে । [রান্নাঘর] | বাবুচিখানা

Baburchi baburchi khanay kaj | baburchi khana
kare. [ranna ghar]

The kite swooped down on the chick. | kite (bird)

চিল মুরগীর ছানার উপর ছোঁ মারল । | চিল

Chil murgeer chhanar upar chhon marla. | chil

Some knaves cheated him. (rogue/cheat) | knave

কতগুলো বদমাস লোক তাকে ঠকাইল/ঠকাল । | বদমাস

Katagulo badmash lok take thakaila/thakalo. | badmash

I have a pain in my knee. | knee

আমার হাঁটুতে ব্যথা আছে । | হাঁটু

Amar hantute baetha achhe. | hantu

Unless he gets a knife he can't work. | knife

ছুরি না পাইলে/পেলে সে কাজ করতে পারে না । | ছুরি

Chhuri na paile/pele she kaj karte pare na. | chhuri

Sharpen the pencil with a pen knife. L. 63 | knife

চাকু দিয়া/দিয়ে পেনসিল কাট । | চাকু

Chaku diya/diye pensil kata. [MEANS] | chaku

I know him. I know the way. | know

আমি তাকে চিনি । আমি রাস্তা চিনি । | চিনা

Ami take chini. Ami rasta chini. | china

I know geography/Bengali/the meaning. | know (a thing)

আমি ভূগোল/বাংলা অর্থ/জানি । | জানা

Ami bhoogal/Bangla/artha jani. | jana

The porter/coolie took my trunk and bedding. | labourer
                                              | porter

কুলি আমার বাক্স ও বিছানা নিয়া/নিয়ে গেল । | কুলি
　　Kuli amar baksha o bichhana niya nıye gela. | kuli

How many labourers/workers will be needed ? | labourer

কয়জন/কত কামলা লাগবে ? | কামলা
　　Kayjan/kata kamla lagbe ? | kamla

He lacks money now. (He is in need of money) lack, | want

তার এখন টাকার অভাব । | অভাব
　　Tar ekhan takar abhab. [GEN.] | abhab

Two ladies are passing down the street. | lady

রাস্তা দিয়া/দিয়ে দুই জন মহিলা যাইতেছে/যাচ্ছে । | মহিলা
　　Rasta diya/dıye duijan mahila jaitechhe/jachchhe.

                                                    | mahila

Light the lamp. Bring a candle. [mom-wax] | lamp, candle

বাতি জ্বালাও । মোমবাতি আন । | বাতি, মোমবাতি
　　Bati jjalao. Mombati ano. | bati, mombati

The man is a landlord/zamindar/zemindar. | landlord

লোকটা জমিদার । | জমিদার
　　Lokta jamidar. | jamidar

A boat has come to our landing place/ghat. | landing place

আমাদের ঘাটে নৌকা আসছে/এসেছে । | ঘাট
　　Amader ghate nauka ashchhe/eshechhe. | ghat

When will you take possession of the land ? | land (property)

কবে জমি দখল করবে ? | জমি
　　Kabe jami dakhal karbe ? | jami

Boys play in this lane. | lane

এ গলিতে ছেলেরা খেলা করে । | গলি
　　E galite chhelera khela kare. | gali

The Bengali language is not difficult at all.	language
বাংলা ভাষা মোটেই কঠিন না ।	ভাষা
Bangla bhasha mote-i kathin na.	bhasha
We use the colloquial form in speaking.	colloquial (language)
আমরা চলিত/চলুতি ভাষায় কথা বলি ।	চলিত/চলতি ভাষা
Amra chalita/chalti bhashay katha bali.	chalita/
	chalti bhasha
The tree is very large. The girl is big.	large, big
এ গাছটা খুব বড় । মেয়েটি বড় ।	বড়
E gachhta khub bara. Meyeti bara.	bara
The last question was very difficult.	last, end
শেষ প্রশ্নটি খুব কঠিন ছিল ।	শেষ
Shesh prasnati khub kathin chhila.	shesh
Costly articles/things last longer.	last, endure, v.
দামী জিনিস বেশী দিন টিকে । [টিকিয়া থাকা]	টিকা
Damee jinish beshee din tike. [tikiya thaka]	tika
He/she came last Monday.	last, past
সে গত সোমবার আসছিল/এসেছিল ।	গত
She gata shombar ashchhila/eshechhila.	gata
He has a lasting job. (permanent)	lasting
তার স্থায়ী চাকরি আছে ।	স্থায়ী
Tar sthayee chakri achhe.	sthayee
Cloth made in the Binny Mills is lasting.	lasting
বিনি মিলের কাপড় টেক্সই হয় ।	টেক্সই
Bini miler kapar teksnai hay.	tekshai
He came five minutes late.	late
সে পাঁচ মিনিট দেরিতে আসল ।	দেরিতে
She panch minit derite ashla.	derite
Don't be late.	be late
দেরি করিও/করো না ।	দেরি করা
Deri kario/kara na.	deri kara

He was late in coming. | be late

তার আসতে দেরি হইল/হল । | দেরি হওয়া

   Tar ashte deri haila/hala. | deri hawa

I haven't seen you lately. | lately

তোমাকে এর মধ্যে দেখি নাই/নি । | এর মধ্যে

   Tomake er maddhe dekhi nai/ni. | er maddhe

He came later. Come after noon. | later, after (prep.)

সে পরে আসচ্ছে/এসেচ্ছে । দুপুরের পরে আস । | পরে

   She pare ashchhe/eshechhe. Dupurer pare ashe. | pare

Seeing him laugh, I laughed. | laugh, n. + v.

তার হাসি দেখিয়া/দেখে আমি হাসলাম । | হাসি, হাসা

   Tar hashi dekhiya/dekhe ami hashlam. | hashi, hasha

The laundryman did not (give) bring the clothes. | laundryman

ধোপা কাপড় দিল না । | ধোপা

   Dhopa kapar dila na. | dhopa

Keep the lavatory clean. [bathroom] | lavatory

পায়খানা পরিষ্কার রাখ । [গোসলখানাটা] | পায়খানা

   Paykhana parishkar rakha. [gasalkhanata] | paykhana

Those who break the law are/get punished. | law

যারা আইন ভাঙ্গে তারা শাস্তি পায় । | আইন

   Jara ain bhange tara shashti pay. | ain

Lay the wood down there. (keep, put). | lay down

সেখানে কাঠগুলি রাখ । | রাখা

   Shekhane kathguli rakha. | rakha

The lazy are not happy. | lazy, idle

অলস লোকেরা সুখী না । | অলস

   Alash lokhera shukee na. | Alash

The boy leaped into the river. | Jeap, jump

ছেলেটি নদীতে লাফাইয়া/লাফিয়ে পড়ল । | লাফান

   Chheleti nadeete lafaiya/lafiye parla. | lafan

Have you learnt your lesson(s) ? | learn, v
তোমার পড়া শিখছ/শিখেছ ? | শিখ
   Tomar para shikhchha/shikhechha ? | shikha

Now is the time for learning. (to learn) | learning
এখন শিক্ষার সময় । | শিক্ষা
   Ekhan shikkhar shamay. | shikkha

Shoes are made of leather. skin of the body. | leather, skin
চামড়া দিয়া/দিয়ে জুতা তৈয়ার হয় । [গায়ের চামড়া] | চামড়া
   Chamra diya/diye juta taiyar hay.[Gayer | chamra
           chamra.]

He/she took leave/he left/departed. | leave, n.
সে বিদায় নিল । | বিদায়
   She biday nila. | biday

Don't leave me alone. | leave, v.
আমাকে একা ছাড়িয়া/ছেড়ে দিও না । [যাওয়া] | ছাড়া
   Amake eka chhariya/chhere dio na [jaoya]. | chhara

May I have two days' leave ? | leave (vacation)
দুইদিনের ছুটি পাইতে/পেতে পারি [কি] ? | ছুটি
   Dui diner chhuti paite/pete pari [ki] ? | chhuti

Go to the left.　The left hand. | left
বাঁ/বাম দিকে যাও ।　বাম হাত । | বাঁ/বাম
   Ban/bam dike jao. Bam hat. | ban/bam

Daddy [has] long legs. | leg, foot
বাবার লম্বা লম্বা পা [   ] । | পা, ঠ্যাং
   Babar lamba lamba pa [achhe]. | pa, theng

I have no leisure.　(free time) | leisure
আমার অবসর নাই/নেই । | অবসর
   Amar abashar nai/nei. | ab(a)shar

Put the juice of three lemons into the water. | lemon
জলে তিনটা লেবুর রস দাও । | লেবু
   Jale tinta lebur rash dao. | lebu

Lend me three taka. | lend
আমাকে তিনটা টাকা ধার দেও/দাও ।   ধার দেওয়া
Amake tinta taka dhar deo/dao.   dhar dewa

He lent (me) some money. | lend
সে কিছু টাকা কর্জ দিল ।   কর্জ দেওয়া
She kichhu taka karja dila.   karja dewa

Leopards are smaller than tigers. | leopard
বাঘের চেয়ে চিতা বাঘ ছোট ।   চিতা বাঘ
Bagher cheye chita bagh chhota.   chita bagh

He talks less now. Why did you give me less ? | less
সে এখন কম কথা কয় । আমাকে কম দিছ/দিয়েছ কেন ?   কম
She ekhan kam katha kay. Amake   kam
       kam dichha/diyechha kena ?

It is a quarter to ten. Three quarters of a seer. | a quarter
                                                                     (less)
পৌনে দশটা বাজে ।   পৌনে এক সের ।   পৌনে
Paune dashta baje. Paune ek sher.   paune

Lessen the amount of rice you eat. L. 30 | lessen
          The water has gone down.
ভাত খাওয়া কমাও ।   জল কমছে ।   কমা ; কমান
Bhat khawa kamao. Jal kamchhe   kama, kaman

Why haven't you learnt your lesson ? | lesson
তোমার পড়া কর নাই/নি কেন ?   পড়া
Tomar para kara nai/ni kena ?   para

Let the little children come to me. (INF.) L. 86 |let, allow
ছোট শিশুদের আমার কাছে আসতে দেও/দাও ।   দেওয়া
Chhota shishuder amar kachhe ashte deo/dao.   dewa

I have received your letter. | letter
তোমার চিঠি পাইছি/পেয়েছি।   চিঠি
Tomar chithi paichhi/peyechhi.   chithi

Bengali letters are easy to write. | letter (alphabet)

বাংলা অক্ষর লিখতে সোজা । | অক্ষর

    B*a*ngl*a* akkhar likhte shoj*a*. | akkhar

How many letter are there in the Bengali alphabet ? | letter

বাংলা বর্ণমালায় কতগুলি বর্ণ ? | বর্ণ

    B*a*ngl*a* barnam*a*lay kataguli barna ? | barna

Take the lid off the kettle/pot/pan. | lid

কেতলির/হাঁড়ির ঢাকনি খুলিয়া/খুলে ফেল । | ঢাকনি/ঢাক্না

    Ketlir/h*a*nir *dha*kni khulyi*a*/khule felo. | *dha*kni/*dha*kn*n*

He/she is a li*a*r and a cheat. | liar

সে মিথ্যুক ও ঠক । | মিথ্যুক

    She mitthuk o *th*ak. | mitthuk

Don't tell lies/don't lie. | lie, v.

মিথ্যা কথা বলিও/বল না । | মিথ্যা কথা বলা

    Mitth*a* kath*a* balio/bala n*a*. | mitth*a* kath*a* bal*a*

A girl went there to lie down (to sleep) | lie down

সেখানে একটি মেয়ে শুইতে/শুতে গেল । | শোয়া

    Shekh*a*ne ek*t*i meye shuite/shute gela. | shooy*a*, shuy*a*

The man saved the boy's life. | life

লোকটি ছেলেটির জীবন বাঁচাইল/বাঁচাল । | জীবন

    Lok*t*i chhele*t*ir jeeban b*a*nchaila/b*a*nch*a*la. | jeeban

Iron is lighter than gold. This is light. | light, adj.

লোহা সোনার চেয়ে হাল্কা । এটা হাল্কা । | হাল্কা

    Loh*a* shon*a*r cheye h*a*lka. Et*a* h*a*lka. | h*a*lk*a*

Light the lamp. Light the candle. | light, kindle, v.
                  [n. *a*lo, আলো]

বাতি জ্বালাও/জ্বাল । মোমবাতি জ্বালাও । | জ্বালা/জ্বালান

    B*a*ti jjal*a*o/jjalo. Mombati jjal*a*o. | jjal*a*, jjal*a*n

Be like a little child. Like him. | like (prep.)

ছোট শিশুর মত হও । তার মত । | মত/সমান

    Chho*t*a shishur mat*a* hao Tar mata. | mata, sham*a*n

I like this.

আমি এটা পছন্দ করি ।

   *A*mi e*ta* pachhanda kari.

like   v.

পছন্দ করা

pachhanda kar*a*

I like the boy. (love)

আমি ছেলেটিকে ভালবাসি ।

   *A*mi chhele*t*ike bh*a*labashi.

like, v.

ভালবাসা

bh*a*lab*a*sha

Lime is needed to build a house. [Gen.]

বাড়ী করতে চুনের দরকার হয় ।

   B*a*ree karte chuner dark*a*r hay.

lime

চুন/চুনা

chun/chun*a*

Draw a straight line. This line is straight.

একটা সরল রেখা টান ।   এ লাইন সোজা ।

   Ek*ta* sharal rekh*a* *ta*na. E l*a*in shoj*a*.

line

রেখা, লাইন

rekh*a*, l*a*in

Man's lips. The bird's beak/bill is long.

মানুষের ঠোঁট ।   পাখীটার ঠোঁট লম্বা ।

   Manusher *thont*. P*a*khee*ta*r *thont* lamb*a*

lip, beak

ঠোঁট

thont

Listen to me. I hear a noise/sound.

আমার কথা শুন ।   আমি শব্দ শুনি ।

   *A*m*a*r kath*a* shuna. *A*mi shabda shuni.

listen, hear

শুনা

shon*a*

He did not listen to me. (mind)

সে আমার কথায় কান দিল না ।   [মান্য করা]

   She *a*m*a*r kath*a*y k*a*n dila n*a*. [m*a*nn*a* kar*a*]

listen to

কান দেওয়া

k*a*n deoya

The little boy is six years-old. Younger/
                 little brother.

ছোট ছেলেটির ছয় বৎসর ।   ছোট ভাই ।

   Chho*ta* chhele*t*ir chhay batshar. Chho*ta* bh*a*i.

little, younger

ছোট

chho*ta*

A little sugar will do.

অল্প চিনি [হলে] চলে ।

   Alpa chini [hale] chale.

a little

অল্প, থোড়া

alpa, thor*a*

Give me a little tea/sugar/water.

একটু চা/চিনি/জল দেও/দাও ।

   Ek*t*u ch*a*/chini/jal deo/d*a*o.

a little

একটু

Ek*t*u

An elephant lives for about a hundred years. | live, exist
হাতী প্রায় একশ' বৎসর বাঁচিয়া/বেঁচে থাকে । | বাঁচিয়া থাকা
Hatee pray ek sha' batshar *banchia/* | *banchia thaka*
benche th*a*ke.

He lives from hand to mouth. | live
সে অনেক কষ্টে জীবন যাপন করে । | জীবন যাপন করা
She anek kash*t*e jeeban japan kar*e.* | jeeban japan kar*a*

He lives with his brother. | lives, stay
সে তার ভাইয়ের সঙ্গে থাকে । | থাকা
She t*a*r bh*a*iyer k*a*chhe th*a*ke. | th*a*ka

We live in a village. | live
আমরা গ্রামে বাস করি । | বাস করা
*A*mr*a* gr*a*me b*a*sh kari. | b*a*sh kar*a*

Who will carry this load ? (responsibility) | load, burden
এ ভার কে বহন করবে ? | ভার, বোঝা
E bh*a*r ke bahan karbe ? | bh*a*r, bojh*a*

He will have to take a loan. | loan
তাকে ধার/কর্জ করতে হবে । [হাওলাত] | ধার/কর্জ
T*a*ke dh*a*r/karja karte habe. [howl*a*t] | dh*a*r, karja

There is a factory in our locality. | locality
আমাদের এলাকায় একটা কারখানা আছে । এলাকা| পাড়া, অঞ্চল
*A*m*a*der el*a*k*a*y ek*t*a karkh*a*n*a* *a*chhe. | el*a*k*a*, p*a*ra

Lock up the house. This lock is new. | lock, v.
ঘরে তালা দেও। এ তালা নূতন । | তালা দেওয়া
Ghare t*a*la deo. E t*a*la nootan. | ch*a*bi deoya

Lock up. I bought a lock. | lock, n.
তালায় চাবি দেও । তালা কিনলাম । | চাবি দেওয়া
T*a*lay ch*a*bi deo. T*a*la kinl*a*m. | t*a*la deoya

Where is your lodging ? | lodging
তোমার বাসা কোথায় ? | বাসা
Tom*a*r b*a*sh*a* kothay ? | b*a*sh*a*

The table is six feet long. The man is very tall. | long, tall
টেবিলটা ছয় ফুট লম্বা । লোকটা খুব লম্বা । | লম্বা
*T*ebi*la*ta chhay fu*t* lamb*a*. Lok*ta* khub lamb*a*. | lamb*a*

Look/see there.   Look this way. | look, see
সেখানে দেখ । এদিকে দেখ । | দেখা
Shekh*a*ne dekha. E dike dekha. | dekh*a*

Look at that man.   Look at me. | look at
ও লোকটার দিকে তাকাও ।   আমার দিকে চাও । | তাকান, চাওয়া
O lok*ta*r dike *ta*ka*o*. *A*ma*r* dike ch*a*o. | *ta*ka*n*, ch*a*oya

Look for my book (s). | look for, search for
আমার বই খুঁজ । | খোঁজা
*A*ma*r* bai khu*n*ja. | kho*n*ja

He looks strange/ill/tired... L. 30 CAUS. | look, appear
তাকে অদ্ভুত/ অসুস্থ/ক্লান্ত···দেখায় । | দেখান
*T*a*ke adbhut/ashustha/kl*a*nta...dekh*a*y. | dekh*a*n

A button on his shirt has become loose. | loose
তার শার্টের বোতাম আল্গা হইয়া গেছে/হয়ে গিয়েছে । | আল্গা
*T*ar sh*a*r*t*er bot*a*m *a*lga haiya | *a*lga
gechhe/haye giyechhe.

He likes to wear loose shirts. It feels loose. | loose
সে ঢিলা শার্ট পরতে ভালবাসে । ঢিলা লাগে । | ঢিলা
She *dh*ila sh*a*r*t* parte bh*a*laba*s*he. dhila lage. | *dh*ila

This son of mine was lost. | lose
আমার এ ছেলে হারাইয়া গেছিল/হারিয়ে গিয়েছিল । | হারান
*A*m*a*r e chhele h*a*r*a*iya gechhila/ | h*a*r*a*n
h*a*riye giyechhila.

A big loss was incurred in the jute trade. | loss
পাট ব্যবসায় অনেক ক্ষতি হইছে/হয়েছে । | ক্ষতি/লোকসান
*P*at baebsh*a*y anek kkhati haichhe/ | kkhati/loksh*a*n
hayechhe.

I love (my) mother. | love, v.
আমি মাকে ভালবাসি । | ভালবাসা
Ami make bhalabashi. | bhalabasha

I love to read books. | love, like, v.
আমি বই পড়তে ভালবাসি । | ভালবাসা
Ami bai parte bhalabashi. | bhalabasha

The table is low. Put it down/below. | low
টেবিলটা নীচু । নীচে রাখ । | নীচ/নীচু
Tebilta neechu Neeche rakha. | neecha/neechu

Keep an eye on your own luggage. | luggage
নিজের মালের উপর নজর রাখ । | মাল
Nijer maler upar najar rakha. | mal

Mother loves me. | mother
মা আমাকে ভালবাসেন । | মা, মাতা
Ma amake bhalabashen | ma. mata

The machine is broken | machine
কলটা ভাঙ্গা । | কল
Kalta bhanga. | kal

The man has become mad. | mad, insane
লোকটা পাগল হইয়া গেছে/হয়ে গিয়েছে । | পাগল
Lokta pagal haiya gechhe/haye giyechhe. | pagal

Today we got no mail. | mail (n.)
আজ আমরা ডাক পাই নাই/নি । | ডাক
Aj amra dak pai nai/ni. | dak

Mail/post this letter. | mail, v.
চিঠিটা ডাকে দাও/পাঠাও । | ডাকে দেওয়া
Chithita dake dao/pathao. | dake deoya

The mailman has brought the mail. | mailman
পিয়ন ডাক আন্‌ছে/এনেছে । | পিয়ন
Piyan dak anchhe/enechhe. | piyan

Rice is the chief diet/food of the Bengalees.	main, chief
ভাত বাঙ্গালীর প্রধান [খাদ্য]/খাওয়া ।	প্রধান
Bh*a*t B*a*ng*a*leer pradh*a*n [kh*a*ddha]/kh*a*oya.	pradh*a*n
This is the main topic of conversation.	main
এটা কথাবার্তার বড় বিষয় ।	প্রধান, বড়
Eta kat*a*a b*a*rt*a*r b*a*ra bishay.	pradhan, b*a*ra
I shall make a table.	make, build
আমি একটা টেবিল তৈয়ার করব ।	তৈয়ারী/তৈরী করা
*A*mi ek*ta* *t*ebil taiy*a*r karb*a*.	taiy*a*r/tairee kar*a*
This is made of wood.	made of
এটা কাঠের তৈয়ারী/তৈরী ।	তৈয়ারী/তৈরী
E*ta* kat*a*er taiy*a*ree/tairee.	taiy*a*ree/tairee
Potters make pots out of earth.	make, build
কুমারেরা মাটি দিয়া/দিয়ে কল্সি বানায় ।	বানান
Kum*a*rera m*a*ti diy*a*/diye kalshi b*a*n*a*y.	b*a*n*a*n
Man wants peace.	man
মানুষ শান্তি চায় ।	মানুষ
M*a*nush sh*a*nti ch*a*y.	m*a*nush
There were many people on the bus/launch···	man (people)
বসে/লঞ্চে অনেক লোক ছিল ।	লোক
B*a*se/lanche...anek lok chhila. [see LOC.]	lok
He manages the school well.	manage
তিনি ভালভাবে স্কুলটি চালান ।	চালান
Tini bh*a*labh*a*be skul*t*i ch*a*l*a*n.	ch*a*l*a*n
Everyone likes mangoes.	mango
সকলে আম পছন্দ করে ।	আম
Shakale *a*m pachhanda kare.	*a*m
His manners are good. (behaviour)	manners
তার চালচলন/ব্যবহার ভাল ।	আচরণ, চালচলন
T*a*r ch*a*lchalan/baebah*a*r bh*a*l*a*.	*a*charan, ch*a*lchalan

Mix manure and earth and put it on the garden. | manure

সার ও মাটি মিলাইয়া/মিলিয়ে বাগানে দেও/দাও । | সার

Shar o mati milaiya/miliye bagane deo/dao. | shar

Many men are going to work. Much water. | many, much

অনেক লোক কাজে যাইতেছে/যাচ্ছে । অনেক পানি/জল । | অনেক

Anek lok kaje jaitechhe/jachchhe. Anek pani/jal | anek

He died many days ago. He has much money. | many

বহু দিন আগে সে মারা গেল । তার বহু টাকা । | বহু

Bahu din age she mara gela. Tar bahu taka. | bahu

Don't talk much. | much

বেশী কথা বলিও/বল না । | বেশী

Beshee katha balio/bala na. | beshee

A good map of Dacca is needed. | map

ঢাকার একটি ভাল ম্যাপ/মানচিত্র দরকার । | ম্যাপ/মানচিত্র

Dhakar ekti bhala mep/manchitra darkar. | mep/manchitra

Don't mark up the book. n. v. | mark, v.

বইয়ে দাগ দিও না । | দাগ দেওয়া

Baiye dag dio na. | dag dewa

He went to the market/bazar. | market

সে বাজারে গেল । | বাজার

She bajare gela.   (bazare) | bajar

Things come from afar to the market. | market (weekly)

হাটে অনেক দূর থেকে জিনিস আসে । | হাট

Hate anek door theke jinish ashe. | hat

He has no wish to marry. | marry, n. v.

তার বিয়া/বিয়ে করার ইচ্ছা নাই/নেই ।   [বিবাহ] | বিয়া/বিয়ে করা

Tar biya/biye karar ichchha nai/nei. | biya/biye kara

[bibaha]

The mason is working. | mason

রাজমিস্ত্রি কাজ করছে/করতেছে । | রাজমিস্ত্রি

Rajmistri kaj karchhe/kartechhe. | raj mistri

Light a match. | match
দিয়াশলাই জ্বাল । | ম্যাচ, দিয়াশলাই
Diyashalai jjala. | diyashalai/mech

I don't know anything about this matter. | matter
এ বিষয়ে আমি কিছু জানি না । | বিষয়
E bishaye ami kichhu jani na. | bishay

What's the matter ? What happened ? | matter
ব্যাপার কি ? | ব্যাপার
Bepar ki ? | bepar

It doesn't matter if he does not pass. | it doesn't matter
সে পাশ না করলেও কিছু যায় আসে না । | কিছু যায় আসে না
She pash na karleo kichhu jay ashe na. | kichhu jay
| ashe na

You may go. [see Inf.] | may, can
তুমি যাইতে/ যেতে পার । | পারা
Tumi jaite/ jete paro. | para

Maybe I won't go home. | maybe
হইতে/হতে পারে আমি বাড়ী যাব না । | হইতে/হতে পারে
Haite/hate pare ami baree jaba na. | haite/hate pare

What does it mean ? What is the meaning | meaning
of this word ? |
এর মানে কি ? এ শব্দের অর্থ কি ? | মানে, অর্থ
Er mane ki ? E shabder artha ki ? | mane, artha

I have no other means. | means
আমার আর কোন উপায় নাই/নেই । | উপায়
Amar ar kona upay nai/nei. | upay

Measure the cloth. Weigh the rice. | v. measure, weigh
কাপড়টা মাপ । চাউলটা মাপ । | মাপা
Kaparta mapa. chawalta map. | mapa

14—

He measured the field. | measure, v.
সে জমিটা মাপ দিল । | মাপ দেওয়া
She jami*ta* m*a*p dila. | m*a*p deoy*a*

He likes meat. | meat, flesh
সে মাংস ভালবাসে । | মাংস
She m*a*ngsha bh*a*lab*a*she. | m*a*ngsha

The doctor gave (him) medicine. | medicine
ডাক্তার ঔষধ দিয়া/দিয়ে গেল । | ঔষধ
*Da*kt*a*r oushad diy*a*/diy*e* gela. | oushad

Meet me in the field. | meet, visit
আমার সঙ্গে মাঠে দেখা কর । | দেখা করা
*A*mar shange m*athe* dekh*a* kara. | dekh*a* kar*a*

Wax melts in fire. | melt
আগুনে মোম গলে । | গলা
*A*gune mom gale. | gal*a*

Memorize the poem. | memorize
কবিতাটা মুখস্থ কর । | মুখস্থ করা
Kabit*ata* mukhastha kara. | mukhastha kar*a*

He mentioned my name. | mention
সে আমার নাম উল্লেখ করছে/করেছে । | উল্লেখ করা
She *a*m*a*r n*a*m ullekh karchhe/karechhe. | ullekh kar*a*

God is a merciful father. | merciful, kind
আল্লাহ/ঈশ্বর দয়ালু পিতা । | দয়ালু
All*a*h/Eeshshar day*a*lu pit*a*. | day*a*lu

Have mercy on me. (show kindness...) | mercy
আমার প্রতি দয়া কর । | দয়া
*A*m*a*r prati day*a* kara. | day*a*

Send him a message. What is the news ? | message, news
তার কাছে একটা খবর পাঠাও । খবর কি ? | খবর, সংবাদ
T*a*r k*a*chhe ek*ta* khabar p*a*th*a*o. Khabar ki ? | khabar, shangb*a*d

What metal is this made of ? | metal
এটা কোন্/কি ধাতু দিয়া/দিয়ে তৈরী ? | ধাতু
    Eta kon/ki dhatu diya/diye tairee ? | dhatu

I don't know the method of doing this sum. | method, rule
এ অংক কষবার নিয়ম জানি না । | নিয়ম
    E anka kashbar niyam jani na. | niyam

He sat in the middle of the crowd. [POSTP.] | in the middle
তিনি ভীড়ের মধ্যে বসলেন । | মধ্যে, মাঝে
    Tini bheerer maddhe bashlen. | maddhe/majhe

He stood in the middle of the room. | in the middle of
      (went and stood)
সে ঘরের মাঝখানে গিয়া দাঁড়াইলা/দাঁড়াল । | মাঝখানে
    She gharer majhkhane giya danraila/danrala.   majh khane

Boys and girls need milk very much. | milk
বালক-বালিকাদের দুধ খুব দরকার । [ছেলেমেয়েদের] | দুধ
    Balak-balikader dudh khub darkar. | dudh
       [chhelemeyeder]

He does not put his mind on his lessons. | mind, n.
পড়ায় তার মন নাই/নেই ।   কাজে মন দেও । | মন
    Paray tar man nai/nei. Kaje man deo.   man

Where is my mirror ? | mirror
আমার আয়না কোথায় ? | আয়না
    Amar ayna kothay ? | ayna

A miserly old man came. | miserly
একজন কৃপণ বুড়া আসূল । | কৃপণ
    Ekjan kripan bura ashla. | kripan

You made a mistake in the account. | mistake
হিসাবে আপনি ভুল করলেন । তুমি করলে | ভুল
    Hishabe apni bhul karlen. tumi karle. | bhul

Don't misunderstand me. | misunderstand
আমাকে ভুল বুঝিও/বুঝ না। | ভুল বুঝা
    *A*make bhul bujhio/bujha n*a*. | bhul bujh*a*

Water does not mix with oil. | mix, int. v.
তেল জলের সঙ্গে মিশে না। | মিশা
    Tel jaler shange mishe n*a*. | mish*a*

Don't mix with bad boys/girls. | mix
খারাপ ছেলে/মেয়ের সঙ্গে মিশ না। | মিশা
    Kh*a*r*a*p chhele/meyer shange misha n*a*. | mish*a*

Mix these two colours. [CAUS.] see GRAM. | mix, (t. v.)
এ রং দুইটা/দুটো মিশাও। L. 30. | মিশান
    E rang dui*ta*/du*to* mish*a*o. | mish*a*n

All my clothes are wet. | wet, moist
আমার সব কাপড় ভিজা। | ভিজা
    *A*m*a*r shab k*a*p*a*r bhij*a*. | bhij*a*

I shall go on Monday. Tomorrow is Monday. | Monday
আমি সোমবারে যাইব/যাব। কাল সোমবার। | সোমবার
    *A*mi shomb*a*re j*a*iba/j*a*ba. K*a*l shomb*a*r [ ]. | shomb*a*r

He has no money on hand. | money
তার হাতে টাকা–পয়সা নাই/নেই। | টাকা-পয়সা
    T*a*r hate *taka*-paysha n*a*i/nei. | *taka*-paysh*a*

People say the mongoose is the snake's foe. | mongoose
লোকে বলে বেজি সাপের শত্রু। | বেজি
    Loke bale beji sh*a*per shatru. | beji

Monkeys imitate men. | monkey
বানর মানুষকে নকল করে। | বানর
    B*a*nar m*a*nushke nakal kare. | b*a*nar

Frogs croak during the monsoon season. | monsoon
বর্ষাকালে বেঙ ডাকে। | বর্ষাকাল
    Barsh*a*k*a*le beng *da*ke. | barsh*a*k*a*l

He went to Dacca last month. | month
সে গত মাসে ঢাকা গেছিল/গিয়েছিল । | মাস
   She gata mashe *Dhaka* gechhila/giyechhila. | mash

The moon has risen in the sky. | moon
আকাশে চাঁদ উঠছে/উঠেছে । | চাঁদ
   Akashe chand uthchhe/uthechhe. | chand

I want more. Better. | more
আমি আরও চাই । আরও ভাল । | আরও
   Ami aro chai. Aro bhala. | aro

You will not be given (any) more. I want a | more
               little more.
তোমাকে আর দেওয়া হবে না । আর একটু চাই । | আর
   Tomake ar deoya habe na. Ar ektu chai. | ar

Get out of bed early in the morning. | morning
খুব সকালে বিছানা হইতে/হতে উঠবে | সকাল
   Khub shakale bichhana haite/hate uthbe. | shakal

The mosque is very big and. beautiful. . | mosque
মসজিদটি খুব বড় ও সুন্দর । | মসজিদ
   Mashjidti khub bara o shundar. | mashjid

Mosquitoes bite. | mosquito
মশা কামড় দেয় ।   [কামড়ায়] | মশা
   Masha kamar dey.   [kamray, v.] | masha

I shall need a mosquito net. | mosquito net
আমার একটা মশারী লাগবে । | মশারী
   Amar ekta masharee lagbe | masharee

My mother loves me very much. | mother
আমার মা আমাকে খুব ভালবাসেন । | মা, মাতা
   Amar ma amake khub bhalabashen. | ma mata

I mount a horse. I ride a car...	mount
ঘোড়ায় চড়ি । গাড়ীতে চড়ি ।	চড়া, উঠা
Ghoray chari. Gareete...chari	chara, utha
There is a mountain/hill there.	mountain
সেখানে পাহাড় আছে ।	পাহাড়
Shekhane pahar achhe.	pahar
We eat with our mouths.	mouth
আমরা মুখ দিয়া/দিয়ে খাই ।	মুখ
Amra mukh diya/diye khai.	mukh
He does not move. Leaves move in the wind.	move (v.i.)
সে নড়ে না । বাতাসে পাতা নড়ে ।	নড়া
She nare na. Batashe pata nare.	nara
Don't move the table. (shake) [CAUS.] L. 30.	move (v.t.)
টেবিলটা নাড়াইও/নড়াইও না ।	নাড়ান/নড়ান
Tebilta naraio/naraio na.	naran/naran
Move away. Move aside.	move away
সরিয়া/সরে যাও । সরিয়া/সরে দাঁড়াও ।	সরা
Shariya/share jao. Shariya/share danrao.	shara
Move these clothes away. (caus. v.) L. 30.	move away (v.t.)
কাপড়–চোপড়গুলো সরাও ।	সরান
Kapar-chopargulo sharao.	sharan
He has much money.	much, many
তার অনেক টাকা আছে ।	অনেক, বহু
Tar anek taka achhe.	anek, bahu
He has too much money. It seems like too much.	much, too
তার বেশী টাকা আছে । বেশী লাগে ।	বেশী/অনেক
Tar beshee taka achhe. Beshee lage	beshee/anek
There is mud on the path.	mud
পথে কাদা আছে ।	কাদা
Pathe kada achhe.	kada

I like music. | music
আমি গানবাজনা ভালবাসি | গানবাজনা
  Ami gan-bajna bhalabashi. | gan-bajna

He must go.   I must stay.   [L. 83] | must
তাকে/তার যাইতে/যেতে হবে। আমার থাকতে হবে। | -তে হওয়া
  Take/tar jaite/jete habe. Amar thakte habe. | -te, haoya

The carpenter wants nails.   Hit the nail. | nail
ছুতার মিস্ত্রি পেরেক চায়। পেরেক মার। | পেরেক
  Chhutar mistri perek chay. Perek mara. | perek

Cut your nails. | nail (finger)
তোমার নখ কাট। | নখ
  Tomar nakh kata. | nakh

What's your name? [give a name, name v.] | name
তোমার নাম কি? [নাম রাখা] | নাম
  Tomar nam ki? [nam rakha, v.] | nam

A narrow path goes between the houses. [L. 61 F.] | narrow
একটা সরু পথ ঘরগুলোর মধ্য-দিয়া/দিয়ে যায়। | সরু
  Ekta sharu path ghargulor maddhe diya/diye jay. | sharu

The English are a courageous nation/people. | nation, caste
ইংরেজ জাতি খুব সাহসী। | জাতি
  Ingrej jatee khub shahashee. | jatee

That man is a native of Bangladesh | native
/Bangladeshee person.
ঐ লোকটি বাংলাদেশী লোক। | দেশী লোক
  Oi lokti Bangladeshee lok. | deshee lok

My house is near the school.   [POSTPOS.] | near
আমার বাড়ী স্কুলের কাছে। | কাছে/নিকটে
  Amar baree skuler kachhe. | kachhe, nikate

Dacca is about 25 miles from my village. | nearly, almost
আমার গ্রাম হইতে/হতে ঢাকা প্রায় পঁচিশ মাইল। | প্রায়
  Amar gram haite/hate Dhaka pray panchish mail. | pray

Keep the necessary papers carefully. | necessary

দরকারী কাগজপত্র যত্ন করিয়া/করে রাখ। | দরকারী

   Darkaree kagaj patra jatna kariya rakha. | darkaree

A crane's neck is very long | neck

সারস পাখীর গলা লম্বা। | গলা

   Sharash pakheer gala lamba. | gala

I need ink. | need

আমার কালি লাগবে/দরকার। | gen. + লাগা

   Amar kali lagbe/darkar. | gen. + laga

Love your neighbour as yourself. | neighbour

প্রতিবেশীকে নিজের মত ভালবাসবে। | প্রতিবেশী

   Pratibesheeke nijer mata bhalabashbe. | pratibeshee

The weaver birds nest is very beautiful. ' | nest

বাবুই পাখীর বাসা খুব সুন্দর। | বাসা

   Babui pakheer basha khub shundar. | basha

The fisherman is weaving/making a net. | net

জেলে জাল বুনতেছে/বুনছে। | জাল

   Jele jal buntechhe/bunchhe. | Jal

I shall never do this (deed, work) again. | never

আমি আর কখনও একাজ করব না। | কখনও না

   Ami ar kakhan-o e kaj karba na. | kakhan-o na

I did not call him, nevertheless he came. (yet) | nevertheless

আমি তাকে ডাকি নাই/নি, তবুও সে আসছে/এসেছে। | তবুও

   Ami take daki nai/nei, tabuo she ashchhe/eshechhe. | tabuo

He has got a new cycle. | new

সে নূতন সাইকেল পাইছে/পেয়েছে। | নূতন

   She nootan saikel paichhe/peyechhe. | nootan

What news is there ? What's the news ? | news

খবর কি ? | খবর/সংবাদ

   Khabar ki ? | khabar, shangbad

He writes for a newspaper. | newspaper

সে খবরের কাগজে লেখে।   খবরের কাগজ

   She khabarer kagaje lekhe.   khabarer kagaj

We shall go to Dacca next month. | next, coming

আগামী মাসে আমরা ঢাকা যাইব/যাব।   আগামী

   *A*gamee m*a*she *a*mr*a* **Dh*a*ka** jaiba/jaba.   *a*gamee

Go to the next shop. | next

সামনের দোকানে যান/যাও।   সামনের

   Sh*a*mner dok*a*ne j*a*n/j*a*o.   sh*a*mner

He did not come that day, he came the next day. | next

সে সেদিন আসল না, পরের দিন আসল। [পর দিন]   পরের

   She shedin *a*shla n*a*, parer din *a*shla. [par din]   parer

My brother works at night. | night

আমার ভাই রাত্রে কাজ করে। [রাতে]   রাত্র, রাত

   *A*m*a*r bhai r*a*tre k*a*j kare. [r*a*te]   ratra, r*a*t

No, I shall not go.   I want no money. | no, not

না, যাইব/যাব না।   আমি কোন টাকা চাই না।   না

   N*a*, jaiba/jaba n*a*.   *A*mi kona *ta*ka ch*a*i n*a*.   n*a*

Nobody spoke a word.   Nobody will come. | nobody

কেহ একটাও কথা বল্ল না। কেহ আসবে না।   কেহ···না

   Keha ek*ta*–o kath*a* balla n*a*. Keha *a*shbe n*a*.   keha...n*a*

I heard a noise. | noise (word)

আমি একটা শব্দ শুনছি/শুনেছি।   শব্দ

   *A*mi ek*ta* shabda shunchhi/shunechhi.   shabda

He talks nonsense. | nonsense

সে বাজে কথা কয়/বলে। [বোকামি]   বাজে কথা

   She b*a*je kath*a* kay/bale.   [bok*a*mi]   b*a*je kath*a*

Don't go on the street in the noonday sun. | noon

দুপুর রৌদ্রে রাস্তায় যাইও/যেও না।   দুপুর

   Dupur roudre r*a*st*a*y j*a*io/jeo n*a*.   dupur

His nose is bleeding. (Blood is coming from ·) | nose
তার নাক দিয়া/দিয়ে রক্ত পড়তেছে/পড়ছে । | নাক
   Tar nak diya/diye rakta partechhe/parchhe. | nak

He went north. (in the direction of the north) | north
সে উত্তর দিকে গেল । [উত্তরে] | উত্তর
   She uttar dike gela. [uttare][LOC.] | uttar

It is not mine. I have no money. | not, no
এটা আমার না । আমার টাকা নাই/নেই । | না
   Eta amar na. Amar taka nai/nei. | na

I do not know him at all. | not at all
আমি তাকে মোটেই চিনি না । | মোটেই না
   Ami take mote-i chini na. | mote-i na

I want a notebook. | notebook
একখানা খাতা চাই । | খাতা
   Ek khana khata chai. | khata

The headmaster noticed it at that time. | notice, see
ঐ সময় হেডমাস্টার এটা/তা লক্ষ্য করলেন । | লক্ষ্যকরা
   Oi shamay hedmastar eta/ta lakkha karlen. | lakkha kara

I did not notice it. (pay attention to) | notice
আমি এটা খেয়াল করি নাই/নি । | খেয়াল/খেল করা
   Ami eta kheyal kari nai/ni. | kheyal/khel kara

Go now, come tomorrow. There is no time now. | now
এখন যাও, কাল আসিও/এস । এখন সময় নাই । | এখন
   Ekhan jao, kal ashio/esha. Ekhan shamay nai. | ekhan

He comes now and then. | now and then
সে যখন তখন আসে । | মাঝে মাঝে, যখন তখন
   She jakhan takhan ashe. | majhe majhe, jakhan takhan

Now-a-days people have no peace of mind. | now-a days
আজকাল লোকের মনে শান্তি নাই/নেই । | আজকাল
   Ajkal loker mane shanti nai/nei. | ajkal

The number of students has increased. m./f. | number

ছাত্র/ছাত্রী সংখ্যা বাড়িয়া গেছে/বেড়ে গিয়েছে । | নম্বর, সংখ্যা

    Chh*a*tra/chh*a*tree shankh*a* b*a*riya | nambar,

                    gechhe/be*r*e giyechhe. | shankh*a*

That old woman is this boy's nurse. [med, nurse]

| nurse, midwife

ঐ বুড়ি এই ছেলের দাই । [নার্স] | দাই

    Oi bu*r*i ei chheler d*a*i. [n*a*rs] | d*a*i

I obey him. | obey

আমি তার কথা মানি । [মান্য করা] | মানা, পালন করা

    *A*mi t*a*r kath*a* m*a*ni. [m*a*nna kar*a*] | m*a*na, p*a*lan kar*a*

John then made no further objections. | object, objection

জন তখন আর কোন আপত্তি করল না । | আপত্তি

    Jan takhan *a*r kona *a*patti k*a*rla n*a*. | *a*patti

I obliged (compelled) him to go. [INF.] | oblige

আমি তাকে যাইতে/যেতে বাধ্য করলাম । | বাধ্য করা

    *A*mi t*a*ke j*a*ite/jete b*a*ddha karl*a*m. | b*a*ddha kar*a*

He did not heed/mind any obstacles. | obstacle

সে কোন বাধা মানল না । | বাধা

    She kona b*a*dh*a* m*a*nla n*a*. | b*a*dh*a*

Don't put obstacles in my way. | put obstacles

আমার কাজে বাধা দিও না । | বাধা দেওয়া

    *A*m*a*r k*a*je b*a*dh*a* dio n*a*. | b*a*dh*a* deoy*a*

He/she obtained permission. | obtain

সে অনুমতি পাইল/পেল । [লাভ করা] | পাওয়া

    She anumati p*a*ila/pela. [*i*abh kar*a*] | p*a*oy*a*

I shall never get such an occasion/a chance again. | occasion

এমন সুযোগ আর পাইব/পাব না । [ঘটনা] | সুবিধা, সুযোগ

    Eman shujog *a*r p*a*iba/pabo n*a*. [gha*t*an*a*] | shubidh*a*, shujog

He comes here occasionally. | occasionally
তিনি এখানে সময় সময় আসেন । | সময় সময়
    Tini ekhane shamay shamay ashen. | shamay shamay

The man's behaviour is odd. It seems odd. | odd, queer
লোকটার আচরণ/ব্যবহার অদ্ভুত । অদ্ভূত লাগে। | অদ্ভুত
    Loktar acharan/baebahar adbhut. adbhut lage. | adbhut

This flower has a nice odour. | odour
এই ফুলের গন্ধ ভাল । | গন্ধ
    Ei fuler gandha bhala. | gandha

Legs of a table ; light of day , my , your , | of (gen.)
           his/her. [GRAM.]
টেবিলের পা ; দিনের আলো ; আমার , তোমার ; তার । | এর,-র
    Tebiler pa ; diner alo , amar , tomar ; tar. | er,-r
        [see GEN. CHART]

Of course, it is true that he did not do this. | of course
অবশ্য এ কথা সত্য যে সে এ কাজ করে নাই/নি । | অবশ্য
    Abassha e katha shatta je she e kaj kare nai/ni. | abassha

Of course I shall go. (certainly) | of course
আমি নিশ্চয় যাইব/যাব । | নিশ্চয়
    Ami nishchay jaiba/jaba. | nishchay

What is his offence ? | offence
তার দোষ কি ? [ত্রুটি] | দোষ
    Tar dosh ki ? [trooti] | dosh

I offered him a taka. (want to give) | offer
আমি তাকে একটা টাকা দিতে চাইলাম । | দিতে চাওয়া
    Ami take ekta taka dite chailam. [L. 85] | dite chaoya

I have often warned him/her. | often
আমি তাকে বারবার সাবধান করছি/করেছি । | বারবার
    Ami take barbar shabdhan karchhi/karechhi. | barbar

Buy a seer of mustard oil.
এক সের সরিষার তেল কিন ।
Ek sher sharish*a*r tel kina.

| oil
তেল/তৈল
tal, tail

His father is old.
তার বাবা বুড়া ।
T*a*r bab*á* bu*r*a.

| old (man)
বুড়া
bu*r*a

The old woman is coming this way.
বুড়িটা এদিকে আসতেছে/আসছে ।
Bu*r*it*a* e dike *a*shtechhe/*a*shchhe.

| old (woman)
বুড়ি
bu*r*i

My pen is old.
আমার কলমটা/পেনটা পুরান ।
*A*m*a*r kalam*ta*/pen*ta* pur*a*n.

| old (thing)
পুরান/পুরাতন
p*u*r*a*n/pur*a*tan

All right, omit two or three pages.
আচ্ছা, দুই তিন পাতা বাদ দেও ।
Achchh*a* dui tin p*a*t*a* b*a*d deo.

| omit
বাদ দেওয়া
b*a*d deoy*a*

Two persons were omitted.
দুইজন বাদ গেছে/গিয়েছে ।
Dui jan b*a*d gechhe/giyechhe.

| be omitted
বাদ যাওয়া
b*a*d jaoy*a*

There is a book on the table. On the head.
টেবিলের উপর বই আছে । মাথার উপরে ।
*T*ebiler upar bai *a*chhe. Math*a*r upare.
একটি বই – ekti bai.

| on, upon, over
উপর, উপরে
upar(e)

I went there once.
সেখানে একবার গেছিলাম/গিয়েছিলাম ।
Shekh*a*ne ekb*a*r gechhil*a*m/giyechhil*a*m.

| once
একবার
ekb*a*r

Once he was very rich.   (at one time)
এক সময় সে খুব ধনী ছিল ।
Ek sh*a*may she khub dhanee chhila.

| once
এক সময়
ek sh*a*may(e)

One day I shall go. I want one.
একদিন যাইব/যাব ।   একটা চাই ।
Ek din j*a*iba/j*a*ba. Ek*ta* ch*a*i.

| one
এক, একটা
ek, ek*ta*

Go to the market/bazar and buy some onions. | onion

বাজারে গিয়া পিঁয়াজ কিনিয়া/কিনে আন । | পিঁয়াজ/পেঁয়াজ

    Bajare giya pinyaj (penyaj) kiniya/   pinyaj, penyaj
                   kine ana.

He only talks.   Only one person came. | only

সে কেবল কথা বলে ।   খালি একজন আসল । | কেবল, খালি

    She kebal katha bale.   Khall ekjan ashla.   kebal,khali

I have only one taka with me. | only

আমার কাছে শুধু একটা টাকা আছে । | শুধু

    Amar kachhe shudhu ekta taka achhe.   shudhu

It is only three o'clock. | only

মাত্র তিনটা বাজছে/বেজেছে । | মাত্র

    Matra tinta bajchhe/bejechhe.   matra

Open the box.   Open the door. | open v., adj untie(d)

বাক্সটা খোল ।   দরজা খোল/খুল । | খোলা

    Bakshata khola.   Darja khola/khula.   khola

What is your opinion ? [unanimous] | opinion

তোমার মত কি ? [এক মত] | মত

    Tomar mat ki ? [ek mat]   mat

I have had no opportunity to go there. | opportunity

সেখানে যাইবার/যাবার সুযোগ পাই নাই/নি । | সুযোগ/সুবিধা

Shekhane jaibar/jabar shujog pai nai/ni.   shujog, shubidha

Don't oppose me.   (prevent) | oppose

আমাকে বাধা দিও না । | বাধা দেওয়া

    Amake badha dio na.   badha deoya

Ram or Rahim will go. | or

রাম বা রহিম কোন একজন যাইবে/যাবে । | বা

    Ram ba Rahim kona ekjan jaibe/jabe.   ba

Oranges grow in Sylhet. | orange

কমলালেবু সিলেটে জন্মে । | কমলালেবু

    Kamala lebu Silete janme.   kamala lebu

The judge passed the orders. Obey his order.	order (n.)
জজ হকুম দিলেন । তার আদেশ পালন করবে ।	হকুম/আদেশ
Jaj hukum dilen. Tar adesh palan karbe.	hukum, adesh

The ordinary people suffered. (common)	ordinary
সাধারণ লোকে কষ্ট পাইল/পেল । [সাদাসিধা]	সাধারণ
Shadharan loke kashta paila/pela.	shadharan
[shadasidha]	

The original picture is in the museum.	original
আসল ছবিটা যাদুঘরে আছে ।	আসল
Ashal chabita jadughare achhe.	ashal

Girls like ornaments.	ornament
মেয়েরা গহনা পছন্দ করে ।	গহনা
Meyera gayna pachhanda kare.	gayna

The orphan boy was brought up here.	orphan, adj.
অনাথ ছেলেটা এখানে মানুষ হয়েছে।	অনাথ
Anath chheleta ekhane manush haiechhe.	anath

Call the other boy. Somebody else.	other
অন্য ছেলেটিকে ডাক । অন্য কেহ ।	অপর, অন্য
Anna chheletike daka. Anna keha.	apar, anna

Such things happen also in other countries.	other (plu.)
অন্যান্য দেশেও এই রকম হয় ।	অন্যান্য
Annanna deshe–o ei rakam hay.	annanna

You ought to do this (work). [L. 76]	ought, proper
এ কাজটা তোমার করা উচিত ।	gen.+ v.n.+ উচিত
E kajta tomar kara uchit.	gen + v.n. + uchit

Go out. Take that out.	out (adv.)
বাইরে যাও । ওটা বাইর কর ।	বাইরে, বাইর
Baire jao. Ota bair kara.	baire, bair

Out of the house.   Out of the [see GRAM. | out of (prep.)
school/from school.   L. 64]

ঘরের বাইরে।   স্কুলের বাইরে। | বাইরে/থেকে
Gharer baire.   Skuler baire, skul theke···   baire/theke

The bird flew over my head. (on) [L. 56] | over, upon
পাখীটা আমার মাথার উপরে উড়ছিল।   উপরে
Pakheeta amar mathar upare urchhila.   upare

I owe him five taka.   v. = dhara ধারা | owe
আমি তার কাছে পাঁচ টাকা ঋণি / ধারি।   ঋণি/ধারি
Ami tar kachhe panch taka rini/dhari.   rini/dhari

Owls search for food at night. | owl
পেঁচা রাতে খাবার খুঁজে।   পেঁচা
Pencha rate khabar khunje.   pencha

Speak for your ownself.   Keep an eye on your | own
own luggage.

তুমি নিজের কথা বল।   আপন আপন মালের   নিজের, আপন
উপর নজর রাখ।
Tumi nijer katha bala.   Apan apan   nijer, apan
maler upar najar rakha.

Where is the owner of this boat ? | owner
এ নৌকার মালিক কোথায় ?   মালিক
E naukar malik kothay ?   malik

She husks paddy and sings.   Buy paddy. | paddy
সে ধান ভানে ও গান গায়।   ধান কিন।   ধান
She dhan bhane o gan gay.   Dhan kina.   dhan

There are over 2oo pages in this book. | page, leaf
এই বইয়ে দু'শর বেশী পাতা আছে।   পাতা
Ei baiye dui shar beshee pata achhe.   pata

He is suffering from a pain in the head. | pain
সে মাথা ব্যথায় কণ্ট পাইতেছে/পাচ্ছে।   ব্যথা
She matha baethay kashta paitechhe/pachchhe.   baetha

How is the pain in your tooth ? | pain
তোমার দাঁতের বেদনা কেমন ?   বেদনা
    Tom*a*r d*a*nter bedan*a* keman ?   bedan*a*

I shall paint the box black. | paint
আমি বাক্সটায় কাল রং দিব/লাগাব ।   রং লাগান/দেওয়া
    Ami b*a*ksha*t*ay k*a*la rang diba/l*a*g*a*ba.   rang l*a*gan/deoy*a*

I do not like red paint/colour. | paint (n.)
আমি লাল রং পছন্দ করি না ।   রং
    Ami l*a*l rang pachhanda kari n*a*.   rang

Who will paint a picture of this house ? | paint, v.
কে এ বাড়ীর একটা ছবি আঁকবে ?   ছবি আঁকা
    Ke e b*a*reer ek*t*a chhabi *a*nkbe ?   chhabi *a*nk*a*

He wants to buy a pair of shoes. | pair
সে একজোড়া জুতা কিনতে চায় ।   জোড়া
    She ek jor*a* jut*a* kinte ch*a*y.   jor*a*

Paper is not cheap now. | paper
কাগজ এখন সস্তা না ।   কাগজ
    K*a*gaj ekhan shasht*a* n*a*.   k*a*gaj

I pardoned him. (excuse, forgive) | pardon
আমি তাকে মাফ/ক্ষমা করলাম ।   মাফ/ক্ষমা করা
    Ami t*a*ke m*a*f/ kham*a* karl*a*m.   m*a*f/ kham*a* kar*a*

He begged/asked pardon. | beg pardon
সে মাফ চাইল/চাল ।   মাফ চাওয়া
    She m*a*f ch*a*ila/ch*a*la.   m*a*f ch*a*oy*a*

Pare the potatoes. | pare, peel
আলুগুলি ছুল/ছুলিয়া/ছুলে ফেল ।   ছুলা
    *A*luguli chhula/chhuliy*a*/chhule fela.   chhul*a*

15—

The primary section is a part of the school. | part
পাঠশালা স্কুলের একটা অংশ । | অংশ, ভাগ
    *Path*shala skuler ek*ta* angsha. | angsha, bh*a*g

I have no particular/special friend. | particular
আমার কোন বিশেষ বন্ধু নাই/নেই । | বিশেষ
    *A*m*a*r kona bishesh bandhu n*a*i/nei. | bishesh

A party of boys is playing there. | party, group
একটা ছেলের দল সেখানে খেলা করতেছে/করছে । | দল
    Ek*ta* chheler dal shekh*a*ne khel*a* kartechhe/karchhe. | dal

He came last week/month. | past, last
সে গত সপ্তাহ/মাসে আসছিল/এসেছিল । [সপ্তাহে] | গত
    She gata shapt*ay*/m*a*she *a*shchhila/ | gata
                 eshechhila. [shapt*a*he]

Boys are playing on the path. | path
ছেলেরা পথে খেলা করতেছে/ করছে । | পথ
    Chheler*a* pathe khel*a* kartechhe/karchhe. | path

He/she has much patience. | patience
তার খুব ধৈর্য্য আছে । | ধৈর্য্য
    T*a*r khub dhairjja *a*chhe. | dhairjja

Be patient and all dangers will pass away. | be/have patience
ধৈর্য্য ধর, সব বিপদ কাটিয়া/কেটে যাইবে/যাবে । | ধৈর্য্য ধরা
    Dhairjja dhara, shab bipad k*a*tiy*a*/ | dhairjja dhar*a*
              ke*t*e j*a*ibe/j*a*be.

The patient is on the way to recovery. | patient (n.)
রোগী/রুগী ভাল হইতেছে/হচ্ছে । | রোগী
    Rogee/rugee bh*a*la haitechhe/hachchhe. | rogee

I want the pattern for that shirt. | pattern, sample
ঐ শার্টের নমুনা চাই । [নক্সা] | নমুনা
    Oi sh*a*rter namun*a* ch*a*i. [naksh*a*] | namun*a*

I paused a while on the way. | pause, stop

রাস্তায় একটু থামলাম ৷ | থামা

    Rastay ektu thamlam. | thama

His pay is fifty taka. (salary) | pay

তার বেতন পঞ্চাশ টাকা ৷ | বেতন, মাইনা

    Tar betan panchash *taka*. | betan, maina

He paid the gardener. [gardener's salary] | pay

সে মালীর মাইনা দিল ৷ টাকা/পয়সা দেওয়া | মাইনা দেওয়া

    She maleer maina dila. taka/paisa deoya, | maina deoya

        [*pay money for something]

Boiled peas are good to eat. [see GRAM.] | peas

মটর সিদ্ধ খাইতে/খেতে মজা ৷ | মটর

    Matar shiddha khaite/khete maja. | matar

Everyone wants peace. [peaceful] | peace

সকলে শান্তি চায় ৷   [শান্ত] | শান্তি

    Shakale shanti chay. [shanta] | shanti

Buy a seer of peanuts. (2 lbs.) | peanut

এক সের চিনা বাদাম কিন ৷ | চিনাবাদাম

    Ek sher chinabadam kina, | chinabadam

The man is peculiar. What a queer car ! | peculiar, odd

লোকটা অদ্ভুত ৷   কি অদ্ভুদ মোটর গাড়ী ! | অদ্ভুত

    Lokta adbhut. Ki adbhut motar gari ! | adbhut

His pen has been lost. | pen

তার কলমটা হারাইয়া গেছে/হারিয়ে গিয়েছে ৷ | কলম

    Tar kalamta haraiya gechhe/hariye giyechhe. | kalam

The people of this country are very good. | people

এ দেশের লোক খুব ভাল ৷ | লোক

    E desher lok khub bhala. | lok

Black pepper is available now. | black pepper

গোল মরিচ এখন পাওয়া যায় ৷ | গোল মরিচ

    Gol marich ekhan paoya jay. | gol marich

Perhaps/maybe he does not know. | perhaps

হইতে/হতে পারে সে জানে না । | হইতে/হতে পারে

Haite/hate pare she jane na. | haite/hate pare

His post/job is permanent. | permanent

তার চাক্রি স্হায়ী । | স্হায়ী

Tar chakri sthayee. | sthayee

He does not do anything without permission. | permission

অনুমতি ছাড়া সে কিছু করে না । | অনুমতি

Anumati chhara she kichhu kare na. | anumati

He permitted me to go. [gave permission] | permit, consent

সে আমাকে যাইতে/যেতে অনুমতি দিল । | অনুমতি দেওয়া

She amake jaite/jete anumati dila. | anumati deoya

A person. Three persons came. | person

একটা লোক ; একজন লোক । তিনজন লোক আসল । | লোক, ব্যক্তি

ekta lok ; ekjan lok. Tin jan lok ashla. | lok, baekti

Send a petition to him. | petition

তার কাছে একটা দরখাস্ত পাঠাও । | দরখাস্ত

Tar kachhe ekta darkhasta pathao. | darkhasta

Call the physician/doctor. | physician

ডাক্তারকে/ডাক্তার ডাক । ডাক্তারকে ডাকিয়া আন/পাঠাও । | ডাক্তার

Daktarke daka. Daktarke dakiya ano. | daktar

Pick up the paper from the ground. Pick flowers. | pick up

মাটি হতে/থেকে কাগজ তুল/তোল । ফুল তোল । | তোলা

Mati hate/theke kagaj tula/tola. Fool toola. | tola

Take a picture (photo). Draw a picture. | picture

ছবি তুল । ছবি আঁক । | ছবি

Chhabi tula. Chhabi anka. [Chhobee] | chhabi

Please give me a piece of paper. | piece

আমাকে এক টুকরো কাগজ দেন/দেও । | টুকরা/টুকরো

Amake ek tukro kagaj den/deo. | tukra/tukro

My pigeon has flown away. | pigeon
আমার কবুতরটা উড়িয়া গেছে/উড়ে গিয়েছে । | কবুতর
Amar kabutarta uriya gechhe/ure giyechhe. | kabutar

Take six pills a day. | pill
দিনে ছয়টা গুলি/বড়ি খাইবে/খাবে । | গুলি/বড়ি
Dine chhayta guli/bari khaibe/khabe. | guli, bari

Put my pillow in the sun. | pillow
আমার বালিশটা রোদে দাও । | বালিশ
Amar balishta rode dao. | balish

Pineapples are very good for the health. | pineapple
আনারস স্বাস্থ্যের জন্য খুব ভাল । | আনারস
Anarash shaststher janna khub bhala. | anarash

Close the first pipe. | pipe
প্রথম নলটা বন্ধ কর । | নল/পাইপ
Pratham nalta bandha kara. | nal, paip

Change the water in the water pipe/hookah. pipe (smoking)
হুকার জল বদলি কর । | হুকা
Hukar jal badli kara. | huku

I have no place to go. | place
আমার যাইবার/যাবার কোন জায়গা নাই/নেই । | জায়গা
Amar jaibar/jabar kona jayga nai/nei | jayga

He likes plain talk.   (words) | plain, clear
তিনি স্পষ্ট কথা ভালবাসেন । | স্পষ্ট
Tini spashta katha bhalabashen. | spashta

He made a plan. | plan
সে একটা মতলব আঁটিল । | মতলব
She ekta matlab antla. | matlab

The plan of the new school is beautiful. | plan
নূতন স্কুলের নক্সাটা সুন্দর । | নক্সা
Nootan skuler nakshata shundar. | naksha

The field is not rough, it is quite plane.   plane, equal

মাঠটা উঁচু নীচু না, একেবারে সমান।   সমান

    Mathta unchu nichu n*a*, ekeb*a*re sham*a*n.   sham*a*n

I can't use a crooked plank.   plank

আমি বাঁকা তক্তা ব্যবহার করতে পারি না। তক্তা   তক্তা

    *A*mi b*a*nk*a* takt*a* baebah*a*r karte p*a*ri n*a*.   takt*a*

Plant/put the rose plant there.   plant, (n.)

এখানে গোলাপের চারা রোও/রুও/লাগাও।   চারা

    Ekh*a*ne gol*a*per ch*a*ra ro-o/ruo/l*a*gao.   ch*a*ra

The farmers are planting paddy seedlings.   plant, v.

কৃষকেরা ধানের চারা রুইতেছে/রুচ্ছে।   রুয়া

    Krishaker*a* dh*a*ner ch*ara* ruitechhe/ruchchhe.   ruy*a*

He has broken the plate.   plate, basin

সে থালাটা/বাসনটা ভাঙ্গিয়া ফেল্ছে/ভেঙ্গে ফেলেছে।   বাসন, থালা

          [থাল, প্লেট]

    She th*ala*ta/bashan*ta* bh*a*ngiya felchhe/

       bhenge felechhe. [th*al*, ple*t*]   b*a*shan, th*ala*

Please help me.   please, kindly

দয়া করিয়া/করে আমাকে সাহায্য করুন।   দয়া করিয়া

    Day*a* kariy*a*/kare *a*make sh*a*hajja karun.   day*a* kariy*a*

He/she is playing. I play.   play, v.

সে খেলতেছে/খেল্ছে। আমি খেলা করি।   খেলা করা/খেলা

    She kheltechhe/khelchhe. *A*mi khel*a* kari.   khela kar*a*/khel*a*

He is pleased/satisfied.   pleased

সে খুশী/সন্তুষ্ট।   খুশী

    She khushee/shantush*t*a.   khushee

He spent his life in pleasure.   pleasure

সে জীবনটা আমোদে কাটাইয়া/কাটিয়ে দিল।   আমোদ

    She jeeban*ta* *a*mode k*a*t*a*iya/k*at*iye dila.   *a*mod

Now I must plough my field(s).

এখন আমার খেতে হাল দিতে হবে ।

Ekhan amar khete hal dite habe.

plough, v.

হাল দেওয়া

hal deoya

The cultivator went to the field with his plough.

কৃষক লাঙল নিয়া/নিয়ে মাঠে গেল ।

Krishak langal niya/niye mathe gela.

plough, n.

লাঙল

langal

The boys are plucking mangoes.

ছেলেগুলো আম পাড়তেছে/পাড়ছে ।

Chhelegula am partechhe/parchhe.

pluck, pick

পাড়া

para

Poets write poetry.

কবিরা কবিতা লেখেন ।

Kabira kabita lekhen.

poet, poetry

কবি, কবিতা

kabi, kabita

A snake's fangs have poison.

সাপের দাঁতে বিষ আছে ।

Shaper dante bish achhe.

poison

বিষ

bish

Policemen stay at the police station.

থানায় পুলিশ থাকে ।

Thanay pulish thake.

police station

থানা

thana

I polish my shoes.

জুতা পালিশ করি ।

Juta palish kari.

polish, v.

পালিশ করা

palish kara

The boy is very polite.

ছেলেটি খুব সভ্য/ভদ্র ।

Chheleti khub shabbha/bhadra.

polite

সভ্য/ভদ্র

shabbha, bhadra

The people of this country are very poor.

এ দেশের লোক খুব গরীব ।

E desher lok khub gareeb.

poor

গরীব

gareeb

This work is possible. If possible, come.

এ কাজ সম্ভব । সম্ভব হইলে/হলে তুমি আস । (ppl.)

E kaj shambhab. Shambhab haile/hale asha.

possible, probable

সম্ভব

shambhab

I shall possibly meet you. (may) | possibly
হয়তো তোমার সঙ্গে দেখা করব । | হয়তো
    Hayto tomar shange dekha karba. | hayto

Go to the post office and bring the mail. | post office
ডাকঘরে গিয়া/গিয়ে চিঠিপত্র নিয়া/নিয়ে আস । | ডাকঘর
Dak ghare giya/giye chithi–patra niya/niye asha. | dakghar

What's in the (metal) pot ? The earthen pot
                      is full of water. | pot
হাঁড়িতে কি ? কল্সি ভরা জল । | হাঁড়ি, কল্সি
    Hanrite ki ? Kalshi bhara jal. | hanri, kalshi

Our potatoes are very small. | potato
আমাদের আলুগুলি খুব ছোট । | আলু
    Amader aluguli khub chhota. | alu

A maund (82 lbs.) of potatoes costs 100 taka. | 82 pounds
এক মণ আলুর দাম একশ টাকা । | মণ
    Ek man alur dam ek sha taka. | man

Buy a seer (2 lbs) of potatoes. | 2 lbs
এক সের আলু কিনিয়া/কিনে আন । | সের
    Ek sher alu kiniya/kine ana. | sher

Pour the milk into the pot. | pour
হাঁড়িতে দুধ ঢাল । | ঢালা
    Hanrite dhud dhala. | dhala

That's a bad practice. [verb] | practice, habit
ওটা খারাপ অভ্যাস । [—করা] | অভ্যাস
    Ota kharap abbhas [—kara] | abbhas

The enthusiasm of boys increases when they
                    receive praise. | praise
ছেলেরা প্রশংসা পাইলে/পেলে তাদের উৎসাহ বাড়ে । | প্রশংসা
    Chhelera prashangsha paile/pele tader | prashangsha
                utshaha bare.

He is preparing his lesson(s). | prepare
সে তার পড়া প্রস্তুত করতেছে/করছে । | প্রস্তুত করা
    She tar para prastut kartechhe/karchhe. | prastut kara

I prepared his tea. | prepare
আমি তার চা তৈরী করলাম । | তৈরী করা
    Ami tar cha tairee karlam. | tairee kara

The boys who were present sang. | present
উপস্থিত বালকেরা গান করল । | উপস্থিত
    Upasthit balakera gan karla. | upasthit

The headmaster was present in the class. | be present
ক্লাসে হেড্‌মাস্টার উপস্থিত ছিলেন । [হাজির] | উপস্থিত হওয়া
    Klase hedmastar upasthit chhilen. [hajir] | upasthit haoya

I shall give the boy a present. | present, gift n.
আমি ছেলেটাকে একটা উপহার দিব । | উপহার দান
    Ami chheletake ekta upahar diba. | upahar dan

At present he lives in Dacca. | at present
বর্তমানে তিনি ঢাকায় থাকেন । | বর্তমানে
    Bartamane tini dhakay thaken. | bartamane

Preserve me from all dangers. | preserve, save
সকল বিপদ হতে আমাকে রক্ষা কর । [বাঁচান] | রক্ষা করা
    Shakal bipad hate amake rakkha kara. | rakkha kara
             [banchan]

The carpenter pressed the plank and | press n.
               straightened it.
ছুতার মিস্ত্রি চাপ দিয়া/দিয়ে তক্তাটা সোজা করল । | চাপা, চাপ দেওয়া
Shutar mistri chap diya/diye taktata shoja karla. | chapa, chap deoya

He/she pressed my hand. | press n.
সে আমার হাত টিপল । | টিপা
    She amar hat tipla. | tipa

What is the price of this cloth ? | price
এ কাপড়ের দাম কত ? | দাম
E kaparer dam kata ? | dam

He took a pricc of taka 5 a yard. | price
সে পাঁচ টাকা গজ দাম নিচ্ছে/নিয়েছে । | দাম
She panch taka gaj dam nichchhe/niyechhe. | dam

Everyone hates pride. | pride
অহংকার সবাই ঘৃণা করে । | অহংকার
Ahangkar shabai ghrina kare. | ahangkar

Who printed the book ? | print, v.
কে বইটা ছাপাইছে/ছাপিয়েছে ? | ছাপান
Ke baita chhapaichhe/chhapiyechhe? | chhapan

Invitation cards are being printed.[ ] | be printed
নিমন্ত্রণ পত্র ছাপান হইতেছে/হচ্ছে । | ছাপান হওয়া
Nimantran patra chhapan haitechhe. | chhapan haoya

It is probable that I shall go there. | probable/possible
আমার সেখানে যাওয়া সম্ভব । | সম্ভব
Amar shekhane jaoya shambhab. | shambhab

What's your profession/business ? | profession
তোমার পেশা/ব্যবসা কি ? | পেশা, ব্যবসা
Tomar pesha/baebsha ki ? | pesha/baebsha

There is no profit/gain in this work. | profit, gain
এ কাজে কোন লাভ নাই/নেই । | লাভ
E kaje kona labh nai/nei. | labh

Businessmen make a good profit. | make a profit
ব্যবসায়ীরা খুব লাভ করে । | লাভ করা
Baebshaira khub labh kare. | labh kara

Promise you will never do this again. | promise
প্রতিজ্ঞা কর, এ কাজ আর করবে না । [অঙ্গীকার] | প্রতিজ্ঞা করা
Pratigga kara, e kaj ar karbe na. [angeekar]
| pratigga kara

What is the pronunciation of this word ? | pronunciation

এ শব্দের উচ্চারণ কি ? | উচ্চারণ

E shabder uchcharan ki ? | uchcharan

There are many proofs that the earth is round. | proof

পৃথিবী যে গোল তার অনেক প্রমাণ আছে । | প্রমাণ [করা]

Prithibee je gol tar anek praman achhe. | praman [kara]

It is proper that we thank Allah/God. [L.76] | proper, fit

আল্লাহকে/ঈশ্বরকে আমাদের ধন্যবাদ দেওয়া উচিত । | উচিত

Allake/Eeshsharke amader dhannabad gen. + inf. + uchit

deoya uchit.

What is his/her proposal ? | proposal

তার প্রস্তাব কি ? | প্রস্তাব

Tar prastab ki ? | prastab

The government protects wild animals. | protect

সরকার বন্য জন্তুগুলি রক্ষা করে । | রক্ষা করা

Sharkar banna jantuguli rakkha kare. | rakkha kara

This is for the use of the public. | public

এটা জনসাধারণের ব্যবহারের জন্য । | জনসাধারণ

Eta janashadharaner baebaharer janna. | janashadharan

Don't publish a secret. | publish

গোপন কথা প্রকাশ করিও/কর না । | প্রকাশ করা

Gopan katha prakash kario/kara na. | prakash kara

He pulled him by the ear. | pull

সে তার কান ধরিয়া/ধরে টানল । | টানা

She tar kan dhariya/dhare tanla. | tana

The water pump is out of order. | pump

পানির কলটা খারাপ । | পানির কল

Panir kalta kharap. | panir kal

It has a pungent taste. It's hot | pungent/hot

এটার স্বাদ ঝাল । | ঝাল

Etar shad jhal. | jhal

His pupil will go to England/Europe. | pupil

তার ছাত্র বিলাত যাইবে/যাবে। | ছাত্র

Tar chhatra bilat jaibe/jabe. | chhatra

These girl students are good in English. | female student

এ ছাত্রীরা ইংরেজীতে ভাল। | ছাত্রী

E chhatreera Ingrejeete bhala. | chhatree

We should take pure milk. (drink) | pure

খাঁটি দুধ খাওয়া উচিত। | খাঁটি

Khanti dudh khaoya uchit. [L.76] | khanti

I did this purposely. (have done) | purposely

এটা আমি ইচ্ছা করিয়া করছি/করে করেছি। | ইচ্ছা করিয়া/করে

Eta ami ichchha kariya karchhi/ | ichchha kariya/kare
kare karechhi.

He pushed me. | push

সে আমাকে ধাক্কা দিল। [জোরে ঠেলা] | ধাক্কা দেওয়া

She amake dhakka dila. [jore thela] | dhakka deoya

Put/place your hand on the book. | put/keep

বইয়ের উপর হাত রাখ। | রাখা

Baiyer upar hat rakha. | rakha

The man has many good qualities/virtues. | quality, virtue

লোকটির অনেক ভাল গুণ আছে। | গুণ

Loktir anek bhala gun achhe. | gun

Don't quarrel. | quarrel

ঝগড়া করিও না। | ঝগড়া করা

Jhagra kario na. | jhagra kara

The queen bee lays eggs. | queen

রাণী মৌমাছি ডিম পাড়ে। | রাণী

Ranee maumachhi dim pare. | ranee

You have (a) queer opinion(s). | queer, odd

তোমার অদ্ভুত মত [আছে] | অদ্ভুত

Tomar adbhut mat [acche]. | adbhut

I did not understand your question. | question, n.

তোমার প্রশ্নটা বুঝি নাই/নি ।   প্রশ্ন

    Tomar prashnata buihi nai/ni. | prashna

He questioned me much about that matter. | question, v.

ঐ বিষয়ে সে· আমাকে অনেক প্রশ্ন করল ।   প্রশ্ন করা

    Oi bishaye she amake anek pras(h)na karla. | pras(h)na kara

Come quickly, don't delay. | quickly

শীঘ্র আস, দেরি কর না ।   শীঘ্র, তাড়াতাড়ি

    Sheegra asha, deri kara na. | sheegra, taratari

Hush/keep quiet ;   don't talk. | be quiet/silent

চুপ কর, কথা বলিও/বল না ।   চুপ করা

    Chup kara, katha balio/bala na. | chup kara

He came quietly. | quietly

তিনি চুপি চুপি আসলেন ।   [চুপে চুপে]   চুপিচুপি/আস্তে আস্তে

    Tini chupi chupi ashlen. [chupe chupe] | chupi/chupi,

                 | aste aste

Speak quietly, don't shout.   [slowly] | quietly/softly

আস্তে আস্তে কথা বল, চেঁচাইও না ।   আস্তে আস্তে

    Aste aste katha bala, chenchaio na. | aste aste

The man is quite blind. | quite

লোকটা একেবারে কানা/অন্ধ ।   [খুব, বেশ]   একেবারে

    Lokta ekebare kana/andha.   [khub, besh] | ekebare

Dust the room with this rag.   (wipe, rub out) | rag

এ নেকড়া দিয়ে ঘরটা মুছিয়া/মুছ✳ ফেল । [✳পুঁছে···]   টেনা/নেকড়া

    E nekra diye gharta muchhiya/ | tena/nekra

      ✳muchhe fela   [✳punchhe]

It rains during the rainy season. | rain, v.

বর্ষাকালে বৃষ্টি হয় ।   বৃষ্টি হওয়া

    Barshakale bristi hay. | bristi haoya

The rains come after summer. (rainy season)   rains, n.

গ্রীষ্মকালের পরে বর্ষাকাল আসে ।   বর্ষাকাল

    Greessha kaler pare barshakal ashe.   barshakal

Raise your hand.   Raise your head.   raise

হাত তুল ।   তোমার মাথা উঠাও ।   তোলা, উঠান

    Hat tula. Tomar matha uthao.   tola, uthan

Men like him are rare.   rare, scarce

তার মত মানুষ খুব কম ।   কম

    Tar mata manush khub kam.   kam

The boy is a big rascal/scoundrel.   rascal

ছেলেটা খুব পাজি/পাজী ।   পাজি

    Chheleta khub paji/pajee. (n., adj.)   paji

Rats make holes in the ground.   rat

ইঁদুর মাটির নীচে গর্ত করে ।   ইঁদুর/ইদুর

    Indur matir neeche garta kare.   indur/indur

At what rate is paddy selling now ? At what   rate
                rate will you buy ?

আজকাল ধানের দর কত ?   কি দরে কিনবে ?   দর

    Ajkal dhaner dar kata ?   Ki dare kinbe ?   dar

Small boys like to eat raw mangoes. [INFIN.]   raw, unripe

ছোট ছেলেরা কাঁচা আম খাইতে/খেতে ভালবাসে ।   কাঁচা

    Chhota chhelera kancha am khaite/   kancha
             khete bhalabashe.

He will reach Dacca by 12 noon.   reach

তিনি দিন বারটার মধ্যে ঢাকায় পৌঁছবেন ।   পৌঁছা

Tini din baratar maddhe Dhakay pounchhben.   pounchha

I can't reach that branch.   reach

আমি ঐ ডালটা লাগ/ নাগাল পাই না !   লাগ/নাগাল পাওয়া

    Ami oi dalta lag/nagal pai na.   lag/nagal paoya

The boy is reading a book.   read, study

ছেলেটি একটা বই পড়:তেছে/পড়ছে ।   পড়া

    Chheleṭi ekṭa bai parṭechhe/parchhe.   para

Read this letter to me. [CAUS. V.] L. 30.   read

আমাকে এই চিঠিটা পড়িয়া/পড়ে শুনাও ।   পড়িয়া শুনান

    Amake ei chiṭhiṭa paria/pare shunao.   paria shunan

He did the work readily.   readily, easily

সে সহজে কাজটা করিয়া/করে ফেলল ।   সহজে

    She shahaje kajṭa kariya/kare fella.   shahaje

He is ready to go. [INFIN.]   ready, willing

সে যাইতে/যেতে প্রস্তুত ।   প্রস্তুত

    She jaite/ jete prastut.   prastut

He was/got ready to go.   be ready

সে যাইবার/যাবার জন্য প্রস্তুত হইল/ছিল।   প্রস্তুত হওয়া

    She jaibar/jabar janna prastut chhila.   prastut haoya

This is a real/genuine pearl/news.   real, genuine

এটা আসল মুক্তা/আসল খবর ।   আসল

    Eṭa ashal mukta/ashal khabar.   ashal

He will really come. (certainly)   really, surely

সে নিশ্চয় আসবে ।   নিশ্চয়

    She nishchay ashbe.   nishchay

What is the reason for his absence ?   reason, cause

    (not coming) [GER./V. N.]

তার না আসবার কারণ কি ? (আসার)   কারণ

    Tar na ashbar karan ki ? [ashar]   karan

I received a book for Christmas.   receive, get

বড় দিনের জন্য একটা বই পাইলাম/পেলাম ।   পাওয়া

    Baradiner janna ekṭa bai pailam/pelam.   paoya

I have a red and blue pencil. | red
আমার একটা লাল ও নীল পেন্সিল আছে । | লাল
*A*mar ek*ta* l*a*l o neel pensil *a*chhe. | l*a*l

I shall refer your case to him. (mention) | refer
আমি তার কাছে তোমার কথা উল্লেখ করব । | উল্লেখ করা
*A*mi t*a*r k*a*chhe tom*a*r kath*a* ullekh karba. | ullekh kar*a*

He refused to play.　　INFIN, | refuse
সে খেলতে রাজি হইল/হল না । | রাজি না হওয়া
She khelte r*a*ji haila/hala n*a*. | r*a*ji n*a* haoy*a*

He was sorry for/regretted his behaviour. | regret, be sorry
সে তার ব্যবহারের জন্য দুঃখিত হইল/হল । | দুঃখিত হওয়া
She t*a*r baebah*a*rer janna dukkhita hala. | dukkhita haoy*a*

He/she goes to school regularly. | regularly
সে রীতিমত স্কুলে যায় । | রীতিমত
She reetimata skule j*a*y. | reetimata

I reject your proposal.　[throw away] | reject
আমি তোমার প্রস্তাব অগ্রাহ্য করি । [ফেলিয়া দেওয়া] | অগ্রাহ্য করা
*A*mi tom*a*r prast*a*b agr*a*jja kari. [feliy*a* deoy*a*] | agr*a*jja kar*a*

I have a relative who lives in Dacca. | relative, n.
আমার এক আত্মীয় ঢাকায় থাকেন । | আত্মীয়, স্বজন
*A*mar ek *a*tteeya *Dh*akay th*a*ken. | *a*tteeya, shajan

Religion ennobles a man. | religion
ধর্ম মানুষকে মহৎ করে । | ধর্ম
Dharma m*a*nushke mahat kare. | dharma

Remain with me. | remain, stay
আমার সাথে থাক/রও । | থাকা/রহা
*A*mar shathe th*a*ka/rao. | th*a*ka, rah*a*

Complete the remainder of the work. | remainder, the rest
বাকী কাজটা করিয়া/করে ফেল । | বাকী
Bakee kajta kariya/kare fela. | bakee

Remember what I said. | remember
আমার কথা মনে রাখিও/রেখ । | মনে রাখা/করা
Amar katha mane rakhio/rekha. | mane rakha/kara

Remove these books. Move away. | remove, move
এই বইগুলি সরাও । সরিয়া যাও । | সরা, সরান
Ei baiguli sharao. Shariya jao. | shara, sharan

House rent in the town is very high. | rent, fare
শহরে ঘর ভাড়া খুব বেশী । | ভাড়া
Shahare ghar bhara khub beshee. | bhara

Repair the broken chair. | repair
ভাঙ্গা চেয়ারটা ঠিক কর । | ঠিক করা
Bhanga cheyarta thik kara. | thik kara

Can you repair a watch ? [L. 84] | repair
তুমি [কি] ঘড়ি মেরামত করতে পার ? | মেরামত করা
Tumi [ki] ghari meramat karte para ? | meramat kara

I repeat, this is mine. | repeat
আমি আবার বলতেছি/বলছি, এটা আমার । | আবার বলা
Ami abar baltechhi/balchhi eta amar. | abar bala

What reply can I give ? (answer) L. 84 | reply
আমি কি উত্তর দিতে পারি ? | উত্তর দেওয়া
Ami ki uttar dite pari ? | uttar deoya

You must grant my request. (comply with) L.83 | request, n.
আমার অনুরোধ তোমার রাখতে হবে । | অনুরোধ
Amar anurodh tomar rakhte habe. | anurodh

I request you, listen to me (mind me) | request, v.
আমি অনুরোধ করি, আমার কথা শুন । | অনুরোধ করা
Ami anurodh kari, amar katha shuna. | anurodh kara

The farmer saved/rescued the king's son. | rescue, save
কৃষকটি রাজার ছেলেকে বাঁচাইল । [মুক্ত/রক্ষা করা] | বাঁচান
Krishakti rajar chheleke banchaila. | banchan
[mukta/rakkha kara]

Respect your parents. (honour) | respect
পিতামাতাকে সম্মান করবে । [বাপমাকে] | সম্মান করা
Pitamatake shamman karbe. [bapmake] | shamman kara

He took the responsibility for doing the work. | responsibility
সে কাজের ভার নিল । [দায়, দায়িত্ব] | ভার
She kajer bhar nila. [day, dayitta] | bhar

You are responsible for this work. | responsible
এ কাজের জন্য তুমি দায়ী । | দায়ী
E kajer janna tumi dayee. | dayee

He has no time to rest. | rest
তার বিশ্রাম করার সময় নাই । | বিশ্রাম করা
Tar bisram karar shamay nai. | bisram kara

The result of your examinations is very good. | result, fruit
তোমার পরীক্ষার ফল খুব ভাল । | ফল
Tomar pareekkhar fal khub bhala. | fal

I shall return after ten days. | return
দশদিন পরে ফিরিয়া/ফিরে আসব । | ফিরিয়া আসা/যাওয়া
Dash din pare firiya/fire ashba. | firiya asha/jaoya

Return the books at your pleasure. | return
যে দিন খুশী বইগুলি ফেরৎ দিও । | ফেরৎ দেওয়া
Je din khushee baiguli ferat dio. | ferat deoya

He works in the hope of getting a reward. GER. | reward
সে পুরস্কার পাইবার/পাবার আশায় কাজ করে । | পুরস্কার
She purashkar paibar/pabar ashay kaj kare. | purashkar

The rice of this field is good/fine. | rice (paddy)
এই ক্ষেতের ধান ভাল । | ধান
Ei kketer dhan bhala. | dhan

Now there is no scarcity of rice. | rice (husked)
এখন চাউলের অভাব নাই/নেই । | চাউল
Ekhan chauler abhab nai/nei. | chaul

Bengalees/Bangalees eat rice. | rice (cooked)
also, Bangladeshis.
বাঙালীরা ভাত খায় । | ভাত
Bangaleera bhat khay. | bhat

No puffed rice is available in this bazar. | rice (puffed)
see L. 82.
এই বাজারে মুড়ি পাওয়া যায় না । | মুড়ি
Ei bajare muri paoya jay na. | muri

Rich people live in big houses. | rich, wealthy
ধনী লোকেরা বড় বাড়ীতে বাস করে । | ধনী
Dhanee lokera bara bareete bash kare. | dhanee

He is a rich man ; he has many servants. | rich man
সে বড়লোক , তার অনেক চাকর আছে । | বড়লোক
She bara lok, tar anek chakar achhe. | baralok

He has come at the right moment. That's right. | right (adj.)
সে ঠিক সময় আসছে/এসেছে । ঠিক কথা । | ঠিক
She thik shamay ashchhe/eshechhe. Thik katha. | thik

What right have you to come here ? | right (n.)
এখানে আসবার তোমার কি অধিকার আছে । | অধিকার
Ekhane ashbar tomar ki adhikar achhe ? | adhikar

Turn to the right. Go to the right. | right (direction)
ডান দিকে ঘুর । ডানে যাও । | ডানদিক
Dan dike ghura. Dane jao. [Loc , Postp.] | dandik

The bell rang. Ring the bell. [CAUS.]	ring, v.
ঘণ্টা বাজল। ঘণ্টা বাজাও।	বাজা, বাজান
Ghanṭa bajla. Ghanṭa bajao.	baja, bajan
The boy rang the bell. [CAUS.] 82.	ring, v.
ছেলেটি ঘণ্টা বাজাইল।	বাজান
Chheleṭi ghanṭa bajaila.	bajan
	82
Where is your wedding ring ?	ring, n.
তোমার বিয়ের আংটি কই ?	আংটি
Tomar biyer angṭi kai ?	angṭi
Ripe mangoes are sweet. (to eat) INF.	ripe
পাক্কা আম খাইতে/খেতে মিষ্ট।	পাকা
Paka am khaite/khete misṭa.	paka
Rise now. When do you rise ?	rise, get up
এখন উঠ। কোন সময় উঠ ?	উঠা
Ekhan uṭha. Kon shamay uṭha ?	uṭha
This river goes by our home/house.	river
এ নদী আমাদের বাড়ীর কাছ দিয়া/দিয়ে যায়।	নদী
E nadee amader bareer kachh diya/diye jay.	nadee
Many people go along this road.	road
এ রাস্তা দিয়া/দিয়ে অনেক লোক যায়।	রাস্তা, সড়ক
E rasta diya/diye anek lok jay.	rasta, sharak
A bird is flying over the roof of the house.	roof
ঘরের ছাদের উপর একটা পাখী উড়তেছে/উড়ছে।	ছাদ
Gharer chhader upar ekṭa pakhee urtechhe/urchhe.	chhad
We eat in this room.	room
আমরা এ ঘরে খাই।	ঘর, কামরা
Amra e ghare khai.	ghar, kamra
I shall stay in my room.	room
আমি আমার কামরায় থাকব।	কামরা
Ami amar kamray thakba.	kamra

The rooster crows in the morning. | rooster
মোরগ সকালে ডাক দেয়/ডাকে। | মোরগ
Morag shakale *dak* dey/*dake*. | morag

Tie the cow with a rope. | rope
দড়ি/রশি দিয়া/দিয়ে গরুটা বাঁধ। | দড়ি, রশি
D*a*ri/rashi diya/diye garu*ta* bandha. | d*a*ri rashi

Good roses grow in our country. | rose
আমাদের দেশে ভাল গোলাপ ফুল জন্মে। | গোলাপ
A*ma*der deshe bh*a*la golap ful janme. | gol*a*p

We must not eat rotten food [INF.] | rot/rotten
পচা খাবার খেতে নাই/নেই। | পচা
Pach*a* kh*a*b*a*r khete n*a*i/nei. | pach*a*

The earth is round. Go round the house. | round (adj., prep.)
পৃথিবী গোল। ঘরের চারিদিকে ঘুর। | গোল, চারিদিকে
Prithibee gol. Gharer ch*a*ridike ghura[Postp.] | gol, ch*a*ridike

Rub the brass basin with sand. (teeth etc.) | rub, scurb
পিতলের বাসন বালি দিয়া/দিয়ে মাজ। | মাজা
Pitaler b*a*shan b*a*li diya/diye m*a*ja. | m*a*ja

Rub it with ashes. (scrub/rub out) | rub
এটা ছাই দিয়া/দিয়ে ঘষ। [ঘষিয়া তোলা] | ঘষা/মাজা
E*ta* chh*a*i diya/diye ghasha. [ghashiy*a* tol*a*] | ghash*a*/m*a*ja

There are few rubber trees in our country. | rubber
আমাদের দেশে অল্প রবার গাছ আছে। | রবার
A*ma*der deshe alpa rab*a*r g*a*chh *a*chhe. | rab*a*r

He follows/abides by the rules. | rule
সে নিয়ম মানিয়া/মেনে চলে। | নিয়ম, রীতি
She niyam m*a*niya/mene chale. | niyam, reeti

That teacher rules his students well. (manages) | rule
ঐ শিক্ষক ছাত্রদের ভালমত শাসন করেন। | শাসন করা
Oi shikkhak chh*a*trader bh*a*la mata | sh*a*shan kar*a*
shashan karen.

He ran to call the doctor. | run

সে ডাক্তার ডাকতে দৌড়াইল/দৌড়াল। | দৌড়ান, দৌড় দেওয়া

She *daktar dak*te dou*raila/doura*la. | dou*ran*, dour deoy*a*

The girl ran away from school. | run away

মেয়েটা ইস্কুল থেকে পালাইয়া/পালিয়ে গেল। | পালান, পালাইয়া যাওয়া

Meye*ta* skul theke p*alaiya/pa*liye gela. | p*alan*, p*alaiya jaoya*

There is no end to man's asking for money. | rupee, taka,
Taka ten. | money

লোকের টাকা চাওয়ার শেষ নাই। দশ টাকা। | টাকা

Loker *taka* ch*aoyar* shesh n*ai*. Dash *taka*. | *taka*

Many sacks of rice have come to the shop. | sack, bag

বস্তা বস্তা চাউল দোকানে আসছে/এসেছে। | বস্তা, ছালা

Bast*a* bast*a* ch*aul* dok*ane a*shchhe/eshcchhe. | bast*a*, chh*ala*

Why is the girl so sad ? | sad

মেয়েটি এত দুঃখিত কেন ? | দুঃখিত

Meye*ti* eta dukkhita kena *?* | dukkhita

Put up the sail of the boat. | sail, n.

নৌকার পাল তুল। | পাল

Nauk*ar* p*al* tula. | p*al*

He get his salary. How much is your pay *?* | salary, pay

সে বেতন পাইছে/পেয়েছে। তোমার মাইনা কত ? | বেতন, মাইনা

She betan p*ai*chhe/peyechhe. Tom*ar* m*aina* kata *?* | betan, m*aina*

We got salt from sea water. | salt

আমরা সমুদ্রের জল থেকে লবণ পাই। | লবণ, নুন, নিমক

*A*mra shamudrer jal theke laban p*ai*. (nimak) | laban, nun

Good morning, good day, peace, greetings. | (salutation)

নমস্কার, সালাম, আদাব। | নমস্কার

Namashk*ar*, sh*al*am, *ad*ab. | namashk*ar*

It is all the same whether you go or not. | same

তোমার যাওয়া না যাওয়া একই কথা। v. n. | একই

Tom*ar* j*aoya* n*a* j*aoya* eki katha. | eki

A lot of sand is needed to build a house. | sand
একটা বাড়ী তৈরী করতে অনেক বালি লাগে। INFIN. | বালি, বালু
   Ekta bari tairee karte anek bali lage. | bali, balu

Everyone was satisfied with his behaviour/conduct. | be satisfied
তার ব্যবহারে সবাই সন্তুষ্ট হইল। [—করা kara v. t.] | সন্তুষ্ট হওয়া
Tar baebahare shabai shantushta haila. | shantushta haoya

He came on Saturday. | Saturday
সে শনিবারে আসছিল/এসেছিল। | শনিবার
   She shanibare ashchhila/eshechhila. | shanibar

Put saucers under the cups. | saucer
পেয়ালার নীচে পিরিজ দাও। | পিরিজ
   Peyalar neeche pirij dao. | pirij

He saved the boy from danger. | save
তিনি ছেলেটিকে বিপদ থেকে বাঁচালেন। | বাঁচান
   Tini chheletike bipad theke banchalen. | banchan

The savour of the curry is fine/excellent. | savour, odour
তরকারির গন্ধটা চমৎকার। | গন্ধ
   Tarkarir gandhata chamatkar. | gandha

What can a carpenter do without a saw ? | saw, n.
করাত ছাড়া ছুতার মিস্ত্রি কি করতে পারে ? | করাত
   Karat chhara chhutar mistri ki karte pare ? | karat

What did you say ? Say it again. | say
কি বলছ/বলেছ ? আবার বল। | বলা, কহা
   Ki balchha/balechha ? Abar bala. | bala, kaha

Honest people are scarce today. | scarce, rare
আজকাল সৎলোক খুব কম। | কম
   Ajkal shatlok khub kam. | kam

He scarcely ever goes to school. | scarcely, hardly
সে প্রায়-ই স্কুলে যায় না। | প্রায়-ই···না
   She pray-i skule jay na. | pray-i...na

If you scatter rice, birds will come. | scatter
ভাত ছড়াইলে/ছড়ালে পাখীরা আসবে। | ছড়ান
    Bhat chharaile/chharale pakheera ashbe. | chharan

She/he studies in this school. | school
সে এই স্কুলে পড়ে। | স্কুল
    She ei skule pare. | skul

Tailor and barbers use scissors. | scissors
দর্জী ও নাপিতে কাঁচি ব্যবহার করে। | কাঁচি, কেচি
    Darjee o napite kanchi baebahar kare. | kanchi, kechi

The mother scolded her daughter/son. | scold
মা মেয়েকে/ছেলেকে বকল। | বকা
    Ma meyeke/chheleke bakla. | baka

The window curtain has become dirty. | screen, curtain
জানালার পরদা ময়লা হইয়া গেছে/হয়ে গিয়েছে। | পরদা
    Janalar parda mayla haiya gechhe/haye giyechhe. | parda

Search for the baby. (seek, look for | search for
শিশুটিকে খুঁজ। | খোঁজা
    Shishutike khunja. | khonja

I have searched the whole house. | search, seek
আমি সমস্ত বাড়ী তালাশ করছি/করেছি। | তালাশ করা
Ami shamasta baree talash karchhi/karechhi. | talash kara

There are six seasons in Bangladesh. | season(s)
বাংলাদেশে ছয়টি ঋতু (আছে)। | ঋতু
    Bangladeshe chhayti reetu achhe. | reetu

He came secretly to me. | secretly
সে গোপনে আমার কাছে আসল/এল। | গোপনে
    She gopane amar kachhe ashla/ela. | gopane

I saw him go. [I see = I understand. q. v.] | see, look
আমি তাকে চলিয়া যাইতে/চলে যেতে দেখলাম। | দেখা
    Ami take chaliya jaite/chale jete dekhlam. | dekha

Trees grow/come from seeds.

বীজ থেকে গাছ হয় ।

Beej theke gachh hay.

seed

বীজ, বীচি

beej, beechi

It seems The man is walking to Dacca.

বোধ হয় লোকটি হাঁটিয়া/হেঁটে ঢাকায় যাইতেছে/যাচ্ছে ।

Bodh hay lokti hantiya/hente Dhakay

jaitechhe/jachchhe.

seem, appear

বোধ হয়

bodh hay

It seems to me he will not come. It seems strange.

আমার মনে হয়, সে আসবে না । অদ্ভুদ লাগে ।

Amar mane hay, she ashbe na.

Adbhut lage. [3rd person]

seem

মনে হওয়া, লাগে

mane haoya, lage

Give me a seer of sugar. (2 lbs)

আমাকে এক সের চিনি দাও/দেন/দিন ।

Amake ek sher chini dao/den/din.

seer

সের

sher

The policeman seized the thief. (hold, catch)

পুলিশ চোরটাকে ধরল ।

Pulish chortake dharla.

seize

ধরা

dhara

Peoples here seldom eat meat.

এখানকার লোকেরা মাংস খুব কম খায় ।

Ekhankar lokera mangsha khub kam khay.

seldom

খুব কম

khub kam

I selected a book from the library.

আমি লাইব্রেরী থেকে একটি বই বাছিয়া নিছি/বেছে

নিয়েছি ।

Ami laibreree theke ekti bai bachhiya

nichhi/bechhe niyechhi.

select, choose

বাছিয়া নেওয়া

bachhiya neoya

The man sold his cow.

লোকটি তার গরু বেচিয়া/বেচে ফেলল ।

Lokti tar garu bechiya/beche fella.

sell

বেচা, বিক্রী করা

becha, bikri kara

Send him for the mail.

তাকে ডাক আনতে পাঠাও ।   INFIN.

Take dak ante pathao.

send

পাঠান

pathan

Make a sentence with this word.	sentence
এই শব্দ দিয়া/দিয়ে বাক্য রচনা কর।	বাক্য
Ei shabda diya/diye bakka rachana kara.	bakka
Separate the rotten potatoes.	separate, v,
পচা আলু আলাদা কর / রাখ।	আলাদা
Pacha alu alada kara/ rakha.	alada
Don't make any separate arrangement for me.	separate, adj
আমার জন্য কোন পৃথক/আলাদা ব্যবস্থা করিও না/করো না।	পৃথক
Amar janna kona preethak/alada baebasta kario na/karo na.	preethak
Call the servant. We have no servant.	servant
চাকরকে ডাক। আমাদের চাকর নাই/নেই।	চাকর
Chakarke daka. Amader chakar nai/nei.	chakar
He serves/works in an office.	serve, work
সে অফিসে চাকরি/কাজ করে।	চাকরি করা
She afishe chakari/kaj kare.	cbakari kara
Set the pot here. (put down, caus. v.) L. 30.	set, place
হাঁড়িটা এখানে বসাও।	রাখা, বসান
Hanrita ekhane bashao.	rakha, bashan
I have come to settle the account.	settle (acct.)
হিসাবটা ঠিক করতে আসছি/এসেছি।	ঠিক করা
Hishabta thik karte ashchhi/eshechhi.	thik kara
Settle your quarrel (or account).	settle
তোমাদের ঝগড়া (বা হিসাব) মিটাইয়া/মিটিয়ে ফেল।	মিটান
Tomader jhagra (ba hishab) mitaiya/mitiye fela.	mitan
He will stay in this country for several years.	several
তিনি এ দেশে কয়েক বৎসর/বছর থাকিবেন/থাকবেন।	কয়েক
Tini e deshe kayek batshar/bachhar thakben.	kayek
Several boys came.	several
কতকগুলি ছেলে আসছিল/এসেছিল।	কতকগুলি
Katakguli chhele ashchhila/eshechhila.	katakguli

Call a cobbler to sew my shoes. | sew

আমার জুতা সেলাই করবার জন্য একজন মুচী | সেলাই করা
ডাকিয়া/ডেকে আন ।

*A*m*a*r ju*ta* shelai karb*a*r janna ekjan | shel*a*i kar*a*
muchee *da*kiya/*de*ke *a*na.

The men are resting in the shade of the tree. | shade

লোকগুলি গাছের ছায়ায় বিশ্রাম করতেছে/করছে । | ছায়া

Lokguli g*a*chher chh*a*yay b*i*sr*a*m kartechhe/karchhe. | chh*a*y*a*

The table shakes. Leaves shake in the wind. | shake

টেবিলটা নড়ে । বাতাসে পাতা নড়ে । [নাড়ান, v. t] | নাড়া, নড়া

*T*ebil*ta* nare. B*a*t*a*she p*a*t*a* nare.

L.82 CAUS. V. (la*r*e) [n*a*ran, v. t.] | n*a*r*a*, nar*a*

Don't shake me when I write. (caus. L. 30, | shake

আমি যখন লেখি, তখন আমাকে নাড়াইও না/নাড়িও না । | নাড়ান

*A*mi jakhan lekhi, takhan *a*m*a*ke n*a*raio n*a*/n*a*rio n*a*. | n*a*ra*n*

This is a shame   Don't shame me. | shame

এটা লজ্জার বিষয় ।   আমাকে লজ্জা দিও না । | লজ্জা

E*ta* lajj*a*r bishay.   *A*m*a*ke lajj*a* dio n*a*. | lajj*a*

The shape of the earth is round. | shape, form

পৃথিবীর আকার গোল । | আকার

Preethibeer *a*kar gol. | *a*ka*r*

I shall get a share of this. | share, part

ইহার এক ভাগ আমি পাইব/পাব । | ভাগ, অংশ

Ih*a*r ek bh*a*g *a*mi p*a*iba/p*a*ba. | bh*a*g,angsha

The knife is sharp. (The knife has an edge.) | sharp

ছুরির ধার আছে । | ধার আছে, (ধারাল)

Chhurir dh*a*r *a*chhe. | dh*a*r *a*chhe (dh*a*ra*l*)

The barber began to shave the donkey. | shave

নাপিত গাধাটিকে কামাইতে লাগল । L. 30. | কামান

Napit gadh*a*tike k*a*maite l*a*gla. | k*a*m*a*n

He/she goes to work at 10 o'clock. | she, he

সে ১০টায় কাজে যায় । | সে, ও

   She dash*t*ay k*a*je j*a*y. | she, o

He has many sheep. (m. f.) | sheep

তার অনেক ভেড়া ভেড়ী আছে । | ভেড়া, ভেড়ী, মেষ

   T*a*r anek bhe*ra* bhe*ree a*chhc. | bhe*ra*, bhe*ree*, mesh

The bedsheet must be changed. (table clo*t*h). | sheet

চাদরটি বদলাইতে/বদলাতে হবে । | চাদর

   Ch*a*dar*t*i badl*a*ite/badl*a*te habe. | ch*a*dar

Large ships travel on the seas. | ship

বড় বড় জাহাজ সমুদ্রে যায় । | জাহাজ

   Ba*ra* b*a*ra j*a*haj shamudre j*a*y. | j*a*h*a*j

The man *w*ore a blue shirt. | shirt

লোকটি একটি নীল রঙের সার্ট পরছিল/পরেছিল । | সার্ট

Lok*t*i ek*t*i neel ranger sh*ar*t parchhila/parechhila. | sh*ar*t

She/he has three pair of shoes. | shoe

তার তিন জোড়া জুতা আছে । | জুতা

   T*a*r tin jo*ra* jut*a a*chhe. | jut*a*

The shoemaker sings while he works. cobbler) | shoemaker

মুচিটা কাজ করতে করতে গান গায় । | মুচি

   Muchi*t*a k*a*j karte karte g*a*n g*a*y. | muchi

The shopkeeper is sitting in his shop. | shop

দোকানদার দোকানে বসিয়া/বসে থাকে । | দোকান

   Dok*a*nd*a*r dok*a*ne bashiy*a*/bashe th*a*ke. | dok*a*n

The man is very short. | short

লোকটি খুব খাটো । | খাটো

   Lok*t*i khub kh*a*to. | kh*a*to

Bring a shorter bamboo. (a bit smaller) | short

আর একটু ছোট বাঁশ আন । | ছোট

   *A*r ek*t*u chho*t*a ba*nsh a*na. | chho*t*a

We ought to love God.   [L. 76] | should, ought
আমাদের ঈশ্বরকে ভালবাসা উচিত । | উচিত
Amader Eeshsharke bhalabasha uchit. | gen. + inf. + uchit

What is that in your hand ? Show me. | show, v.
তোমার হাতে ওটা/সেটা কি ? আমাকে দেখাও । | দেখান
Tomar hate ota/sheta ki ? Amake dekhao. | dekhan

He bought shrimp in the market/bazar. | shrimp
সে বাজারে চিংড়ী মাছ কিনছে/কিনেছে । | চিংড়ী
She bajare chingri machh kinchhe/kinechhe. | chingri

Shun the company of bad boys. | shun, give up
দুষ্ট ছেলেদের সঙ্গ ছাড় । [এড়ান] | ছাড়া
Dushta chheleder shanga chhara. [eran] | chhara

Don't shut the doors and windows. | shut, close
দরজা, জানালা বন্ধ করিও/করো না । | বন্ধ করা
Darja janala bandha kario/kara na. | bandha kara

He is sick. | sick, ill
তার অসুখ হইছে/হয়েছে । তিনি/সে অসুস্থ । | অসুখ, অসুস্থ
Tar ashukh haichhe/hayechhe. Tini/she ashustha. | ashukh, ashustha

The boy/girl is very sickly/thin. | sickly, thin
ছেলেটি/মেয়েটি খুব রোগা । | রোগা
Chheleti/meyeti khub roga. | roga

Some sort of sickness is in that family. | sickness, disease
ঐ বাড়ীতে কোন একটা রোগ থাকে । | রোগ
Oi bareete kona ekta rog thake. | rog

Come, let's walk along the river bank. | side
চল, নদীর ধারে বেড়াই । [দিক] | ধার, কিনার
Chala, nadeer dhare berai. [dik] | dhar, kinar

Come, sit beside me. (at my side) (postp.) | side, beside
আস/এস আমার পাশে বস । | পাশে
Asha/esha, amar pashe basha. | pashe

Who has signed this paper ?	sign (v.)
এ কাগজে কে সই করছে/করেছে ?	সই দেওয়া/করা
E kagaje ke shai karchhe/karechhe ?	shai deoya/kara
I don't know whose signature this is.	signature
এই স্বাক্ষর/সই কার তা আমি জানি না ।	স্বাক্ষর, সই
Ei shakkhar/shai kar ta ami jani na.	shakkhar, shai
Be silent, don't talk.	silent, be
চুপ কর়ো ; কথা বলিও/বলো না । চুপ রও ।	চুপ করা
Chup karo ; katha balio/balo na. Chup rao.	chup kara
Silver things are dear/costly.	silver
রূপার জিনিস দামী ।	রূপা
Roopar jinish damee.	roopa
This task is very easy.	simple, easy
এ কাজটি খুব সোজা ।	সোজা
E kajti khub shoja.	shoja
It's not easy to learn English.	simple, easy
ইংরেজী শিখা সহজ না ।	সহজ
Ingrejee shikha shahaj na.	shahaj
The man is very simple. (sincere)	simple, frank
লোকটি খুব সাদাসিধে/সরল ।	সরল, সাদাসিধে
Lokti khub shadashidhe/sharal.	sharal, shadashidhe
Stealing is a sin. We should not sin. L. 95 d	sin
চুরি করা পাপ । পাপ করতে নাই/নেই ।	পাপ
Churi kara pap. Pap karte nai/nei.	pap
He has been ill since Sunday last. L. 64	since, from [Postp.
গত রবিবার থেকে/হতে তার অসুখ হইছে/হয়েছে ।	থেকে, হতে
Gata Rabibar theke/hate tar ashukh	theke, hate
haichhe/hayechhe.	
The man likes to sing.	sing
লোকটি গান গাইতে ভালবাসে ।	গান গাওয়া
Lokti gan gaite bhalabashe.	gan gaoya

Boats float in the water. They do not sink. | sink, drown

নৌকা জলে ভাসে ; ডুবিয়া/ডুবে ষায় না । | ডুবা, ডুবিয়া যাওয়া

Nauka jale bhashe ; dubia/dube jay na. | duba, dubia jaoya

She/he was drowned. | sink

সে ডুবল/(ডুবিয়া গেল)/ডুবে গেল । | ডুবা

She dubla/dubia/dube gela. | duba

I have no sister(s). (I haven't any······) | sister

আমার কোন বোন নাই/নেই । | বোন

Amar kona bon nai/nei. | bon

Sit down a little while. [L. 29 fut. imp.] | sit

একটু/একটুখানি বস/বসুন/বসেন । | বসা

Ektu/ektukhani basha/bashun/bashen. | basha

Her/his skin is rough. (leather) | skin (n)

তার গায়ের চামড়া খসখসে । | চামড়া

Tar gayer chamra khashkhashe. | chamra

The skin of an orange. Tiger's skin. | skin, n.

কমলা লেবুর ছাল ।   বাঘের ছাল । | ছাল

Kamala lebur chhal. Bagher chhal. | chhal

At that time the moon was in the sky. | sky

তখন আকাশে চাঁদ ছিল । | আকাশ

Takhan akashe chand chhila. | akash

Sleep restores/gives us back lost energy/strength. | sleep n.

ঘুম হারান শক্তি ফিরাইয়া/ফিরিয়ে দেয় । | ঘুম

Ghum harana shakti firaiya/firiye dey. | ghum

Don't sleep any more. | sleep, v.

আর ঘুমাইও না/ঘুমিও না । | ঘুমান

Ar ghumaio na/ghumio na. | ghuman

Speak slowly/softly/quietly. | slowly, softly

আস্তে আস্তে কথা বল । | আস্তে আস্তে

Aste aste katha bala. | aste aste

He/she walks slowly. | slowly
সে ধীরে ধীরে হাঁটে । [আস্তে আস্তে] | ধীরে ধীরে
She dheere dheere hante [aste aste] | dheere dheere

The small bird sat on the branch. | small, little
ছোট পাখীটি ডালের উপর বসল । | ছোট
Chhota pakheeti daler upar bashla. | chhota

The girl/boy is smart. | smart, clever
মেয়েটি/ছেলেটি চতুর । [চালাক] | চতুর
Meyeti/chheleti chatur. [chalak] | chatur

The gardenia has a sweet smell (odour). | smell n.
গন্ধরাজের সুগন্ধ আছে । | গন্ধ
Gandharajer shugandha achhe. | gandha

He/she smelled the flower. | smell v.
সে ফুলটির গন্ধ শুঁকল । | গন্ধ শুঁকা/পাওয়া
She fultir gandha shukla. | gandha shuka/ paoya

Why are you smiling ? A pretty smile | smile (n.+v.)
broke out on her/his face. |
তুমি হাসতেছ/হাসছ কেন ?   তার মুখে | হাসি, হাসা
একটি সুন্দর হাসি ফুটল । |
Tumi hashtechha/hashchha ken ? Tar | hashi n., hasha v.
mukhe ekti shundar hashi futla. |

The floor of the room is smooth.(even, equal) | smooth
ঘরের মেঝেটা সমান । | সমান
Gharer mejheta shaman. | shaman

There are many snakes in Bangladesh. | snake
বাংলাদেশে অনেক সাপ আছে । | সাপ
Bangladeshe anek shap achhe. | shap

He/she did not study, so he/she was punished. | so, therefore
সে পড়ে নাই/নি, সেই জন্য সে শাস্তি পাইছে/পেয়েছে । | সেইজন্য, তাই
She pare nai/ni, shei janna she shasti |
paichhe/peyechhe. | shei janna, tai

Do this work in this way. | so, in this way
এই কাজটি এই ভাবে কর । | এমনে, এইভাবে
Ei kajti ei bhabe kara. | emne, ei bhabe

Why do you talk so much ? I want this much. | so/this much,
এত কথা বল কেন ? এতটা চাই । | এত, এতটা
Eta katha bala kena ? Etata chai. | eta, etata

Soak this towel. (and bring it back). | soak, wet
এই তোয়ালেটা ভিজাইয়া/ভিজিয়ে আন । | ভিজান
Ei toyaleta bhijaiya/bhijiye ana. | bhijan

Use soap when you bathe. Bathe with soap. | soap
সাবান দিয়ে/দিয়া স্নান কর / গোসল কর। | সাবান
Shaban diye/diya snan kara / gosal kara. | shaban

This butter is soft. | soft
এই মাখন নরম । | নরম
Ei makhan naram. | naram

The soil in this garden is very good. (ground) | soil, earth
এই বাগানের মাটি খুব ভাল । | মাটি
Ei baganer mati khub bhala. | mati

British soldiers were in France. | soldier
ইংরেজ সৈন্যরা ফ্রান্সে ছিল । | সৈন্য, সৈনিক
Ingrej shainnara Franse chhila. | shainna, shainik

I want some butter. Some animal has eaten it. | some
কিছু মাখন চাই । কোন জন্তু ইহা খাইছে/খেয়েছে । | কিছু, কোন
Kichhu makhan chai. Kona jantu iha | kichhu, kona
khaichhe/kheyechhe.

Somebody has taken away my knife. | somebody
কেহ আমার ছুরি নিয়া গেছে/নিয়ে গিয়েছে । | কেহ, কোন লোক
Keha amar chhuri niya gechhe/niye giyechhe. | keha, kona lok

17—

I came to know this somehow. L. 84 | somehow
আমি কোন রকমে ইহা জানতে পারলাম । | কোন রকমে
Ami kona rakame iha jante parlam. | kona rakame

He comes to our house sometimes. (occasionally) | sometimes
সে সময় সময় আমাদের বাড়ীতে আসে । | সময় সময়
She shamay shamay amader bareete ashe. | shamay shamay

How many sons/daughters have you ? | son
তোমার কয়জন ছেলেমেয়ে ? | ছেলে, (পুত্র)
Tomar kayjan chhele/meye ? | chhele (putra)

They are singing a song. | song
তারা গান গাইতেছে/গাচ্ছে । | গান
Tara gan gaitechhe/gachchhe. | gan

Do it soon ; don't delay. | soon, quickly
শীঘ্র কর ; দেরী করিও/করো না । | শীঘ্র
Sheeghra kara ; deri kario/karo na. | sheeghra

He (his body) is covered with sores. | sore, wound
তার শরীর ভরা ঘা । | ঘা
Tar shareer bhara gha. L. 35 | gha

He/she wasn't sorry. (regret) | sorry, be
সে দুঃখিত হয় নাই/নি । | দুঃখিত হওয়া
She dukhita hay nai/ni. | dukhita haoya

I don't like that sort of book. | sort, kind
আমি ঐ রকম বই পছন্দ করি না । | রকম
Ami oi rakam bai pachhanda kari na. | rakam

The soul [is] immortal. | soul
আত্মা অমর [ ] । | আত্মা
Atta amar [ ]. | atta

I heard the sound of the bell. | sound, word
ঘণ্টার শব্দ শুনছি/শুনেছি । | শব্দ
Ghantar shabda shunchhi/shunechhi. | shabda

We eat more soup in winter. | soup
শীতকালে আমরা বেশী সুরা/ঝোল খাই । | সুরা, সুরুয়া
   Sheet kale amra beshee shura/jhol khai.   shura, shuruya

All mangoes are not sour. | sour (adj.)
সব আম টক/চুকা না । | টক, চুকা
   Shab am tak/chuka na.   tak, chuka

There is a field to the south of our house. | south
আমাদের বাড়ীর দক্ষিণে একটি মাঠ আছে । | দক্ষিণ দিক)
   Amader bareer dakkhine ekti math achhe. dakkhin (dik)

Cultivators sow crops after ploughing the field. | sow (seed)
চাষীরা হাল দিয়া/দিয়ে শস্য বুনে । | বোনা, বুনা
   Chasheera hal diya/diye shashsha bune.   bona, buna

Give me a little space. | space, place
আমাকে একটু জায়গা দাও । | জায়গা
   Amake ektu jayga dao.   jayga

Don't speak any more. Speak slowly/softly. | speak
আর কথা কইও/কয়ো না । আস্তে আস্তে কথা কও । কথা বলা/কহা
   Ar katha kaio/kayo na. Aste aste katha kao.   kaha
            [katha bala]

Where did I put my spectacles ? (glasses) | spectacles
আমার চশমা কোথায় রাখলাম ? | চশমা
   Amar chashma kothay rakhlam ?   chashma

He became speechless (surprised) | speechless, be, become
সে অবাক হইয়া/ হয়ে গেল । | অবাক হওয়া
   She abak haiya/haiye gela.   abak haoya

Con't you spell this easy word ? (make) | spell, build
এ সহজ শব্দ বানান করতে পার না ? | বানান
   E shahaj shabda banan karte para na ?   banan

He spends all that he earns. (make expense) | spend
সে যা রোজগার করে তা খরচ করে ।   খরচ করা/ব্যয় করা
   She ja rojgar kare ta kharach kare. kharach kara/bae kara

I spent three month in Dacca. | spend time

ঢাকায় ৩ মাস কাটাইছি/কাটিয়েছি । | সময় কাটান

    Dhakay 3 (tin) mash *kata*ichhi/*kati*yechhi. shamay *katan*

It's good to put spices in the curry. | spice

তরকারীতে মশলা দেওয়া ভাল । | মশলা

    Tark*a*reete mashl*a* deoy*a* bh*a*la. | mashl*a*

You have spoiled my picture. The milk has spoiled. | spoil, waste

তুমি আমার ছবি নষ্ট করছ/করেছ । দুধ নষ্ট   নষ্ট করা/হওয়া

                  হইছে/হয়েছে ।

    Tumi *a*m*a*r chhabi nash*t*a karchha/   nash*t*a kar*a*/haoy*a*

    karechha.   Dudh nash*t*a haichhe/hayechhe.

I put two spoonfuls of sugar in a cup of tea. | spoon

এককাপ চায়ে আমি দুই চামচ চিনি দেই/দিই । | চামচ

    Ek k*a*p ch*a*ye *a*mi dui ch*a*mach chini dei/dii. | ch*a*mach

We like all kinds of sports. (games) | sport, play

আমরা সব রকম খেলা ভালবাসি । | খেলা

    *A*mr*a* shab rakam khel*a* bh*a*lab*a*shi. | khel*a*

In Bangladesh spring lasts two months. | spring (time)

বাংলাদেশে বসন্তকাল দুই মাস থাকে । | বসন্তকাল

    B*a*ngl*a*deshe bashantak*a*l dui m*a*sh th*a*ke. | bashantak*a*l

He was standing at the foot of the stairs. | stairs, ladder

সে সিঁড়ির নীচে দাঁড়াইছিল/দাঁড়িয়েছিল । | সিঁড়ি

    She shi*n*rir neeche d*a*nr*a*ichhila/d*a*nriyechhila. | shi*n*ri

They say that stale bread is tasty. | stale

বাসি রুটি নাকি খাইতে/খেতে ভাল । | বাসি

    B*a*shi ru*t*i n*a*ki kh*a*ite/khete bh*a*la. | b*a*shi

Postage stamps are sold at post offices. | stamp, postage

পোস্ট অফিসে ডাক টিকিট বিক্রি হয় । | ডাক টিকিট

    Pos*t* afishe *dak tikit* bikri hay. | *dak tikit*

Stand in the corner.

কোনায় দাঁড়াও ।

Konay danrao.

stand, v.

দাঁড়ান

danran

Stand it up. (Intrans. stand up/erect.)

ইহা খাড়া কর ।(খাড়া হও।

Iha khara kara.(khara hao.

stand (cause)

খাড়া করা

khara kara

Many stars can be seen in the sky today. L. 82

আজ আকাশে অনেক তারা দেখতে পাওয়া যাইতেছে/যাচ্ছে ।

Aj akashe anek tara dekhte paoya jaitechhe/jachchhe.

star

তারা

tara

He/she started to sing. L. 93, Infin.

সে গান করতে শুরু করল ।

She gan karte shuru karla.

start, begin, v.

শুরু করা, আরম্ভ করা

shuru kara, arambha kara

He/she (has) started on his/her journey in the morning.

তিনি সকালে রওনা হইছেন/হয়েছেন ।

Tini shakale raona haichhen/hayechhen.

start a journey

রওনা হওয়া

raona haoya

Stay here. I stayed there three (3) months.

এখানে থাক । সেখানে তিন মাস রইলাম ।

Ekhane thaka Shekhane tin mash railam.

stay, remain

থাকা, রহা

thaka, raha

Thou shall not steal. Don't steal.

চুরি করবে না ।

Churi karbe na. L. 29

steal

চুরি করা

churi kara

He sat on the step(s).

সে ধাপে বসল ।

She dhape bashla.

step (n.)

ধাপ

dhap

They beat him with sticks.

তারা তাকে লাঠি দিয়া/দিয়ে মারল ।

Tara take lathi diya/diye marla.

stick (n)

লাঠি

lathi

The stamp did not stick to the envelope.

খামে টিকিট লাগে নাই/নি ।

Khame tikit lage (anta) nai/ni.

stick, be joined

লাগা,(আঁটা)

laga,(anta)

Stick/paste a stamp on the envelope. L. 30. | stick, afix
খামে টিকিট লাগাও । | লাগান
Khame *tikit* lagao. [caus. v.] | *lagan*, v. t

Still he hasn't finished the work. | still, up to now
সে এখনও কাজটি শেষ করে নাই/নি । | এখনও
She ekhan-o *kajti* shesh kare n*ai*/ni. | ekhan-o

He/she is very stingy. | stingy
সে খুব কৃপণ । | কৃপণ
She khub kripan. | kripan

He has an upset stomach/a stomach ache. | stomach
তার পেটের অসুখ । তার পেট ব্যথা করে । | পেট
T*a*r pe*t*er ashukh. T*a*r pe*t* baeth*a* kare. | pe*t*

The stones of some fruits are very hard. | stone (fruit)
কোন ফলের বীচি খুব শক্ত । | বীচি
Kona faler becchi khub shakta. | beechi

There are no stones in the soil of this country. | stone (n.)
এদেশের মাটিতে পাথর নাই/নেই । | পাথর
E desher m*a*tite p*a*thar n*ai*/nei. | p*a*thar

Stop, don't come farther. | stop (v.)
থাম, আর সামনে আসিও না/এসো না । | থামা
Th*a*ma, *a*r sh*a*mne *a*shio n*a*/esho n*a*. | tham*a*

Stop this boy. Stop the car. L. 30 | stop (caus.)
এই ছেলে[টি]কে থামাও । গাড়ী থামাও । | থামান
Ei chhele[*t*i]ke th*a*ma*o*. G*a*ree th*a*ma*o*. | tham*a*n

How much rice is there in the store-house ? | store-house,barn
গুদামে কত চাউল আছে ? [গোলা] | গুদাম
Gud*a*me kata ch*a*ul *a*chhe ? [gol*a*] | gud*a*m

I live on the first storey/floor. | storey, floor
আমি এক তালায় থাকি । | তালা, তলা
*A*mi ek t*a*lay th*a*ki. [Loe.] | tala, t*a*la

He knows fine stories.

সে ভাল ভাল গল্প জানে ।

She bhala bhala galpa jane.

| story, tale
| গল্প
| galpa

Water is boiling on the stove.

চুলার উপরে জল ফুটতেছে/ফুটছে ।

Chular upare jal futtechhe/futchhe.

| stove
| চুলা
| chula

Draw a straight line. Stand up straight.

সোজা রেখা টান । খাড়া হও ।

Shoja rekha tana. Khara hao.

| straight, easy
| সোজা, খাড়া, সিধা
| shoja, khara, shidha

He looks strange/queer/odd.

তাকে অদ্ভুত দেখায় ।

Take adbhut dekhay.

| strange
| অদ্ভুত
| adbhut

The man has great strength.

লোকটির অনেক শক্তি আছে । [লোকের]

Loktir anek shakti achhe. [loker]

| strength
| শক্তি, বল
| shakti, bal

Our headmaster is a strict man.

আমাদের হেড্‌মাস্টার কড়া লোক ।

Amader hedmastar kara lok.

| strict, harsh
| কড়া
| kara

Don't strike the dog.

কুকুরটাকে মারিও/মেরো না ।

Kukurtake mario/mero na.

| strike, hit
| মারা
| mara

Give me a piece of string.

আমাকে এক টুকরা সুতা দাও । [সরু দড়ি]

Amake ek tukra shuta dao. [sharu dari]

| string, thread
| মোটা সুতা
| mota shuta

This cloth is very strong.

এই কাপড় খুব মজবুত ।

Ei kapar khub majbut.

| strong (thing)
| মজবুত
| majbut

The number of students is increasing. (m., f.)

ছাত্র/ছাত্রী সংখ্যা বাড়তেছে/বাড়ছে ।

Chhatra/chhatree shankkha bartechhe/barchhe.

| student, pupil
| ছাত্র, ছাত্রী
| chhatra, m
| chhatree,

The boy/girl studies well. (fall) | study, read
ছেলেটি/মেয়েটি ভালমত পড়ে। [ছেলে/মেয়ে] | পড়া
   Chheleṭi/meyeṭi bhala mata paṛe. [chhele/meye]   paṛa

Is he/she as stupid as that ? [such a] | stupid
সে এত বোকা ?   [এত] | বোকা
   She eta bokā ?   [eta]   bokā

He has put a substitute in his place. (at work) | substitute
সে তার কাজের বদলী দিছে/দিয়েছে। | বদলী
   She tar kajer badlee dichhe/diyechhe.   badlee

Never do this kind of thing again. | such
এই রকম কাজ আর করিও না/করো না। | এমন, এ রকম
   Ei rakam kaj ar kario/kara na.   eman, e rakam

He/she went away suddenly. | suddenly
সে হঠাৎ চলিয়া/চলে গেল। | হঠাৎ
   She haṭhat chaliya/chale gela.   haṭhat

He/she takes too much sugar in his/her tea. | sugar
সে চায়ে খুব বেশী চিনি খায়। | চিনি
   She chaye khub beshee chini khay.   chini

He will go to Shillong in the summer. | summer
সে গ্রীষ্মকালে শিলং যাবে। | গ্রীষ্মকাল
   She greeshsha kale Shillong jabe.   greeshsha kal

The clouds have covered the sun. | sun
মেঘ সূর্য[কে] ঢাকিয়া ফেলছে/ঢেকে ফেলেছে। | সূর্য
Megh shoorjja[ke] dhakiya felchhe/dheke felechhe.   shoorjja

Rest on Sunday. | Sunday
রবিবারে বিশ্রাম করবে/করিও। | রবিবার
   Rabibare bisram karbe/kario.   Rabibar

Put the washed clothes/quilt···in the sun. | sunshine
ধোয়া কাপড়/লেপ ···রৌদ্রে দাও। | রোদ, রৌদ্র
   Dhoya kapar/lep···raudre dao   rod, raudra

I suppose he will not come. (think)	suppose
আমি মনে করি সে আসবে না। (আমার মনে হয়)	মনে করা
Ami mane kari she ashbe na. (amar mane hay)	mane kara
He/she will surely come. I am sure. (certainly)	surely
সে নিশ্চয় আসবে। আমি নিশ্চয় জানি।	নিশ্চয়
She nishchay ashbe. Ami nishchay jani.	nishchay
I was surprised at his words/at what he said.	surprised, be
আমি তার কথা শুনিয়া/শুনে অবাক হইলাম/হলাম।	অবাক হওয়া
Ami tar katha shuniya/shune abak hailam/halam.	abak haoya
Sweep the school house.	sweep
স্কুলঘর ঝাটা দাও।	ঝাড়, ঝাটা দেওয়া
Skul ghar jhata dao.	jharu, jhata deoya
This mango is very sweet.	sweet
এই আম[টা] খুব মিঠা।	মিঠা, মিষ্টি, মিষ্ট
Ei am[ta] khub mitha.	mitha, mishti, mishta
He/she doesn't want to eat sweets/candy.	sweets
সে মিষ্টি খাইতে/খেতে চায় না।	মিষ্টি, মিঠাই
She mishti khaite/khete chay na.	mishti, mithai
The ducks are swimming in the water.	swim
হাঁসগুলি জলে সাঁতার দিতেছে/দিচ্ছে।	সাঁতার দেওয়া
Hanshguli jale shantar ditechhe/dichchhe.	shantar deoya
Put it on the table. On the table. Loc./POSTP.	table
টেবিলে রাখ। টেবিলের উপরে।	টেবিল, মেজ
Tebile rakha. Tebiler upare.	tebil, mejh
The tailor works all day.	tailor
দরজী সারাদিন কাজ করে।	দরজী
Darjee sharadin kaj kare.	darjee
Take the money/time/leave/medicine ·····.	take
টাকা/সময়/ছুটি/ঔষধ······নেও/নাও।	নেওয়া, নিয়া যাওয়া
Taka/shamay/chhuti/oushadh···neo/nao.	neoya, niya jaoya

A palm tree is higher than a betel nut tree. | tall, high
তাল গাছ সুপারী গাছের চেয়ে উঁচু। [লম্বা] | উচ্চ, উঁচু
Tal gachh shuparee gachher cheye unchu/ uchcha. [lamba] | uchcha, unchu

There are many fishes in this tank. | tank (pond)
এ পুকুরে অনেক মাছ আছে। | পুকুর, পুষ্করিণী
E pukure anek machh achhe. | pukur, pushkarinee

Water has no taste. Taste (it). | taste (n., v.)
জলের/পানির কোন স্বাদ নাই/নেই। স্বাদ নেও। | স্বাদ (নেওয়া)
Jaler/panir kona shad nai/nei. Shad neo. | shad (neoya)

It's time for tea/for eating/taking tea. | tea
চা খাইবার/খাবার সময় হইছে/হয়েছে। | চা
Cha khaibar/khabar shamay haichhe/hayechhe. | cha

Who teaches you ? | teacher
তোমাকে কে শিখায়/শিক্ষা দেয় ? | শিখান, শিক্ষা দেওয়া
Tomake ke shikhay/shikkha dey ? | shikhan, shikkha deoya

Our teacher is very strict. | teacher
আমাদের মাস্টার/শিক্ষক বড় কড়া। | মাস্টার, শিক্ষক
Amader mastar/shikkhak bara kara. | mastar, shikkhak

Sheila is a teacher in this school. | teacher (fem.)
শীলা এ স্কুলে শিক্ষয়িত্রী/শিক্ষিকা। | শিক্ষয়িত্রী/দিদি
Sheela e skuler shikkhayitree/shikkhika. | shikkhayitree/didi

The cloth is torn.   (Pass., L. 82) [torn | tear, break
কাপড়[টা] ছিঁড়া গেছে/ছিঁড়ে গিয়েছে।[ছিঁড়া | ছিঁড়া, চিরা
Kapar[ta] chhinra gechhe/chhinre giyechhe[ohhinra, chira
                                          chinra.
Tell (me) who has beaten you ? Tell me...... | tell, say
বল, কে তোমাকে মারছে/মেরেছে ? আমাকে বল…। | বলা
Bala ke tomake marchhe/merechhe ? Amake bala… | bala

Test the boy.   He took a test.

ছেলে[টি]র পরীক্ষা নেন/নেও । সে পরীক্ষা দিচ্ছে/দিয়েছে ।

Chhele[ti]r pareekkha nen/neo.

She pareekkha dichhe/diyechhe.

test, v.

পরীক্ষা নেওয়া

pareekkha neoya

Meat is better than fish.   Postp.

মাছের চেয়ে মাংস ভাল ।

Machher cheye mangsha bhala.

than (prep.)

চেয়ে, থেকে

cheye, theke

I don't want that.   I don't want that book.
That's good.

আমি সেটা চাই না । সেই বই চাই না । তা বেশ !

Ami sheta chai na. She bai chai na. Ta besh !

that (adj., pro.)

সে, সেটা, তা

she, sheta, ta

He was arrested for the crime of theft.   (pass.)

চুরির অপরাধে তাকে ধরা হইল/হল ।

Churir aparadhe take dhara haila/hala.

L. 82

theft

চুরি

churi

Nobody is there.   Go there.

সেখানে কেহ নাই/নেই । সেখানে যান ।

Shekhane keha nai/nei. Shekhane jan.

there

সেখানে, ওখানে

shekhane, okhane

I have recovered ; therefore I shall not
stay in bed.

আমি সুস্থ হইছি/হয়েছি, সেই জন্য বিছানায় থাকব না ।

Ami shustha haichhi/hayechhi, shei
janna bichhanay thakba na.

therefore

সেই জন্য, তাই

shei janna, tai

Take these away.   Take all these books.

এ গুলি নিয়া/নিয়ে যাও । এই সব বই নেও ।

E guli niya/niye jao. Ei shab bai neo.

these

এই সব, এগুলি

ei shab, e guli

Blood is thick.   This book is thick.

রক্ত ঘন ।   এই বই মোটা ।

Rakta ghana. Ei bai mota.

thick

ঘন, মোটা

ghana, mota

He is a thief and mixes with thieves

সে চোর ও চোরদের সঙ্গে মিশে ।

She chor o chorder shange mishe.

thief

চোর

chor

This paper is very thin. | thin

এ কাগজ খুব পাতলা । পাতলা

E kagaj khub patla. patla

You won't get such a thing anywhere. | thing

এমন জিনিষ কোথাও পাইবে না/পাবে না । জিনিষ

Eman jinish kothao paibe/pabe na. jinish

I think that you will be able (to do it). | think, suppose

আমি মনে করি যে তুমি পারবে ।   clauses | মনে করা

Ami mane kari je tumi parbe.   L. 132 mane kara

Don't think about that. | think

সেই বিষয়ে চিন্তা করিও/করো না । ভাবা, চিন্তা করা

Shei bishaye chinta kario/karo na. bhaba, chinta kara

I thirst. (I am/feel thirsty.) | thirst

আমার পিপাসা পাইছে/পেয়েছে/লাগে । পিপাসা

Amar pipasha paichhe/peyechhe/lage. pipasha

This boy is very good.   This is mine. | this
(adj. ; pron.)

এই ছেলে[টি] খুব ভাল ।   এইটা আমার । এই, এটা

Ei chhele[ti] khub bhala Eita amar. e(i), e(i)ta

He has no thought for tomorrow. | thought (n.)

কাল কি হবে সে বিষয়ে তার কোন চিন্তা নাই/নেই । চিন্তা

Kal ki habe she bishaye tar kona chinta nai/nei. chinta

Throw the ball to me. | throw (v.)

বল[টা] আমার কাছে ফেক/ছুঁড় । ফেকা, ছুঁড়া

Bal[ta] amar kachhe feka/chhura. feka, chhura

Throw that cigarette away. L. 11, 105 | throw away

তোমার হাত থেকে ও সিগারেট[টা] ফেলিয়া/ফেলে দাও । ফেলা

Tomar hat theke o sigaret[ta] feliya/fele dao. fela

He will come on Thursday. | Thursday

সে বিসূদবারে আসবে । [ব্রহস্পতিবার], বিসূদবার

She bishudbare ashbe. [brihashpatibar], bishudbar

Tie these together. | tie, bind
এইগুলি এক সঙ্গে বাঁধ । | বাঁধা
  Ei guli ek shange *ba*ndha. | *ba*ndha

The tiger is the king of the forest. | tiger
বাঘ বনের রাজা । | বাঘ
  *Ba*gh·baner ra*ja*. | *ba*gh

Wait till 5 o' clock. Till tomorrow. L. 61a, 79, 108 | till, up to
পাঁচটা পর্যন্ত অপেক্ষা কর/দেরি কর । কাল পর্যন্ত । | পর্যন্ত
*Pa*nch*ta* parjanta apekkha/deri kara. *Ka*l parjanta. | parjanta

There's no more time left. Sometime later. | time
আর সময় নাই/নেই । কিছু কাল পরে । | সময়, কাল
  *A*r shamay n*a*i/nei. Kichhu *ka*l pare. . | shamay,k*a*l

I told you many times. Time and again. | time (repetition)
তোমাকে অনেক বার বলছি/বলেছি । বার বার । | বার
  To*ma*ke anek b*a*r balchhi/balechhi. B*a*r b*a*r. | b*a*r

Being weary, he sat under a tree. (under a tree) | tired, weary
ক্লান্ত হইয়া/হয়ে সে গাছ তলায় বসল । (গাছের তলায়) । | ক্লান্ত
  Kl*a*nta haiy*a*/haye she g*a*chh tal*a*y bashla. | kl*a*nta
    (G*a*chher tal*a*y) L. 101 + 61d

Toast/bake the bread. Bake/roast the meat. | toast, bake
রুটি সেঁক । মাংসটা সেঁক । | সেঁকা
  Ru*ti* she*n*ka. M*a*ngsha*ta* she*n*ka. | she*n*ka

It's not good to smoke tobacco. L. 77 v. n. | tobacco
তামাক খাওয়া ভাল না । | তামাক
  T*a*mak khaoy*a* bh*a*la n*a*. | t*a*m*a*k

There's no work today. | today
আজ কোন কাজ নাই/নেই । | আজি, আজ, আজকে
  *A*j kona k*a*j n*a*i/nei. | *a*ji, *a*j, *a*jke

They went to Dacca together. | together
তারা এক সঙ্গে ঢাকায় গেল । | এক সঙ্গে, একত্রে
  T*a*ra ek shange *Dha*k*a*y gela. | ek shange, ek*a*tre

I shall go to Barisal tomorrow. | tomorrow
আমি আগামী কাল বরিশাল যাইব/যাব । | আগামী কাল
   Ami *a*gamee k*a*l Barish*a*l j*a*iba/j*a*ba. | *a*gamee k*a*l

Tonight there will be a storm. Come tonight/at night. | tonight
আজ রাত্রে ঝড় হবে । রাত্রে আস/এস । | আজ রাত্রে, রাত্রে
   Aj r*a*tre jhar habe. R*a*tre *a*sha/esha. | *a*j r*a*t*r*e, r*a*tre

You talk too much. | too, too much
তুমি খুব বেশী কথা বল/কও । | খুব বেশী
   Tumi khub beshee kath*a* bala/kao. | khub beshee

His/her tooth must be extracted/pulled out. | tooth
তার দাঁত তুলতে হবে । | দাঁত
   T*a*r d*a*nt tulte habe. | d*a*nt

What is the total expense/cost ? | total
মোট কত খরচ হইছে/হয়েছে ? | মোট
   Mo*t* kata kharach haichhe/hayechhe ? | mo*t*

Look at/towards me. Look that way. L. 59 | towards, at
আমার দিকে চাও । ঐ দিকে দেখ । | দিকে
   Am*a*r dike ch*a*o. Oi dike dekha. | dike

The towel got dirty. L. 19 | towel
তোয়ালে ময়লা হইছে/হয়েছে । | তোয়ালে
   Toy*a*le mayl*a* haichhe/hayechhe. | toy*a*le

He lives in the town. | town
সে শহরে বাস করে/থাকে । | শহর, নগর
   She shahare b*a*sh kare/th*a*ke. | shahar, nagar

Translate this sentence into English. | translate
এই বাক্য[টি] ইংরেজীতে অনুবাদ কর । | অনুবাদ করা
   Ei b*a*kka[*t*i] Ingrejeete anub*a*d kara. | anub*a*d kar*a*

Treacle/molasses must be bought. [must buy] | treacle, syrup
গুড় কিনতে হবে । | গুড়
   Gu*r* kinte habe. | gu*r*

Climb up the tree.

গাছে উঠ/চড় ।

Gachhe utha/chara.

| tree

গাছ

gachh

He took money by playing a trick.

সে চালাকি করিয়া/করে টাকা নিল ।

She chalaki kariya/kare taka nila.

| trick

চালাকি

chalaki

The man is very tricky/clever/cunning.

লোক[টা] খুব চালাক ।

Lok[ta] khub chalak.

| tricky, shrewd

চালাক

chalak

This is a trifling mistake. A trifling
matter/a trifle.

এ ভুল[টা] সামান্য । তুচ্ছ বিষয় । [ছোট]

E bhul[ta] shamanna. Tuchchha
bishay. [chhota]

| trifling, small

সামান্য, তুচ্ছ

shamanna, tuchchha

He/she has a lot of trouble (inconvience)

তার অনেক কষ্ট । [অসুবিধা]

Tar anek kashta. (ashubidha)

| trouble (n.)

কষ্ট

kashta

Don't trouble (hurt) your parents.

পিতামাতাকে কষ্ট দিও না ।

Pita matake kashta dio na.

| trouble (v.)

কষ্ট দেওয়া

kashta deoya

Where are my payjamas/trousers/pants ?

আমার পায়জামা/প্যাণ্ট কোথায় ?

Amar payjama/pent kothay ? (pajamas)

trousers

পায়জামা, প্যাণ্ট

payjama, pent

This is true. What you say is true.

ইহা সত্য । তুমি যা বল, তা সত্য ।

Iha shatta. Tumi ja bala, ta shatta.

| true

ঠিক, সত্য

thik, shatta

Trust in God.

ঈশ্বরে বিশ্বাস কর । ঈশ্বরের উপর নির্ভর কর ।

Eeshshare bishshash kara. Eeshsharer
upar nirbhar kara.

| trust, believe

বিশ্বাস করা

bishshash kara

He is a trustworthy servant. | trustworthy

সে বিশ্বস্ত চাকর । | বিশ্বস্ত

   She bishshasta ch*a*kar. | bishshasta

Try again and again. | try

বারে বারে/বার বার চেষ্টা কর । | চেষ্টা করা

   B*a*re b*a*re/b*a*r b*a*r chesht*a* kar*a*. | chesht*a* kar*a*

He/she will go on Tuesday. | Tuesday

সে মঙ্গলবারে যাইবে/যাবে । | মঙ্গলবার

   She mangalb*a*re j*a*ibe/j*a*be. | mangalb*a*r

Turn this way. I feel giddy. Walk about. | turn, v.

এই দিকে ঘুর । মাথা ঘুরে । ঘুরিয়া বেড়ান । | ঘুরা

   Ei dike ghura. M*a*th*a* ghure. Ghuriy*a* ber*a*n. | ghur*a*

Turn the table. (causative v.) L. 30. | turn (caus.)

টেবিল[টা] ঘুরাইয়া/ঘুরিয়ে দাও । | ঘুরান

   *T*ebil[*ta*] ghur*a*iya/ghuriye d*a*o. | ghur*a*n

The book costs two taka and a half. | two & a half

বই[টা]র দাম আড়াই টাকা । [বইয়ের] | আড়াই

   Bai[*ta*]r d*a*m *ara*i taka. [bai-er] | *ara*i

I have no umbrella. | umbrella

আমার ছাতা নাই/নেই । | ছাতা, ছাতি

   *A*mar chh*a*ta nai/nei. | chh*a*ta, chh*a*ti

The dog is lying under the table. L. 47 | under, below

টেবিল[টা]র নীচে কুকুর[টি] শুইয়া/শুয়ে আছে । | নীচে, নিম্নে

*T*ebil[*ta*]r neeche kukur[*ti*] shuiy*a*/shuye *a*chhe. | neeche, nimne

What is the price of this undershirt ? | undershirt

এই গেঞ্জি[টা]র দাম কত ? | গেঞ্জি

   Ei genji[*ta*]r d*a*m kata ? | genji

I don't understand what you say. | understand

তুমি যা বল তা আমি বুঝি না । | বুঝা

   Tumi j*a* bala, t*a* *a*mi bujhi n*a*. | bujh*a*

I shall not let you go unless you sing. | unless, if not

L. 115 & 86

তুমি গান না গাইলে তোমাকে যাইতে/যেতে দিব না । না···ইলে
Tumi gan na gaile tomake jaite/jete diba na. na ··ile

I shall not let you go unless you sing. | unless

তুমি যদি গান না গাও তবে তোমাকে যাইতে/যেতে দিব না । যদি···ন্য
Tumi jadi gan na gao, tabe tomake jadi···na
jaite/jete diba na.

Boys and girls like to eat unripe mangoes. | unripe, raw

ছেলেমেয়েরা কাঁচা আম খাইতে/খেতে ভালবাসে । কাঁচা
Chhele meyera kancha am khaite/khete bhaiabashe. kancha

His/her father is unwell/ill/sick. | unwell

তার বাবা অসুস্থ ।   তার বাবার অসুখ । অসুস্থ, অসুখ
Tar baba ashustha. Tar babar ashukh. ashustha, ashukh

Come up.   Put it on the table. [L. 57.] | up, upon

উপরে আস/এস ।   ইহা টেবিলের উপরে রাখ । উপরে
Upare asha/esha.   Iha tebiler upare rakha. upare

Count up to twenty. (as far as) L. 61a, 79, 108 up to, till

কুড়ি পর্য্যন্ত গোণ/গুণ । পর্য্যন্ত
Kuri parjjanta gona/guna. parjjanta

Up to now he has not come. (yet) | up to now

সে এখনও আসে নাই/নি । এখনও
She ekhan-o ashe nai/ni. ekhan-o

Up to then he was singing.(still) | up to then

সে তখনও গান গাইতেছিল/গাচ্ছিল । তখনও
She takhan-o gan gaitechhila/gachchhila. takhan-o

I have a piece of urgent business. | urgent

আমার একটি জরুরী কাজ আছে । জরুরী, দরকারী
Amar ekti jaruree kaj achhe. jaruree,darkaree

18 —

Use this paper.	use, treat
এই কাগজ ব্যবহার কর । [কাজে লাগান]	ব্যবহার করা
Ei kagaj baebahar kara. [kaje lagan]	baebahar kara
The soap has been used up.	use up
সাবান ফুরিয়া গেছে/ফুরিয়ে গিয়েছে ।	ফুরান, শেষ হওয়া
[খরচ করিয়া ফেলা]	
Shaban furaiya gechhe/ furiye giyechhe.	furan, shesh
[kharach kariya fela]	haoya
Useful tning. Business-like man.	useful
কাজের জিনিস । কাজের লোক ।	কাজের
Kajer jinish. Kajer lok.	kajer
These are all useless words.	useless words
এই সব বাজে কথা ।	বাজে কথা
Ei shab baje katha.	baje katha
Don't buy useless things.	useless thing
বাজে জিনিষ কিনিও/কেন না ।	বাজে জিনিষ
Baje jinish kinio/kena na.	baje jinish
He ıs a useless person. He/she is absolutely useless.	useless person
ও একজন অকেজো লোক । ও একেবারে অকেজো ।	অকাজের লোক
O ek jan akejo lok. O/she ekebare akejo.	akejo, akajer lok
I want three days' leave.	vacation, leave
আমি তিন দিনের ছুটি চাই ।	ছুটি
Ami tin diner chhuti chai.	chhuti
There are various kinds of fishes in the river.	various kinds
নদীতে নানা রকম মাছ আছে ।	নানা রকম
Nadeete nana rakam machh achhe.	nana rakam
It is necessary to eat fresh vegetables. L. 80	vegetable
টাটকা সব্জী খাওয়া দরকার । [শাক-সব্জি]	সব্জী
Tatka shabjee khawa/khaoya darkar.	shabjee

No sentence is possible without a verb. | verb
ক্রিয়া ছাড়া বাক্য হয় না । | ক্রিয়া
Kriya chhara bakka hay na. L. 62, 19 | kriya

He/she is a very good boy/girl. | very
সে খুব ভাল ছেলে/মেয়ে । | খুব; অতি
She khub bhala chhele/meye. | khub, ati

I am very/quite well. You've done well ! Fine ! | very, quite
আমি বেশ ভাল । বেশ করছ/করেছ । বেশ তো ! | বেশ
Ami besh bhala. Besh karchha/karechha. Besh to ! | besh

I'll go to Padrishibpur via Barisal. (by way of) | via
আমি বরিশাল হইয়া/হয়ে পাত্রীশিবপুর যাব/যাইব । | হইয়া, হয়ে
Ami Barishal haiya/haye Padreeshibpur | haiya, haye
L. 101. jaiba/jaba.

The name of our village is Ulukhola. | village
আমাদের গ্রামের নাম উলুখোলা । | গ্রাম, গাঁ
Amader gramer nam Ulukhola. | gram, gan

In which quarter of the village do you live ? (stay) | village, qtr.
তুমি গ্রামের কোন পাড়ায় থাক ? | পাড়া
Tumi gramer kon paray thaka ? | para

Meet me in the evening. loc., L. 65 | visit, meet
আমার সঙ্গে সন্ধ্যায় দেখা করিও/করো । | দেখা করা
Amar shange shandhay dekha kario/karo. | dekha kara

What wages do you want/get ? | wages (daily)
কত মজুরী চাও/পাও ? | মজুরী
Kata majuree chao/pao ? | majuree

They receive wages once a month. | wages, pay
তারা মাসে একবার বেতন পায় । | বেতন, মাইনা
Tara mashe ek bar betan pay. | betan, maina

Wait ! why do you delay ? দেরী কর কেন ? | wait, delay
সবুর কর/দেরি কর/অপেক্ষা কর ! Deri kara kena ? | দেরি, সবুর
Shabur kara/deri kara/apekkha kara ! | deri, shabur

He woke up from his sleep. | woke

সে ঘুম হতে/থেকে জাগল । | জাগা

   She ghum bate/theke jagla.   *jaga*

Don't wake him/her up.   L. 30. CAUS. | wake (caus.)

তাকে জাগাইও না/জাগিও না । | জাগান

   Take jagaio/jagio na.   *jagan*

I can't walk farther.   Don't walk there. | walk

আর চলতে পারি না ।   সেখানে হাঁটিও/হেঁটো না । | হাঁটা/চলা

   Ar chalte pari na. Shekhane hantio/hento na.   hanta, chala

This wall broke. | wall

এ দেওয়াল[টা] ভাঙ্গিয়া গেছে/ভেঙ্গে গিয়েছে । | দেওয়াল

   E deoyal[ta] bhangiya gechhe/bhenge giyechhe.   deoyal

He is wandering/walking in the garden. | wander about

সে বাগানে বেডাইতেছে/বেড়াচ্ছে । [ঘুরিয়া বেড়ান] | বেড়ান

   She bagane beraitechhe/berachchhe. [ghuriya beran] beran

I want to go to Dacca. I asked for his permission. | want (v.)

আমি ঢাকায় যাইতে/যেতে চাই । তার অনুমতি চাইলাম । | চাওয়া

   Ami Dhakay jaite/jete chai. Tar anumati chailam.   chaoya

It's too warm today.   Warm (it) up. |warm, hot

আজ বেশী গরম হইছে/হয়েছে ।   গরম কর । | গরম

   Aj beshee garam haichhe/hayechhe. Garam kara. |garam

The clothes have been washed. I had the clothes washed. wash

কাপড় ধোয়া হইছে/হয়েছে । কাপড় ধোয়াইছি/ধুয়েছি ।   ধোয়া, কাচা

   Kapar dhoya haichhe/hayechhe.   dhoya, kacha

   Kapar dhoyaichhi/dhuyechhi.

The laundryman/washerman didn't come. | washerman

ধোপা আসে নাই/নি । | ধোপা

   Dhopa ashe nai/ni.   *dhopa*

Don't waste your money/time.   (spoil, ruin) | waste, destroy

টাকা/সময়···নষ্ট করিও/কর না । | নষ্ট করা

   Taka/shamay...nashta kario/kara na.   nashta kara

What's the time by the watch ?

ঘড়িতে কয়টা বাজে ?

Gharite kayta baje ?

| watch, clock

| ঘড়ি

ghari

We drink water. Wash (it) in water.

আমরা পানি/জল খাই। জলে সাফ কর।

Amra pani/jal khai. Jale shaf kara.

| water

| পানি, জল

pani, jal

Where's the (earthen) water pot/jug ?

জলের কলসী কোথায় ?

Jaler kalshee kothay ?

| water pot

| কলসী, কলস

kalshee, kalash

By which path/way shall I go ?

কোন পথ/দিক দিয়া/দিয়ে যাইব/যাব ?

Kon path/dik diya/diye jaiba/jaba ?

| way, path

| পথ, দিক

path, dik

Why do you look so weak ?

তোমাকে এত দুর্বল দেখাইতেছে/দেখাচ্ছে কেন ?

Tomake eta durbal dekhaitechhe/
dekhachchhe kena ?

| weak

দুর্বল, কাহিল

durbal, kahil

Why didn't you wear (your) shoes ?

জুতা পর নাই/নি কেন ?

Juta para nai/ni kena ?

| wear

| পরা

para

I am very weary/tired. I have become.

আমি বেশ ক্লান্ত হইয়া গেছি/হয়ে গিয়েছি।

Ami besh klanta haiya gechhi/haye giyechhi.

| weary, tired

| ক্লান্ত

klanta

There was a wedding in that home. (marriage)

এই বাড়ীতে বিয়া হইছে/হয়েছে।

Ei bareete biya haichhe/hayechhe.

| wedding

বিবাহ, বিয়া, বিয়ে

bibaha, biya, biye

I shall go on Wednesday.

বুধবার দিন আমি যাইব/যাব।

Budhbar din ami jaiba/jaba.

| Wednesday

| বুধবার

Budhbar

Where will you be next week ?

সামনের সপ্তাহে তুমি কোথায় থাকবে ?

Shamner shaptahe tumi kothay thakbe ?

| week

| সপ্তাহ

shaptaha

Weigh it correctly/well, don't give (me) less. | weigh
ভালমত ওজন কর, কম দিও না । | ওজন করা
Bhala mata ojan kara, kam dio na. | ojan kara

Do this work well. Study hard. | well (adv.)
এ কাজ ভালমত কর । ভালমত পড় । [ঠিকমত] | ভালমত/করিয়া
E kaj bhala mata kara. Bhala mata   bhala mata/kariya
para. [thik mata]

He reached Dacca all right.(well) Do it well. | well
সে ভালমত ঢাকায় পৌঁচ্ছে/পৌঁছেছে । ভাল রকমে কর । ভাল রকমে
She bhala mata Dhakay pounchchhe/   bhala rakame
pounchheche. Bhala rakame kara.

He is well now. It doesn't look well/good. | well (adj.)
সে এখন সুস্থ । ইহা/তা ভাল দেখায় না । | সুস্থ, ভাল
She ekhan shustha. Iha/ta bhala dekhay na. shustha, bhala

Go west. The sun goes down in the west. | west
পশ্চিম দিকে যাও । সূর্য পশ্চিম দিকে নামে । | পশ্চিম দিক
Paschimdike jao. Shoorja paschim dike name.   paschim dik

All my clothes are wet. | wet, moist
আমার সব কাপড় ভিজা । | ভিজা
Amar shab kapar bhija. | bhija

What's your name ? Give him what he wants. | what ?
তোমার নাম কি ? সে যা চায় তা দেও । L. 132. | কি ?/যা...তা
Tomar nam ki ? She ja chay, ta deo. | ki ?/ja..
...ta
Whatever I have is your gift. | whatever
আমার যা কিছু আছে সব তোমার দান । L. 132. | যা কিছু, যা
Amar ja kichhu achhe, shab tomar dan. | ja kichhu, ja

I shall go when you call me. [when-then]L.132.|when
তুমি যখন আমাকে ডাকবে, তখন আমি যাইব/যাব । | যখন
Tumi jakhan amake dakbe, takhan ami jaiba/jaba. jakhan

When (at what time) will you come/go ? | when ?

তুমি কখন আসবে/যাবে ?   L. 133 | কখন ?

Tumi kakhan ashbe/jabe ? | kakhan ?

When (on what day) will you come/go ? | when ?

তুমি কবে আসবে/যাবে ? [কোনদিন। | কবে ?

Tumi kabe ashbe/jabe ? [kondin. | kabe ?

I shall go where (–ever) you go. [where-there] | where

তুমি যেখানে যাও, সেখানে আমিও যাইব/যাব। | যেখানে

Tumi jekhane jao, shekhane ami-o jaiba/jaba. | jekhane

Where is your home ? | where ?

তোমার বাড়ী কোথায়/কই ? | কোথায়, কই ?

Tomar baree kothay/kai ? | kothay, kai ?

Which do you want ? Which table do you want ? | which ?

তুমি কোন্টা চাও ? কোন্ টেবিল চাও ? | কোন্টা, কোন্ ?

Tumi konta chao ? Kon tebil chao ? (pron., adj.) | konta, kon ?

While going to Dacca I saw a steamer. | while

ঢাকা যাইতে যাইতে ষ্টীমার দেখছি/দেখেছি। [যখন] | –ইতে –ইতে

Dhaka jaite jaite sreemar dekhchhi/ | -ite -ite
dekhechhi. [jakhan]

He/she wears white clothes. | white

সে সাদা কাপড় পরে। | সাদা

She shada kapar pare.   L. 132. | shada

Who called me ? Ask him who came.   132. | who ?

কে আমাকে ডাক দিল ? তাকে জিজ্ঞাসা কর কে আসছে ? | কে ?

Ke amake dak dila ? Take jiggasha kara ke ashchhe. | ke ?

Tell the boy who calls for me to sit down. 133 | who

যে ছেলে আমাকে ডাকে তাকে বসতে বল। | যে

Je chhele amake dake take bashte bala. | je

What do you do all day ? | whole day

সারাদিন কি কর ? | সারাদিন

Sharadin ki kara ? | sharadin

He plays the whole day. I want all/the whole of it. | whole, all
সে সমস্ত/সারা দিন খেলে। সমস্ত চাই। | সমস্ত
She shamasta/shara din khele. Shamasta chai. | shamasta

The bread has become wholly bad. | wholly
রুটি[টা] একেবারে নষ্ট হইয়া/হইয়ে গেছে। | একেবারে
Ruti[ta] ekebare nashta haichhe হইয়া গেছে। | ekebare

Whom do you want ? | whom ?
তুমি কাকে চাও ? | কাকে ?
Tumi kake chao ? | kake ?

He, whom you want, is not at home. · Rel. cl. | whom ?
তুমি যাকে চাও সে বাড়ী নাই/নেই। L. 132. | যাকে ?
Tumi jake chao, she baree nai/nei. | jake ?

Whose book did you take ? | whose ?
তুমি কার বই নিছ/নিয়েছ ? | কার ?
Tumi kar bai nichha/niyechha ? | kar ?

He, whose book you took, hasn't come. Rel. cl. | whose ?
তুমি যার বই নিছ/নিয়েছ সে আসে নাই/নি। | যার ?
Tumi jar bai nichha/niyechha, she ashe nai/ni. | jar ?

Why didn't you tell me ? | why ?
তুমি আমাকে বল নাই/নি কেন ? | কেন, কি জন্য ?
Tumi amake bala nai/ni kena ? | kena, ki janna ?

The wicked will be/get punished. | wicked
দুষ্টরা শাস্তি পাইবে/পাবে। দুষ্ট ছেলে/মেয়ে। | দুষ্ট
Dushtara shasti paibe/pabe. Dushta chhele/meye. | dushta

I was annoyed at the girl's/boy's wickedness. | wickedness
ছেলে[টি]র/মেয়ে[টি]র দুষ্টামিতে আমি বিরক্ত হলাম। | দুষ্টামি
Chhele[ti]r/meye[ti]r dushtamite ami birakta halam. | dushtami

That door is very wide, Wide road. | wide
ঐ দরজা খুব চওড়া। চওড়া রাস্তা! | চওড়া
Oi darja khub chaora. Chaora rasta. | chaora

His wife is very good. Son's wife.	wife
তার স্ত্রী খুব ভাল। ছেলের স্ত্রী =বৌ।	স্ত্রী ; বৌ, বউ
Tar stree khub bhala. Chheler stree =)	stree, bau
bau = daughter-in-law (young)	

I am willing/ready to go. Infin.	willing, ready
আমি যাইতে/যেতে ইচ্ছুক।	ইচ্ছুক
Ami jaite/jete ichchhuk.	ichchhuk

The wind is blowing.	wind, breeze
বাতাস বইতেছে/বইছে।	বাতাস
Batash baitechhe/baichhe.	batash

Wind the clock. loc.	wind, v. (clock)
ঘড়িতে চাবি দাও।	চাবি দেওয়া
Gharite chabi dao.	chabi deoya

Open/close the window.	window
জানালা খোল/বন্ধ কর।	জানালা
Janala knola/bandha kara.	janala

Here it does not rain during winter.	winter
এখানে শীতকালে বৃষ্টি হয় না।	শীতকাল
Ekhane sheetkale brishti hay na.	sheetkal

Wipe (your) face/the water/the table.	wipe
মুখ/জল/টেবিল···মুছিয়া/মুছে ফেল।	মুছা, পোছা
Mukh/jal/tebil···muchhiya/muchhe fella.	muchha, pochha

The wire snapped/broke/tore.	wire
তার ছিঁড়িয়া গেছে/ছিঁড়ে গিয়েছে।	তার
Tar chhinriya geehhe/chhinre giyeehhe.	tar

Three wise men came.	wise
তিনজন জ্ঞানী ব্যক্তি/লোক আসলেন/এলেন।	জ্ঞানী
Tin jan genee baekti/lok ashlen/elen.	genee

He does as he wishes. Do as you wish. rel. cl. | wish (n.)

সে ইচ্ছামত চলে/করে ।   তোমার যা ইচ্ছা কর । | ইচ্ছা

She ichchha mata chale/kare. Tomar | ichchha
ja ichchha kara.

I wish to be good.   (desire) Infin. | wish (v.)

আমি ভাল হইতে/হতে ইচ্ছা করি । | ইচ্ছা করা

Ami bhala haite/hate ichchha kari. | ichchha kara

Come with me.   L. 44 | with

আমার সঙ্গে আস/এস । | সঙ্গে, সাথে

Amar shange asha/esha. | shange, shathe

Who is inside/within ? Who is in the room ? | within, in

ভিতরে কে ?   ঘরের মধ্যে কে? L. 41, 43 | ভিতরে, মধ্যে

Bhitare ke ? Gharer maddhe ke ? | bhitare, maddhe

I shall not go anywhere without him. | without (Postp.)

তাকে ছাড়া আমি কোথাও যাব না । L. 62 | ছাড়া

Take chhara ami kothayo jaba na. | chhara

We cannot live without water.   L. 62 | without (Postp.)

জল/পানি ছাড়া আমরা বাঁচতে পারি না । | ছাড়া

Jal/pani chhara amra banchte pari na. | chhara

He does me harm without reason.   L. 61b | without (Postp)

সে বিনা কারণে আমার ক্ষতি করে । | বিনা

She bina karane amar kkhati kare. | bina

That woman is a widow. | woman

ঐ/সেই স্ত্রীলোক[টা] বিধবা । | স্ত্রীলোক

Oi/she streelok[ta] bidhaba. | streelok

What a wonderful sight ! | wonderful

কি চমৎকার দৃশ্য ! | চমৎকার

Ki chamatkar drishsha ! | chamatkar

We bought fifty taka's worth of wood. | wood

আমরা পঞ্চাশ টাকার কাঠ কিনলাম । | কাঠ

Amra panchash takar kath kinlam. | kath

What does this word mean ? [these words] | word ,

এই কথার/শব্দের মানে কি ?   কথা, শব্দ

    Ei kathar/ shabder mane ki ?   katha/shabda

Where do you work ? He is working (at a job). | work (n., v.)

কোথায় কাজ কর ?   সে চাকরি করে।   কাজ করা/চাকরি করা

    Kothay kaj kara ? She chakari kare.   kaj/chakari kara

There are many people in the world. | world, earth

জগতে অনেক মানুষ আছে। [পৃথিবী]   জগৎ

    Jagate anek manush achhe. [prithibee]   jagat

Write a letter.   I wrote a letter. | write

একটি চিঠি লেখ।   একটি চিঠি লিখলাম।   লেখা

    Ekti chithi lekha.   Ekti chithi likhlam.   lekha

You have a wrong idea.   You are wrong. | wrong, mistake

তোমার ভুল ধারণা আছে।   তোমার ভুল হইছে/হয়েছে।   ভুল

    Tomar bhul dharana achhe.   Tomar bhul   bhul
        haichhe/hayechhe.   L. 19

Three feet make a yard.   I want 3 yards of cloth. | yard

তিন ফুটে এক গজ।   তিন গজ কাপড় চাই।   গজ

    Tin (৩) fute ek gaj.   Tin gaj kapar chai   gaj

He/she is five years of age. | year

তার পাঁচ বৎসর বয়স।   বৎসর

    Tar panch batshar bayash.   batshar

The flower is yellow,   (in colour) | yellow

ফুলটির/ফুলের রং হলদে।   হলদে/হলুদ

    Fultir/fuler rang halde.   halde, halud

Yes, I'll go.   yes

হা/হ্যা/হ, যাব।   [হঁা]   হা, হ্যা, হ

    Ha/he/haw, jaba.   [hen]   ha, he, haw

I came yesterday. | yesterday

আমি কাল/গতকাল আসছি/এসেছি।   কাল/গতকাল

    Ami kal/gatakal ashchhi/eshechhi.   kal, gatakal

He/she hasn't come yet. (upto now, still) | yet

সে এখন-ও আসে নাই/নি । [তখন-ও] | এখন-ও

She ekhan-o ashe nai/ni. [takhan-o] | ekhan-o

The man is young. He is young. (a youth | young (adj.)

লোকটি অল্প বয়সের । সে জোয়ান লোক । | অল্প বয়সের/[বয়স্ক]

Lokti alpa bayasher. She joyan lok. | alpa bayasher/ [bayashka]

The dog gave birth to some pups. L. 19 | young (n.)

কুকুরের কতগুলি বাচ্চা হইছে/হয়েছে । | বাচ্চা

Kukurer kataguli bachcha haichhe/bayechhe. | bachcha

That young woman/lady teaches in a school. | young, adj.

(16 to 30 years) | জোয়ান=jowan

সে জোয়ান মহিলা স্কুলে পড়ায় । | যুবক , যুবতী

Shei jowan mahila skule paray. | jubak (m), jubatee (f.)

302

১০ দশ dash	৮০ আশি ashi
১১ এগার egara	৯০ নব্বই nabbai
১২ বার bara	১০০ একশ ek sha
১৭ তের tera	১০০০ এক হাজার ek hajar
১4 চৌদ্দ choudda	Use এক কুড়ি তিন—23.
১৫ পনর panara	ek kuri tin
১৬ ষোল shola	চল্লিশ ও পাঁচ—45
১৭ সতর shatara	challish o panch
১৮ আঠার athara	৪০ চল্লিশ challish
১৯ উনিশ unish	৫০ পঞ্চাশ panchash
২০ কুড়ি kuri	৬০ ষাট sha(i)t
৩০ ত্রিশ trish	৭০ সত্তর shattar

Secondary Vocabulary

absence n. অনুপস্থিতি anupasthiti
absent adj. অনুপস্থিত anupasthit ; হাজির না hajir na
abuse n./v. গালি gali ; গালি দেওয়া gali dewa
accept v. গ্রহণ করা ; নেওয়া ; গ্রাহ্য করা grahan kara, newa,
accident দুর্ঘটনা durghatana   grajja kara
account n. হিসাব hishab
accuse দোষী করা, নিন্দা করা doshee kara, ninda kara
accusative case কর্ম কারক karmma karak
ache n. v. ব্যথা, ব্যথা করা baetha, baetha kara
acquire/get লাভ করা, পাওয়া labh kara, paoya
across, come যাইতে যাইতে হঠাৎ দেখতে পাওয়া jaite jaite hathat
act n. (work) কাজ [কার্য] kaj [karja]   dekhte paoya
add v. যোগ দেওয়া jog deoya
adverb ক্রিয়া বিশেষণ kriya bisheshan
agree মিল হওয়া mil haoya.
aim লক্ষ্য lakkha ; উদ্দেশ্য uddeshsha.
alas ! হায় ! hay !
alive জীবিত jeebita
alley/lane গলি gali
allow/let —তে দেওয়া, অনুমতি দেওয়া —te dewa, anumati dewa
alms ভিক্ষা bhikkha
already এর মধ্যে er maddhe
also/too ও, o ; আরও aro
although যদিও jadio
always সব সময়ে shab shamaye
amount মোট mot
a/an [see : definitive particles in gram.]
anxious চিন্তিত chintita

approach v. কাছে আসা kachhe asha

April এপ্রিল Epril

argue v. তর্ক করা tarka kara

argument n. তর্ক tarka

arm [বাহু bahu] হাত hat

as যেমন jeman

ashamed লজ্জিত lajjita

at – LOCATIVE CASE

attend উপস্থিত হওয়া upasthit haoya

author লেখক lekhak

avoid এড়ান erana

awake জাগিয়া উঠা jagiya utha

awaken জাগান jagana

away দূরে doore

back, in—of পাছে pachhe ;   পিছনে pichhane

bank/shore তীর teer ;   নদীর ধার nadeer dhar

banquet বড় খানা bara khana

bathroom গুসলখানা gusal khana ;   পায়খানা paykhana = toilet

beef গরুর মাংস garur mangsha

belief বিশ্বাস bishshash

belong এটা আমার eta amar – this is mine.

best সবচেয়ে ভাল shab cheye bhala

better আরও ভাল aro bhala

Bible বাইবেল Baibel

blanket কম্বল kambal

blown, কিল kil ;   ঘুষি ghushi

blue নীল neel

board তক্তা takta

bone হাড় har ;   [হাড্ডি haddi]

bottle বোতল botal

bottom, at—তলে tale ;   তলায় talay L. 61

boundary সীমা sheema

broad চওড়া chawra

brush বুরুশ burush

burst ফাটা *fata* ; ফাটান *fatana*

bus বাস্ *bas*

bare (bodied) খালি গা khali *ga*, ... foot খালি পা khali *pa*

can n. টিন *tin*

cargo মাল *mal* [baggage, luggage]

case [gram.] কারক *karak*

carrot গাজর *gajar*

center/—re কেন্দ্র kendra

certain make স্থির sthir করা kara

chain শিকল shikal ; চেন chen

chalk চক্ chak খড়ি মাটি khari *mati*

charge/duty ভার *bhar* ; take charge—নেওয়া neoy*a*

Christmas বড়দিন bara din

circle চক্র   chakra =চক্র = wheel, ring

claim দাবী d*a*bee ; দাবী করা d*a*bee kar*a*, v.

climb up চড়া char*a* ; উঠা *utha*

coffee কফি kafi

coin রেজগি rejgi ; পয়সা paysh*a*

college কলেজ kalej

composition রচনা rachan*a* ; compose – kar*a*

complete adj. পূরা pur*a* ; সম্পূর্ণ shampoorna

condition(s) অবস্থা abasth*a*(= state, mood, circumstances.

conduct v. চালান chalan*a* ; নিয়া যাওয়া niy*a* ja*o*ya

connect বাঁধা bandh*a* ; লাগান lagan ; জোড়া দেওয়া jor*a* deoya

consult পরামর্শ নেওয়া/করা par*a*marsha neoy*a*/kara

compare v. তুলনা করা tulan*a* kara

control v. দমন করা daman kar*a* ; শাসন করা sh*a*shan kar*a*

cool adj. অল্প ঠাণ্ডা alpa *thanda*

cost n. দাম d*a*m ; দাম কত ? d*a*m kata ? What is the—?

crow কাক k*a*k

cubit এক হাত ek hat—18 inches

cultivation চাষ   ch*a*sh

dad বাবা baba

dare সাহস করা shahash kar*a* ; সাহসী shahashee adj.

dative case সম্পাদন কারক shamp*a*dan k*a*rak

decide স্থির করা sthir kara ; সঙ্কল্প করা shankalpa kara

decorate সাজান shajan

decrease কমা kama' ; কমান kamana   L. 30.

deed কাজ k j ; (paper) দলিল dalil

dense ঘন ghana

depart চলিয়া যাওয়া chaliya jaoya

depend on—উপর নির্ভর করা—upar nirbhar kara

dig খুঁড়িয়া তোলা khunriya tola ; কোদলান kodlan

direct adv. সোজা shoja ; চালান chalana v.)

dirt ময়লা mayla

dismiss বিদায় দেওয়া/করা biday deoya/kara

document দলিল dalil.

down adv. নীচে neeche

drive away তাড়াইয়া দেওয়া taraiya deoya

drop,v. পড়া para ; ফেলিয়া দেওয়া feliya dewa =let............drop=
ছাড়িয়া দেওয়া chhariya deoya, t. v.

drown ডুবিয়া মরা dubiya mara ; — dewa t. v.

during the day দিন থাকতে din thakte ; দিনের মধ্যে diner maddhe.

duty উচিত কাজ uchit koj =কর্তব্য kartabba

educate শিক্ষা দেওয়া shikkha dewa ;—tion শিক্ষা shikkha

effort,n. চেষ্টা chesta

either হয়·····না হয় hay......na hay

end v. শেষ করা shesh kara (=fiinish

engine যন্ত্র jantra ; কল kal

enjoy আনন্দ পাওয়া ananda paoya

event ঘটনা ghatana

example দৃষ্টান্ত drishtanta ; উদাহরণ udaharan.

v.except বাদ দিয়া bad diya (L. 61, 62)

excuse,n. ওজর ojar ; নানা কারণ nana karan

exercise,n. ব্যায়াম beyam

expect,v. আশা করা asha kara

fail,v. ফেল করা fel kara ; পাশ না করা pash na kara

facial feature চেহারা chehara

famous বিখ্যাত bikkheta ; নামজাদা namjada

farm জমি jami ; জমাই jamai, ক্ষেত kkhet, বাগান bagan=garder

farther আরও দূরে aro doore

feather পালক palak

fee ফী fee ; fees বেতন betan

ferry, n. খেয়ার নৌকা kheyar nauka

festival পর্ব parba ; উৎসব utshab ; পর্বদিন parbadin

few অল্পই alpa-i ; খুব-ই কম khub-i kam

first প্রথম pratham

flood বন্যা banna ; বান ban

foam ফেনা fena

fog কুয়াশা kuyasha

follow পরে আসা/যাওয়া pare asha/jaoya

fourth চতুর্থ chaturtha

frock/dress ফ্রক frak ˙

gallon 4 quarts=almost 4 seers

gap ফাঁক fank

gas গ্যাস gesh

gate গেট get ; দরজা darja (door)

gate-keeper/watchman দারোয়ান darowan

gender লিঙ্গ linga ৲ mfn পুং Pung— ; স্ত্রী stree— ; ক্লীব kleeb—

genitive সম্বন্ধ বাচক/—বোধক shambandha bachak/—bodhak

gentle বিনীত bineeta ; শান্ত shanta কোমল komal

geography ভূগোল bhoogol

good-bye নমস্কার namashkar ; আদাব adab ; সালাম salam

government সরকার sharkar, adj. সরকারী sharkaree

grain/seed দানা dana

grammar ব্যাকরণ bekaran

grind গুঁড়া করা gunra kara

guard চৌকি দেওয়া chawki dewa ; রক্ষা করা rakkha kara

green=raw=unripe

hand, v. হাতে করিয়া দেওয়া hate kariya deoya ; তুলিয়া দেওয়া tulia deoya

harvest, n. ফসল fashal ; শস্য shashsha

v. hate ঘৃণা করা grina kara

heal,t. v. সুস্থ করা shushtha kara/i. v. ; সারিয়া যাওয়া shoriya jaoya
hoe,n. নিড়ানি nirani
holiday ছুটি chhuti ; ছুটির দিন chhutir din
holy পবিত্র pabitra
horse ঘোড়া ghora
hospital হাসপাতাল hoshpatal
humble নম্র namro
husband স্বামী shamee

I আমি ami
identical একই eki ; এক রকম ek rakam
illness রোগ rog ; বেমো bemo
imagine কল্পনা করা kalpana kara
inch ইঞ্চি inchi.
income আয় ay ;/expenditure ব্যয় bae
in fact আসলে ashale
innocent নির্দোষ nirdosh ; দোষী না doshee na
interest. n. জানবার/করবার /দেখাবার ইচ্ছা janbar/karbar/dekhbar
invent,v. t. আবিষ্কার করা abishkar kara   ichchha

jar বয়ম bayam
job কাজ kaj ; চাকরি chakari
just/right/proper ন্যায্য neyjja ; উচিত uchit ; ঠিক thik

kerosene কেরোসিন keroshin
kick লাথি মারা lathi mara
king রাজা raja
knock against ধাক্কা/মারা dhakka mara [pass. —khawa]
knot,n. v. গিঁট gint ; গিঁট দেওয়া gint deoya

labour/work কাজ kaj ; -er মজুর majur (worker)
ladder কাঠের সিঁড়ি kather shinri; মই mai [bamboo+ rope —]
lantern হারিকেন hariken
launch লঞ্চ lanch
lead.v. নিয়া যাওয়া niya jaoya ; সঙ্গে নেওয়া shange neoya

leaf/page পাতা pata

level adj সমান shaman

liable/responsible দায়ী dayee

lie.v. পড়িয়া থাকা pariya thaka

liquid adj. তরল taral ; watery পানসে panshe

living/livelihood জীবিকা jeebika

luck ভাগ্য bhagga (lot) ; কপাল kapal (fate)

magazine পত্রিকা patrika

mechanic মিস্ত্রী mistree

meditate চিন্তা করা chinta kara ; ধ্যান করা dhen kara

medium মধ্য maddha ; মধ্যম maddham

memory স্মরণ শক্তি sharan shakti

mend মেরামত করা meramat kara ; ঠিক করা thik kara

merchant দোকানদার dokandar

merely মাত্র matra কেবল kebal

at midnight মধ্য/দুপুর রাত্রে maddha/dupur ratre

n.might বল bal ; (strength) শক্তি shakti

n.might/power ক্ষমতা kkhamata [may : L. 86]

mile মাইল mail

mill কল kal

minute মিনিট minit

mischief দুষ্টামি dushtami

mischievous দুষ্ট dushta

v.miss, not hit না লাগা na laga ; না মারা na mara

moisten/wet ভিজা bhija : ভিজানা bhijana [caus.] L. 30.

a Muslim মুসলমান Mushalman

Muslim religion ইসলাম Islam

most সবচেয়ে··· shab cheye···

motive/intention উদ্দেশ্য uddessha

motor মোটর motar ; —car মোটর গাড়ী motar garee

mouse ছোট ইন্দুর chhota indur

movie সিনেমা sinema [cinema]

murder খুন khun ; verb=খুন করা khun kara

nature স্বভাব shabhab (character)

necessity/need দরকার darkar ;   অভাব abhab=lack)

needle ছুঁচ chhunch.

neither......ও না.... o na ; নয় নয় nay...nay

next week আগামী সপ্তাহ agamee shaptaha(-e)

the next day পরদিন par din

nice বেশ besh ;   ভাল bhala ; চমৎকার chamatkar

none কেহ-ই না keha-i na ; একটি-ও না ekti-o na

nothing কিছু ই না kichhu-i na

noun বিশেষ্য bisheshsha

nowhere কোথাওনা kotha-o na

null বাতিল batil

objective case কর্ম কারক karma karak

object বিষয় bishay ;   জিনিষ jinish ;   উদ্দেশ্য uddeshsha = purpose

object (GRAM.) কর্মপদ karma pad

ocean মহাসাগর maha shagar

off/from থেকে theke ;   হতে hate L.64

offend/hurt কষ্ট দেওয়া kashta deoya

office (room) অফিস afish ;   আফিস afish

be at one একমত হওয়া ek mat haoya (agree)

all one একই কথা ek-i-katha/jinish the same)

one by one একে একে eke eke

one another পরস্পর parashpar

opposite বিপরীত bipareet

orphan অনাথ { ছেলে/মেয়ে } anath { chhele/meye }

I owe him taka 10 আমি তার কাছে দশ টাকা ধারি ami tar kachhe dash taka dhari

packet প্যাকেট peket

pan হাঁড়ি hanri ;   (lg) ডেকচি dekchi (pot); চাটু chatu

pants প্যান্ট pent ;   পা(য়)জামা pa(y)jama [thin]

parcel পার্শেল parsel

pass,v. যাওয়া jaoya ;   নিকট দিয়া যাওয়া nikat diya jaoya

patch,n. তালি tali ;   v. —দেওয়া —dewa

paw থাবা thaba

pay for ...জন্য টাকা দেওয়া...janna taka dewa

peevish রাগী ragee

perfect adj. বেশ besh ; পাকা paka ; যার দোষ নাই jar dosh nai

perspiration ঘাম gham ;   verb : ঘামা ghama

pin,n. আলপিন alpin

pinch,n. চিমটি chimti ; of salt এক—লবণ ek—laban

please,v. সন্তুষ্ট করা shantushta kara

plenty of অনেক anek ; বহু bahu

pocket পকেট paket

pond/tank পুকুর pukur

position/situation অবস্থা abastha ;   post চাকরি chakari

v.possess দখল করা dakhal kara (L. 12, 16, 17)

possessive case সম্বন্ধ পদ shambandha pad (L. 12, 16, 17)

v.pray প্রার্থনা করা prarthana kara

principal/chief প্রধান pradhan

progress উন্নতি unnati ; উন্নতি করা unnati kara. v.

pronoun সর্বনাম sharbanam

prose গদ্য gadda

proud অহংকারী ahankaree   মানী manee

public road সরকারী রাস্তা sharkaree rasta ;   rasta

in public প্রকাশে prakashe   , লোকদের সামনে lokder shamne

pumpkin কুমড়া kumra ;   white) কদু kadu , লাউ lau

a pull/attraction টান tan

purple বেগুনী রং begunee rang

purpose,n. উদ্দেশ্য uddeshsha ; মতলব matlab

pus পুঁষ puj ; পুঁজ punj

quart=¼ gallon প্রায় তিন পোয়া almost ⅜ seers pray tin powa

a quarter এক পোয়া ek powa ; ½ less পৌনে poune

quit school···স্কুল ছাড়া .... skul chhara

raddish মূলা moola

rap ধাক্কা মারা dhakka mara

ration রেশন reshan ;

razor ক্ষুর kkhur

v.realize সত্য করিয়া তোলা shatta kariya tola=understand

v.realize (money) টাকা আদায় করা taka aday kara

receipt রসিদ rashid

recess (school) টিফিন tifin

recipe নিয়ম niyam

v. recite মুখস্থ বলা mukhastha bala

recognize/know চিনা china

recommend সুপারিশ করা shuparish kara

reduce/make less কমা kama ; কমান kamana, t. v. CAUS. V.

v. relate/tell কহা kaha ; বলা bala

v. release ছাড়িয়া দেওয়া chhariya deowa

v. remind মনে করিয়া দেওয়া mane kariya dewa

reputation সুনাম shunam ; যশ jash

v. resign কাজ/চাকরি ছাড়িয়া দেওয়া kaj/chakari chhariya dewa

v. resolve সঙ্কল্প করা shankalpa kara ; স্থির করা sthir kara

v. respond উত্তর/জবাব দেওয়া uttar/jabab deoya (answer)

restaurant রেস্তোরাঁ restoran

v. revolve/turn ঘুরা ghura

ribbon ফিতা fita

ride. v. —এ যাওয়া—e-y-te jawa ; চড়িয়া যাওয়া chariya jaoya

v. ridicule/joke with ঠাট্টা করা thatta kara

rifle বন্দুক banduk

riot n. দাঙ্গা danga , হাঙ্গামা hangama

v. ripen পাকা paka ; পাক হওয়া pak howa

v. roam/wander ঘুরিয়া বেড়ান ghuriya berana

roast, v. পাক করা pak kara ; পাকান pakan; সেকা ===bake

v. rob চুরি করিয়া নেওয়া churi kariya neoya

robber ডাকাত/ডাকাইত dakat/dakait

v. roll/turn ঘুরা ghura , ঘুরান ghurana t. v.

root মূল mool (origin) ; শিকড় shikar (of plant)

rough (to touch) কর্কশ karkash ; অসমান ashaman

roughly speaking মোটামুটি বলতে গেলে motamuti balte gele

route রাস্তা rasta

row, n. লাইন lain

row, v. দাঁড় টানিয়া চালান danr taniya chalana

ruination সর্বনাশ ! sharbanash ! (exag. exclam.)

rude/uncivil অভদ্র abhadra

rule,v. শাসন করা shashan kara ; ruler কর্ত্তা kaitta

rumour গুজব gujab ; হুজুক hujuk ; জনরব janarab

v.rust মরিচা (ধরা বা পড়া) maricha (dhara/para) ; জং jang

sacred/holy পবিত্র pabitra

safe adj. নিরাপদ nirapad ; in safety —e

sail পাল pal ; verb —tuliya dewa

-for the sake of জন্য janna (for)

salve মলম malam ; মালিশ malish

sap/juice রস rash

scaffold/platform মাচান/মাচা machan/macha

scale n. পাল্লা palla

scarcity অভাব abhab

scene(ry) দৃশ্য drishsha

scheme/plan পরিকল্পনা parikalpana

science বিজ্ঞান biggan

scour পরিষ্কার করা parishkar kara , ঘষা ghasha

scratch,v. আঁচড়ান anchran , চুলকান chulkana itch)

scream,v. চিৎকার করা chitkar kara , চেঁচান chenchana

sea/bay সমুদ্র shamudra , সাগর shagar

season ঋতু reetu, spring, summer, rainy, autumn,dewy, winter q. v

seat চেয়ার cheyar (chair)

secret গোপন কথা gopan katha ; adj. গোপন gopan

second adj. দ্বিতীয় dditeeya

seek/search for খোঁজা khonja ; চাওয়া chawa —want

seem strange অদ্ভুত লাগে adbhut lage

    cold ঠাণ্ডা লাগে thanda lage

    easy সহজ ,, shahaj lage

    hard কঠিন ,, kathin lage

    so it seems এইরকম তো লাগে ei rakam to lage

self, I myself আমি নিজে ami nije

    my own work আমার নিজের কাজ amar nijer kaj

erve সেবা করা sheba kara ; অন্যের জন্য কাজ করা anner janna kaj

hallow/not deep গভীর না gabheer na   kara

shame,v. লজ্জা দেওয়া lajja dewa ; (exclam.) ছি ছি ! chhi chhi !

share,v. অংশ নেওয়া angsha newa

shed/barn গুদাম gudam

shelf তাক tak

shine.v. উজ্জ্বল হওয়া ujjal howa

shiver,v. কাঁপা kanpa

shoot গুলি করা guli kara ; ছোড়া chhora

shore/bank তীর teer

shout চিৎকার করা chitkar kara ; চেঁচান chenchana

shove ধাক্কা দেওয়া dhakka dewa ; ঠেলা দেওয়া *thela dewa*

shun এড়ান erana ; ছাড়িয়া দেওয়া chhariya dewa

shy/coy লাজুক lajuk

sight/scene দৃশ্য drishsha

sign n চিহ্ন chinha (chinna) ; লক্ষণ lakkhan

similar to/like মত mata [L. 51]

simply/merely কেবল kebal

a single boy একটি মাত্র ছেলে ekti matra chhele

singular number এক বচন ek bachan

sir স্যার sar ; জনাব janab ; মহাশয় mahashay

slap,v. চাপড়/চড় মারা chapar/char mara

sleeve হাতা hata

slip আছাড় দেওয়া/খাওয়া achhar dewa/khaowa

smoke n. ধূম dhoom ; ধূমা dhooma ; v.—pan kara

society সমাজ shamaj

sore/wound ঘা gha

sorrow দুঃখ dukhkha ; খেদ khed

sound আওয়াজ awaj ; শব্দ shabda

spade কোদাল kodal ; কুদাল kuddal

sparrow চড়াই পাখী charai pakhee

speechless অবাক abak ; (be) – হওয়া —haowa

spell,v. বানান করা banan kara

spider মাকড়সা makarsha ; মাকড় makar

spill ঢালিয়া ফেলা *dhaliya fela*

spit,v. থুথু ফেলা thu thu fela

spot/mark দাগ dag ; place স্থান stan

spread ছড়ান chharana ;—out বিছান bichhana

sprinkle ছিটান chhitana

stare,v. তাকান takan

starve না খাইয়া/কম খাইয়া কষ্ট পাওয়া n ঃ khaiya/kam khaiya kashta paoya

state/condition অবস্থা abastha

station স্টেশন steshan

statue মূর্তি moorti

steamer স্টীমার steemar

stench/bad odour দুর্গন্ধ durgandha (stink)

storm ঝড় jhar ; তুফান tufan

a stranger অজানা লোক ajana lok

straw খড় khar

street/road রাস্তা rasta

succeed v. সফল হওয়া shafal howa

success সফল চেষ্টা shafal chesta

sueccssful সফল shafal

such a one/a certain...অমুক amuk

suck চোষা chosha

suffer কষ্ট পাওয়া kashta paowa ; দুঃখ ভোগ করা dukhkha bhog kara

suffice/be enough বস্ হওয়া bas haoya/বস ! —চলবে chalbe ; যথেষ্ট হওয়া jathesta haoya

sugarcane আখ akh , গেণ্ডারী gendaree

sum/total মোট mot

supper রাত্রের খাওয়া/খানা ratrer khaoya/khana

supply/give দেওয়া dewa

surface/top উপরের ভাগ uparer bhag

surname পদবী padabee

suspect দোষী মনে করা doshee mane kara ; সন্দেহ করা shandeha kara

swallow,v. গিলা gila

swamp/flooded area বিল bil/beel

sweat,n. v. ঘাম gham ; ঘামা ghama

tail লেজ lej

take care of—এর যত্ন নেওয়া ...er jatna newa

take down নামান namana

take fire আগুন লাগা agun laga

take leave of এর কাছে বিদায় নেওয়া —er kachhe biday newa

take notice সাবধানে দেখা shabadhane dekha ·

talk/speak কথা কহা katha kaha ; আলাপ করা alap kara

tame adj পোষা posha.

tap (water) জলের কল jaler kal

tap water কলের জল kaler jal/pani

(it is tasty) স্বাদ ভাল sshad bhala

temple মন্দির mandir

tendency/pull টান tan

tense (gram.) কাল বাচক বিভক্তি kal bachak bibhakti

term (school) টার্ম tarm

thanks ধন্যবাদ dhannabad ; v. — দেওয়া —dewa

that is মানে mane

then তখন takhan

third তৃতীয় triteeya

those এইগুলি, এই সব/সকল ei guli, ei shab/shakal

though/although যদিও jadio [L. 109. 118. 125]

thousand হাজার hajar

thread সুতা shoota

through [see : diya, diye, bhitar diya in gram. and across in

be through শেষ হওয়া shesh howa   vocab.]

ticket টিকিট tikit

till v. চাষ দেওয়া chash dewa ; লাঙল দেওয়া langal dewa

tin/can টিন tin, adj. টিনের tiner

tip আগা aga ; ডগা daga (n.)

get tired ক্লান্ত হওয়া klanta haoya

title নাম nam ; উপাধি upadhi

to [gram. কাছে kachhe ; dative L. 11 ; 46 Loc.

toast টোস্ট tost সেঁকা রুটি shenka ruti

toe পায়ের আঙুল payer angul

toilet গুসলখানা gusal khana ; পায়খানা paykhana

tomato টম্যাটো tameto ; তেমুতি temuti

tongue জিব jib ; জিহ্বা jihba (jibba)

too/also [gram.—defin. particle L. 118]

top উপরের ভাগ uparer bhag ; মাথা matha

topsy-turvy ওলট-পালট olat-palat

torch/flash light টর্চ লাইট tarch lait

torn ছিঁড়া chhinra

touch ছোঁয়া chhonya ; স্পর্শ করা sparsha kara, হাত দেওয়া hat

towel, dish ঝাড়ন jharan   dewa লাগা laga

toy খেলনা khelna

train ট্রেন tren ; রেল গাড়ী rel garee

trap ফাঁদ fand

travel v. বাসে/ট্রেনে/জাহাজে/প্লেনে ··· যাওয়া bashe/trene/jahaje

treat/use ব্যবহার করা baebahar kara   plene··jaoya

treatment ব্যবহার baebahar , চিকিৎসা chikitsha (med.)

trial/judgement বিচার bichar

trip/journey অল্প ভ্রমণ alpa bhraman ; সফর shafar

truck/lorry ট্রাক trak

trunk বাক্স baksha (box)

truth সত্য কথা shatta katha ; সত্য shatta

truthful সৎ shat , সত্যবাদী shattabadee

tumult/uproar/disturbance গোলমাল golmal

turn/chance n. পালা pala

turn upside down উল্টান ultana

ugly কুৎসিত kutshit ; বিশ্রী bisree ; সুন্দর না shundar na

unbearable অসহ্য ashajja

unconscious অজ্ঞান aggan, (aggen)

uncover খোলা khola [adj. uncovered, open]

under/below L. 47 নীচে neeche

undress কাপড় খোলা/ছাড়া kapar khola/chhara

uneducated অশিক্ষিত ashikkhita

unemployed বেকার bekar

uneven অসমান ashaman ; সমান না shaman na

unfair অন্যায় annay ; অসৎ ashat

unfaithful নিমকহারাম nimak-haram , bishshashee na

unhappy অসুখী ashukhee ; সুখী না shukhee na

unjust অন্যায় annay

unknown অজানা ajana ; jana na

v.unscrew পেঁচ খোলা pench khola

un—[most words are positive words + না na]

until [see : until,till পর্যন্ত parjanta ; L. 61. 79. 108]

untrue মিথ্যা mittha

unwilling নারাজ naraj ; রাজী না raji na

up/straight খাড়া khara

upside down উল্টা ulta ; v. turn—উল্টান ultana

upstairs উপরে upare ; উপর তালা upar tala তলা tala

v.urge জেদ করা jed kara

v.urinate প্রস্রাব করা prasrab kara

vacant/empty খালি khali

vaccination টিকা tika

vain/fru tless বৃথা britha ; ব্যর্থ baertha

value মূল্য moolla ; দাম dam (price)

valuable দামী damee ; অমূল্য amoolla (priceless)

veil/curtain পরদা parda ; ঘোমটা ghomta (face)

victory জয় jay; বিজয় bijoy

view/scene দৃশ্য drishsha

vine লতা lata

virgin/maiden/unwed girl কুমারী kumaree

virtue/quality গুণ gun

voice স্বর shar

v.vomit বমি করা bami kara

watch,v. পাহাড়া/চৌকি দেওয়া pahara/chauki dewa

wax মোম mom

weather আবহাওয়া abhaoya

v. weave বুনা buna

weed আগাছা agachha ; জঙ্গল jangal, n.

weep/cry কাঁদা kanda

welfare মঙ্গল mangal

well, n. কূপ koop ; কুয়া kuya

wheat গম gam

wheel চাকা chaka

whether/if যদি jadi ; কি না/ki na L. 115, 125

a while কিছুক্ষণ kichhu kkhan

wick শলিতা shalita

will/wish ইচ্ছা ichchha

wing ডানা dana ; পাখা pakha

worse আরও খারাপ aro kharap

worst সবচেয়ে খারাপ shab cheye kharap

wound/hurt, n. ঘা gha

writing/written লেখা lekha

yard/courtyard উঠান uthan

you (sing, pl.) তুমি tumi ; তোমরা tomra [see pron. chart]

NUMBERS

১ এক ek	১৭ সতর shatara
২ দুই dui	১৮ আঠার athara
৩ তিন tin	১৯ উনিশ oonish
8 চার char	২০ কুড়ি kuri, বিশ bish
৫ পাঁচ panch	৩০ ত্রিশ trish
৬ ছয় chhay	8০ চল্লিশ challish
৭ সাত shat	৫০ পঞ্চাশ panchash
৮ আট at	৬০ ষাট shat, shait
৯ নয় nay	৭০ সত্তর shatur

১০ দশ dash

১১ এগার egara

১২ বার bara

১৩ তের tera

১৪ চৌদ্দ choudda

১৫ পনর panara

১৬ ষোল shola

১৭ সতর shatara

১৮ আঠার athara

১৯ উনিশ unish

২০ কুড়ি kuri

৩০ ত্রিশ trish

৮০ আশি ashi

৯০ নব্বই nabbai

১০০ একশ ek sha

১০০০ এক হাজার ek hajar

Use এক কুড়ি তিন—23.

ek kuri. tin

চল্লিশ ও পাঁচ—45

challish o panch

80 চল্লিশ challish

৫০ পঞ্চাশ panchash

৬০ ষাট sha(i)t

৭০ সত্তর shattar

INDEX

(LESSON NUMBERS)

ইয়া iya 101. introduction 1. intensive. particle ই i 110, 117, 119. interrogative sentences 21, 22, 133. it is 18.

jadi, if 115, 125. jana 84. janna 55, 74, 80. jaoya 82, 88, 104. je 123, 124. joy 94.

kachhe 11, 46. kachh theke 61e. karane 60. katha 71. keep doing 89. ki কি 21, 121, 133.

laga (sentences) 93. law, permission by 95 d. let 86. like 90. locative 65—70, 81, 83, 133, 134. love 90.

maddhe 41. manner 63, 101, 102, 103. mata 51. material, genitive of 39. may 84. means 63, 101, 102, 103. measurement, genitive of 40. mood (see infin., conditioral clauses, ppl. in ইলে ile. must 83.

na/nay, না/নয় 20, 22, 23, 79, 108, 116. neeche 47. need 80. negative 13, 16, 20, 22, 79, 108, 116...., negative conditional 116. neoya, take 105. nice 96. nikate 46. nominative absolute 113. nominative appositive 35. nominative case 6, 8, 13, 15, 61a, 75—77, 79, 82, 87—91. nominative verbal noun 75, 76, 77. noun as subject 5, in apposition 8.

objective/objective case/accu. 8, 9, 10, 13, 14, 30, 34, 36, 78, 83, 86, 113, 134. object, indirect 10, 11. objective of verbal noun 78. order 5, 8, 10, 13 – 15, 91. ought 76. ought, should 76. own 16.

pachhe 42. palatals 2. paoya get 88. par 53, 80. para 84, 95 d. pare 53. parjanta 61a, 79, 108. participle 95a, 95b, 95e, 98, 99—119. participle, infin. as 95a, 95b, 95e. participle in ইয়া iya ঃ I conjunction 98. II diff. between ইয়া iya and ইতে···ইতে, ite··· ·ite 99. III shows cause, reason 100. IV adverbial use 101. V manner 102. VI by means of 103. VII with যাওয়া jaoya, দেওয়া deoya, continued action, to intensify 104. VIII with দেওয়া deoya and নেওয়া neoya

20—